Carthage:

A Mosaic of Ancient Tunisia

Edited by

Aïcha Ben Abed Ben Khader and

David Soren

Photographs by Martha Cooper

This book is based on an exhibition presented by

The American Museum of Natural History

in collaboration with

Bardo National Museum, Tunis

Carthage National Museum, Tunis

Archeological Museums, El Jem, Sousse, Sfax, Nabeul

The American Museum of Natural History

in association with

W.W. Norton & Company

New York   ·   London

Authors

Preface: David Soren

An American Overview
  David Soren

Carthage: Tunisia in Prehistory
  Mounira Riahi-Harbi

The Berbers of the Pre-Roman Period
  Mansour Ghaki

Punic Civilization

Kerkouane: A Punic City at Cape Bon

Tunisia After Classical Antiquity: A Personal View
  M'Hamed Hassine Fantar

From the Fall of Carthage to the Arrival of the Moslems
  Hédi Slim

The African Mosaic in Antiquity
  Aïcha Ben Abed Ben Khader

Authors of Catalogue Notices

Jenina Akkari-Weriemmi, Attachée de recherche, Institut National d'Archéologie et d'Art (INAA), Tunisia   JAW

Nayla Attya-Ouertani, Chargée de recherche, INAA, Tunisia   NAO

Zeineb Ben Abdallah, Chargé de recherche, INAA, Tunisia   ZBA

Aïcha Ben Abed Ben Khader, Chargée de recherche et Conservateur du Musée National du Bardo   ABABK

Ouassila Ben Osman-Bairem, Chargée de recherche, INAA, Tunisia   OBOB

Habib Ben Younes, Chargé de recherche, INAA, Tunisia   HBY

Alya Ben Younes-Krandel, Attachée de recherche, INAA, Tunisia   ABYK

Fethi Chelbi, Chargé de recherche, INAA, Tunisia   FC

Zohra Cherif, Attachée de recherche, INAA, Tunisia   ZC

Abdelmajid Ennabli, Maître de recherche, Conservateur du Musée et du site de Carthage   AE

Mongi Enneifer, Conservateur en chef des Musées de Tunisie   ME

M'Hamed Hassine Fantar, Directeur de recherche, INAA, Tunisia MF

Mansour Ghaki, Chargé de recherche, INAA, Tunisia MG

Mustapha Khanoussi, Chargé de recherche, INAA, Tunisia MK

Leila Ladjimi-Sebai, Chargée de recherche, INAA, Tunisia LLS

Mounira Riahi-Harbi, Maître de recherche et Sous Directeur, INAA, Tunisia MR

Hédi Slim, Maître de recherche et Directeur du Centre des Études Classiques et Byzantines, INAA, Tunisia HS

Latifa Slim, Chargée de recherche, INAA, Tunisia LS

American Consultants

Margaret A. Alexander, University of Iowa

David Grose, University of Massachusetts

Priscilla Molinari, University of Arizona

John Leonard, University of Arizona

Steven Krebs, University of Arizona

Richard Jensen, University of Arizona

Arielle Kozloff, Curator of Ancient Art, Cleveland Museum of Art

The exhibition on which this book is based has been funded in part by the National Endowment for the Humanities and is supported by an indemnity from the Federal Council on the Arts and Humanities. This catalog has been funded in part by a grant from the Samuel H. Kress Foundation.

First American Edition 1987

Library of Congress 87-71760
ISBN 0-913424-11-0

All photographs by Martha Cooper, 1987, except where noted:
Photographs by Mohammed Kefi: Catalogue 13, 14, 15, 61, 72
Photograph by Noelle Soren: Figure 6
Photograph by David Soren: Figure 7
Photograph by Julian Whittelessey: Figure 43

Design: Mark La Riviere, Homans Design, Inc.
Typsetting by Unicorn Graphics.
Printing by South Sea International Press.

The American Museum of Natural History
Central Park West at 79th Street
New York, New York   10024

W. W. Norton & Company, Inc.
500 Fifth Avenue
New York, New York   10110

W. W. Norton & Company Ltd.
37 Great Russell Street
London   WC1B3NU

I 2 3 4 5 6 7 8 9 0

Published simultaneously in Canada by Penguin Books Canada Ltd., 2801 John Street, Markham, Ontario L35 1B4.

Printed in Hong Kong.

Acknowledgments for maps.
The Mediterranean in antiquity, page 14.
Copyright © 1964 by Deutscher Taschenbuch Verlag GmbH & Co.

Map of the Punic Wars, page 32.
Excerpt from *Anchor Atlas of World History* edited by Hermann Kinder and Werner Hilgemann. Copyright © by Penguin Books, Ltd. Reprinted by permission of Doubleday & Company.

Contents

Dedication

To President Habib Bourguiba, Tunisia's greatest freedom fighter, with our hope for peace and warm relations always between our people and for all mankind.

Foreword

The Trustees and Staff of the American Museum of Natural History are
honored to bring *Carthage: A Mosaic of Ancient Tunisia* to the museum-
going public of our country. The exhibit contains the largest collection
of Tunisian objects ever shown in the United States. It represents
contributions from five Tunisian museums and uncounted hours of
scholarly work by dozens of Tunisian archaeologists, as well as those of
our American colleagues.

The story of ancient Carthage and her environs is vast and complex—
only vaguely perceived by most of us and understood by only a few. The
goal of this exhibit has been to present an accurate panorama of
Carthage's varied and splendid artistic achievements against a backdrop
of the events of the times and the struggles that surged across this part of
the African landscape.

Through *Carthage: A Mosaic of Ancient Tunisia*, the public may gain an
understanding of and empathy with an ancient city and its resilient,
creative people of long ago. It is presented as a gift of our two countries
to the cultural patrimony of the world.

Thomas D. Nicholson
Director, American Museum of Natural History

With this archaeological exhibition, *Carthage: A Mosaic of Ancient Tunisia*,
Tunisia sends a warm greeting to the American people. Thanks to the
generous cooperation of the American Museum of Natural History,
Tunisia, a friend to all peoples, is able here to tell the American public

something of its lands, people, struggles, and achievements and to show a rich portion of its heritage. Here, then, are some of the principal landmarks in Tunisia's fertile history, offered as a guide for the reader and visitor seeking to understand Tunisia's contributions to world civilization.

M'Hamed Hassine Fantar
Directeur Général de l'Institut National d'Archéologie et d'Art

Preface

Carthage: A Mosaic of Ancient Tunisia evolved from a desire of Thomas D. Nicholson, Director of the American Museum of Natural History in New York, to make a wider public aware of the extraordinary ancient culture and artistic treasures of Tunisia. Recent excavations by Tunisian and international teams resulted from a Tunisian appeal to UNESCO to save Carthage. Since 1973, a great deal of new information has been amassed, while discoveries in the hinterland of Tunisia also continued in a spectacular vein, especially in the area of mosaics.

The project was executed as a collaborative effort between the United States and Tunisia. Its format allows for a brief overview designed to acquaint the lay American public with the general outline of Carthage's history and cultural achievement, paying particular attention to the Berbers, the Punic people (Phoenician settlers), and the Romans. The second part, edited by Aïcha Ben Abed Ben Khader and supervised by M'Hamed Fantar, provides a Tunisian assessment of their own ancient land. Part three is the catalogue of the objects proper, prepared by the leading Tunisian specialists in consultation with American art historians.

We gratefully acknowledge the unfailing support of the Tunisian Ministry of Culture, the Embassy of the United States of America, and the United States Information Service in Tunis. Our thanks go to the numerous individuals who have been responsible for helping to develop and coordinate the exhibition, particularly Richard Schoonover, Director, and Robert Krill, Cultural Affairs Officer, USIS, Tunis; Margaret A. Alexander, Co-Director, *Corpus des Mosaiques de Tunisie*; Mongi Boulouednine, Chef de Service, INNA; Khemais Ben Amor and Mohammed el Aid, Supervisors, Musée du Bardo; Patricia Payne, Director, and Ann Mhenni, AMIDEAST, Tunis; Mohammed Kefi and

Noelle Soren, for excellent photos; Danielle and Elizabeth Krill, for assistance in Tunisia; the Hilton Hotel and Hertz Rent-a-Car in Tunis.

We also wish to thank our translators Vicki Reich, Ralph C. Whittum, Jr., and Diana Vergis. The manuscript was edited with the enormous contributions of Nancy Creshkoff and Colleen Mehegan. Thanks to Professors Albert Leonard, Jr., and Norman Yoffee for critical advice on the American material.

David Soren

Carthage
An American Overview

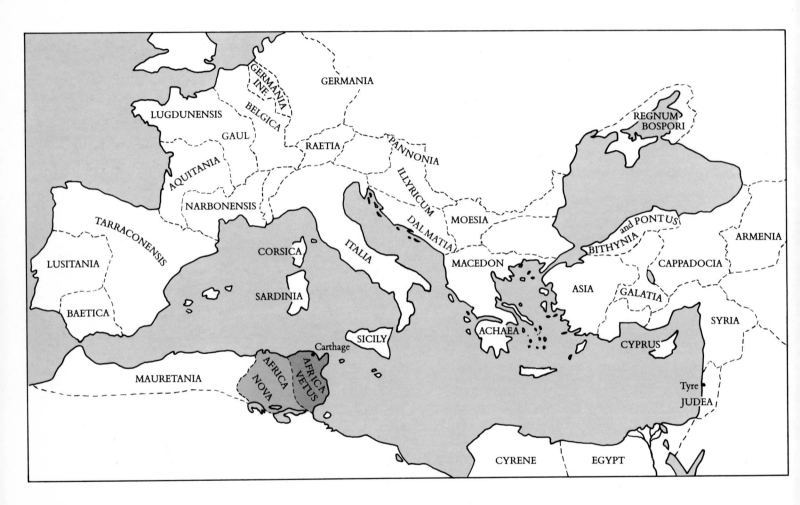

Figure 2. The Mediterranean in
antiquity.

Introduction

Carthage! The name conjures up images of Roman soldiers attacking lofty citadels, mighty ships sailing out to high adventure, and altars reeking with incense and the blood of human sacrifice. Gustave Flaubert visited Carthage in 1858—and was captivated by it. His novel *Salammbô*, finished in 1862, creates a "mirage of antiquity" based on his extensive reading, study, and fantasy.[1]

Today we better understand the city, its influence, and its legacy due to efforts of the Tunisian government and the National Institute of Archaeology and Art (INAA). Realizing that all vestiges of the ancient city would be lost in the wake of modern construction, the Tunisians approached UNESCO in the early 1970s. Soon distinguished archaeologists from many nations were vying for sites. The French took the Byrsa, the city's acropolis, an area investigated by French archaeologists since Flaubert's visit. Americans and British moved in on the ancient ports and the sanctuary of human sacrifices. The Germans excavated ancient Carthaginian houses near the seafront. Americans dug up the Roman ruins by the supermarket to the west of the main road. Canadians worked north of the theater. Nearby were Tunisians, Italians, Danes, and Swedes. French, Dutch, American, and Tunisian archaeologists explored the hinterland.[2]

Many of the recent discoveries as well as some classic earlier discoveries are presented here. The book tells primarily of three groups—the Libyans (now called Berbers), the Phoenicians (Punic people), and the Romans—and their struggles for supremacy over North Africa. Their successors, the Vandals and the Byzantines, appear as well. The Libyans (sometimes called the indigenous group) were in Tunisia first; their roots go back to the ninth millennium before Christ. The Phoenicians gradually took control and founded the city we know as Carthage in 1186 B.C.—the traditional date (Figure 2). The actual date is probably the later ninth century B.C. or even the eighth century. They named their city simply New City (Kart-Hadasht). Later, the Greeks called it Carchedon, and the Romans called it Carthago. The Phoenician colonizers (who came from the Tyre area in modern Lebanon) were known to the Romans as the *Poeni* (adj. *punicus*). In Latin, the name was usually accompanied by a word such as *foedifragi* (treacherous ones, treaty-breakers), which suggests what a biased opinion of the Punic people we get from the Romans. Therefore, the Punic Wars were for the Romans "*bella punica.*"

The list of Carthaginian contributions is long. The Carthaginians developed sophisticated agricultural techniques that were passed on to western civilization and that made Tunisia the breadbasket of the Roman Empire. They built magnificent ships that led to the creation of the Roman navy. Carthage's location at the tip of Tunisia made the city an international center for education and commerce. They invented true mosaics—a revelation of recent Tunisian and German excavations. They were respected and bold explorers, perhaps reaching England and Ireland. They produced military geniuses, some far superior to Roman military leaders (Figure 3).

The story of Carthage has inspired writers from Virgil to Chaucer and Marlowe and such musical composers as Berlioz and Purcell. Flaubert's *Salammbô* dealt romantically with a revolt in Carthage of mercenaries between the first two Punic Wars. Thea Von Harbou and Fritz Lang brought Flaubert to the movie screen in the German science fiction film *Metropolis* (1926), which compared the horrifying treatment of dehumanized laborers of the future to the Carthaginian rite of human sacrifice.

Figure 3. Plan of Tunisia showing ancient cities and modern counterparts.

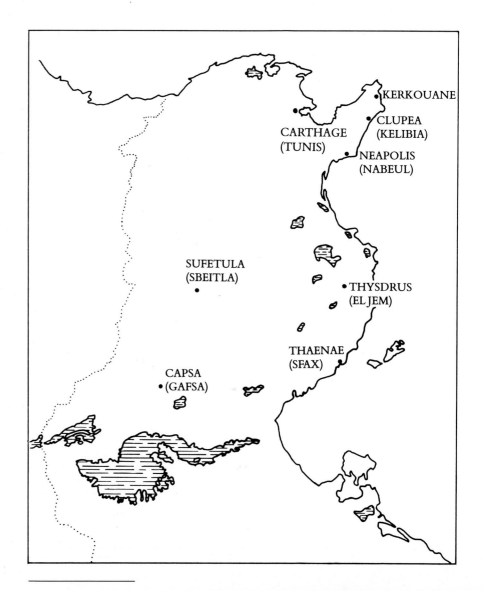

The names of some individual Carthaginians have become almost household words: Princess Elissa, known as Queen Dido and beloved of the Trojan wanderer Aeneas, and Mago, famous as an agricultural pioneer. Perhaps the best known is the great general of the Second Punic War, Hannibal, visionary and Roman-fighter. For centuries after his death, early in the second century B.C., a Roman feeling threatened or fearful could cry out, "Hannibal is at the gates"—and everyone would know what he meant.

Carthage was destroyed by the Romans in 146 B.C., but rose again—literally from the ashes. The city then became a colony for veterans who had served Roman Emperor Augustus.

The first through early third centuries A.D. saw Carthage become a splendid city again under Roman domination. In the third and fourth, as unrest and instability grew in the political, economic, and religious life of the Empire, Carthage became a center of Christianity and Christian controversy among various sects and people's movements. The fifth century brought a Vandal invasion led by King Gaiseric. In the sixth, Belisarius began the Byzantine occupation that would endure fitfully until yielding to the growing might of Islam in the next century. This invasion was to change the direction and appearance of Tunisia for good, and dynasties such as the Aghlabids brought a new golden age of culture and beauty.

From 1574 to 1881, the country was ruled by the Turks. It finally became a French protectorate and remained so until the successful revolution led by Habib Bourguiba and the Neo-Destour Party in 1956, when it became an independent republic, which it is today under President Bourguiba.

Throughout recent history, Tunisia has played a major role in Arab international affairs while still maintaining close relations outside the Islamic orbit. Although Tunisia's capital is now Tunis, Carthage is still a major international center and a resort that teems with elegant hotels, restaurants, sun worshippers, and cinema goers. The Queen Dido Hotel is located on the spot where Queen Dido is said to have laid out her city, acquired, according to tradition, from a Berber king. It now looks out over the Carthage Museum and the UNESCO-sponsored excavations. To the modern visitor, it is quite evident that—contrary to the demand of the Roman censor Cato—*Carthago non delenda est*: Carthage must not be destroyed!

The Landscape of Tunisia

Tunisia is the smallest of the North African countries and is bordered to the west by Algeria and to the east by Libya. The importance of Carthage in antiquity was due to its strategic location close to Sicily and Italy and near the mouth of the Medjerda River (then the Bagradas)—often depicted on Roman coins. The river runs through an incredibly fertile valley—the nourishing spine of Tunisia. This is the heart of the wheat- and olive-growing areas, and it was a source of food supplies for Rome. Starting near what was the Roman military camp of Timgad in eastern Algeria, the river continues through the ancient Libyan/Berber city of Dougga (Thugga) and northeast to Carthage and Utica, both of which were bustling ports, Punic and (later) Roman cities and strongholds and commercial centers.

Northeastern Tunisia is a mountainous promontory culminating in great sandstone and limestone quarries at Cape Bon. The Phoenician settlers used massive ashlar blocks from these quarries to link up curtains of rubble walls in a technique known as *opus Africanum*. The northwest has more mountains and a rainier and windier climate. The quarries, first exploited by the Libyans, include those at Chemtou near the Algerian border. These yielded a beautiful yellow and sometimes even pinkish marble (*giallo antico*) much prized by the Romans.

The eastern coast area (*Sahel* in Arabic) between Sousse (ancient Hadrumetum) and the fishing port of Mahdia to the south has a pleasant climate and attracts many tourists, especially from Germany. Mahdia was the site of a shipwreck in the early first century B.C.; bronze sculptures by major Hellenistic Greek artists (such as Boethos of Chalcedon) poured into the sea just off the coast. Mahdia was also part of a pottery-making region where an elegant African Red Slip Ware was produced in antiquity.[3]

Communities like Dougga and Thuburbo Maius in the Medjerda and Miliana River valleys are well-watered, fertile centers tucked amid rolling hills. Southward the land becomes increasingly arid and expansive. It is traveled today by semi-nomadic Berbers as well as tourists in search of the exotic. Desert towns delight the eye with colorful brickwork and oases. Gafsa (a traditional Berber stronghold) features flashy and gay native rugs, and one finds troglodyte houses in Matmata. The latter were featured in *Star Wars*, which was filmed in southern Tunisia by George Lucas. Young Luke Skywalker's home planet is known in the film as Foum Tatouine, which is really the name of a town in the foothills of the Sahara Desert. The Sand People in the same movie wear Berber robes (burnouses) from the area.

Countless peoples have roamed this varied land—Libyans, Phoenicians, Romans, Byzantines, Vandals, Arabs, Turks, French, and others. Today's Tunisian family seeking a pleasant evening might dine at one of numerous French restaurants (almost all urban Tunisians speak some French) and then go home to watch Italian television transmitted from Sicily.

The Libyans and the Berbers

The original settlers were Berbers, known in Tunisia as Libyans.[4] They were semi-nomads who lived off the land, tended flocks, and carried their wealth with them as they migrated seasonally to warmth, shelter, and food. According to Tunisian prehistorian Mme. Mounira Harbi-Riahi, the Berbers inhabited central Tunisia in the Capsian period—the ninth or eigth millennium B.C. (Capsa was the ancient name of Gafsa.) The term *Capsian* was formulated on the basis of 1909 investigations of the Gafsa site.

The Capsians lived in what the Tunisians call *rammadyat* near water sources (often by *oueds*, similar to washes in the American desert southwest). They often took refuge in natural outcroppings on mountainsides. Their land stretched for about a hundred miles north and east of Gafsa—an area particularly rich in flint. They used bones and flint to make tools and weapons. Remains can be found as far west as western Algeria and as far south as the northern Sahara. The Capsians, sometimes referred to as the Proto-Mediterraneans, began to spread across the Mahgreb (Morocco, Algeria, and Tunisia) in the eighth millennium. Rock engravings and sculptures like those found at El Mekta (near Gafsa) have been found and seem to date from the seventh millennium B.C. Elephants, rhinos, giraffes, and even buffaloes represented in this art stress the importance of hunting. Many of today's Berbers are descendants of these Capsians and inhabit Tunisia's rural areas. (The term *Berber* is a misnomer, since it is derived from the Greek *barbaros* and Latin *barbarus* and means any group that is foreign, strange, and savage.)

Many Tunisian Berbers speak their own dialects. They have no written literature, although numerous ancient Libyan inscriptions have been found. Many others know Arabic and/or French, and many have become assimilated into modern Tunisian life.

Today's Berbers prepare a popular Tunisian wheat dish beloved by Arabs throughout the Mahgreb. It is couscous and consists of a specially produced wheat product that is steamed over a spicy stew, usually containing lamb, vegetables, and tomatoes. Berbers may still also be seen gathering the snails that affix themselves to the walls of archaeological sites; in so doing, they are continuing a tradition that dates back to the Capsian period.

In ancient times, the Romans referred to Berber villages, little groupings around water sources, as *castella*. A Berber confederation (*aguellid*) under a powerful chieftain was not to be taken lightly by an enemy. Tunisia contained many aguellid refuges or strongholds (Ksour or Bordj).

Libyan chieftains might be distinguished by plumed crowns and jewelry such as pins (*fibulae*). Recent discoveries at Chemtou (Simitthus) have provided an invaluable guide to what the well-dressed Berber leader wore. Simitthus was founded by the Numidian Massyles, who may have been members of a larger confederation known as the Misciri. The cemetery (necropolis) provided material from the period between the fourth century B.C. and the Roman conquest. Tombs of the chamber type or the circular style (*bazinas*) occur, and there is also a series of squarish monuments on podia. The tombs have projecting entry walls (*antae*) and contain two chambers. A sanctuary was erected between 150 and 100 B.C. on one of the city's main hills—probably during the reign of Micipsa, son of Massinissa. A colossal altar, visible from a great distance, capped the hill. The altar combines Greco-Roman, Punic, and Egyptian motifs, and it was the first monument that used the famous Chemtou marble known as *marmor numidicum*.

Findings in 1979 included a funerary stele, probably from the first century B.C., now in the Chemtou Museum (Figure 4).[5] A horseman with full

Figure 4. Funerary stele of Numidian horseman dating to the first century B.C. and found in the region of Chemtou.

Figure 5. Votive relief of the seven Berber gods dating to the third century A.D. Bardo Museum. (Catalogue 3)

Figure 6. Libyo-Punic
Mausoleum at Dougga, probably
dating to the second century B.C.

beard is wearing a diadem and dressed in a long-sleeved tunic cut off at the thigh. An elegant mantle is bound over his right shoulder by a round fibula like those worn by Berber women today, and his stockings resemble those worn throughout the Mahgreb. His regal bearing and diadem give evidence that we are being given a rare glimpse of a Numidian Berber chieftain.

A 1967 Chemtou find sheds light on ancient Berber religion.[6] A bizarre stele dating roughly to the second or first century B.C. shows eight frontally facing divinities, each with what appears to be a full-blown Afro hairdo. Seven male gods and one goddess perhaps indicate what the Berber pantheon was like. An even more unusual companion piece is the bas relief of the seven Libyan gods from the Beja area; it dates perhaps to the third century A.D. (Figure 5). This piece, possibly the most unusual Berber monument in Tunisia, illustrates the cultural assimilation of the Berbers to the later Romans. It contains a dedication to seven Berber divinities, each with its own attributes; the dedication is written in Latin and signed by two citizens with Roman names. Names such as Bonchor (surrounded by two goddesses), Macurgam (with his serpent wand), and Matilam (to whom the ram was sacrificed) sound strange to us but must represent a thriving religious practice in Tunisia's hinterland during the height of the Roman occupation.

The Berbers were and still are noted for belief in demons, mystical potions, and spells. Villagers of Berber origin in El Fahs (near the ruins of Thuburbo Maius and Tunis) speak of love spells baked into cakes and of the Arbetha, a creature of the night who snatches children away on dark and stormy nights.

Although each aguellid differed in its customs, most were patriarchal, and polygamy was practiced. Many Berber groups are still patriarchal and polygamous. A man with seven children will not uncommonly say that he has five boys and two "other" rather than say that he has two girls. On the other hand, older women frequently command considerable respect and may wield influence in a community that generally respects its elders.

The Phoenicians and Romans have received most of the attention in the study of ancient Tunisian history, but the "indigenous ones" played an enormous role too. Both Phoenicians and Romans depended on their support. Berbers must have come into contact with Phoenician traders and settlers by the eighth century B.C., if not earlier. They gradually began to assimilate Phoenician customs and religion. Fiercely independent, upon occasion they would unify under a charismatic tribal leader (*Mas*) such as Massinissa.

When this occurred, Phoenicians and (later) Romans rushed to win over the Mas. Massinissa became so powerful in the eastern area of what is now Algeria after the Second Punic War that his influence at one time spread all across the interior of North Africa. Yet many of his communities worshipped Carthaginian deities alongside of the traditional Berber pantheons, and he modeled his government on that of Carthage.

After winning two Punic Wars, the Romans courted Berber tribes during the second century B.C. to extend their influence over lands outside of Punic control. The crafty Berber Micipsa, one of Massinissa's three sons, was familiar with Greek, Roman and Punic cultures. He allied himself with the Roman armies and was soon supplying them with hired soldiers, wheat, marble, wood, copper and even elephants. Micipsa helped the Romans get a stranglehold on his region even before the end of the Roman Republic. He may have developed Dougga (Thugga) and built a sanctuary there (Figure 6). The city later became an important Roman community. Right in the middle of town and dominating the view to the south is a monumental tower tomb nearly three stories high, the Libyo-Punic Mausoleum, which dates from the epoch of Massinissa and his sons, the period of the great Berber hegemony over the North African hinterland. This extraordinary structure is the best surviving example of its type and contains an inscription (today in the British Museum) in a script that shows the influence of both the Libyan and Punic peoples. We do not know to whom the mausoleum was dedicated, but it was built by someone probably of Punic origin; the architect has signed the work as Ateban, son of Iepmatath.[7]

Hundreds of tower tombs dotted the ancient Tunisian landscape, but this one appears to be the oldest and is the most interesting. A second Libyo-Punic inscription from Dougga (now in the Bardo Museum) was built into a Byzantine fort near the Roman forum. It appears to refer to a temple erected to Massinissa in about 140 B.C. and supports the theory that the mausoleum, with its regal lion atop, honored one of the princes of this royal family.

Massinissa's grandson was the legendary Berber warlord Jugurtha. Jugurtha had a Roman education, thanks to Scipio Aemilianus, the Roman general who destroyed Carthage. He also had dreams of establishing a Numidian empire and replacing that of Carthage. Feuding with Micipsa's two sons, Jugurtha attacked the Berber capital city of Cirta (today's Constantine in eastern Algeria) in 112 B.C. Many Roman citizens were slaughtered. Jugurtha, fearing reprisals, went to Rome to apologize and plead his case—in Latin—before the Senate. But he continued to be troublesome for the Romans throughout Algeria and Tunisia. The Roman general Marius, a leader of Rome's working classes, led a counterattack, storming the Berber center of Gafsa in 107 B.C. Mauretanian tribes attacked from the west. Jugurtha's dream of an empire evaporated. He was taken to Rome, thrown into prison in the Tullianum on the slope of the Capitoline Hill, and finally strangled.

The last great Berber chieftains of classical antiquity were members of the aguellid of Jugurtha and unusual individuals indeed. Freed from the Carthaginian yoke and friendly with the Romans, Juba I enjoyed a luxurious life at his capital of Zama, about one hundred miles southwest of Tunis and the site of the last great battle of the Second Punic War more than one hundred years earlier. When the Roman political scene degenerated into chaos and civil wars in the first century B.C., Juba took the side of the famous general Pompey the Great and fought against the partisans of Pompey's rival Julius Caesar in the waning days of the Roman Republic. With the beginning of the Roman Empire under Augustus in 31 B.C., young Juba II became the emperor's ward and brings our portrait of ancient Berbers to a distinguished and surprisingly sophisticated and refined ending.

So eclectic were his tastes, talents, and interests that he knew Greek and Latin, more languages than most Roman citizens knew. Even more amazingly, he married the beautiful daughter of Antony and Cleopatra, sent the first expedition to the Canary Islands, and searched for the source of the Nile!

After the Roman destruction of Carthage in 146 B.C., Provincia Africa was created. Its southern limit was marked by the Fossa Regia or Fossa Scipionis. This border ran along the valley of the Oued Khalled. Dougga was barely excluded; it remained under Libyan control but had numerous Punic sanctuaries. Partly because so many Libyan communities had supported Pompey, Caesar extended the Fossa (literally, a ditch) farther to the south, and Dougga was officially under Roman control as part of a new province Africa Nova. Africa Nova included areas as much as a hundred miles south of Gafsa and a large secction of present-day eastern Algeria. In 26 B.C., Emperor

Figure 7. Berber woman of El Jem making pottery in the Neolithic tradition.

Augustus combined Old Africa (Africa Vetus) and the Caesarian extension into one entity, Africa Proconsularis. For a time, the great Libyan empires were under control.

Although Berber tribes continued to play an important role in later Roman and even Islamic history in Tunisia, they are a small, peaceful, and partially assimilated group today. One can happen upon some unlikely contrasts of the old and new worlds. On the cramped, winding streets of El Jem, a Tunisian teenager listens to the Rolling Stones on a transistor radio, and a Berber woman makes pottery—using the simple, generations-old coiling technique to make functional low-fired housewares (Figure 7). Clay is obtained on a quick camel trip to the local oued. The equipment and ingredients are basic: a bread oven, flat pieces of wood, clay, ash for temper and perhaps a tiny bit of ground-up straw. The locals call this "women's pottery" to distinguish it from the flashier and more commercial wares turned out by the men, who have more sophisticated equipment. As her neighbors' son warms to Mick Jagger's music, this woman with her tattoos and native dress follows a tradition virtually unchanged since the Neolithic Period.

Figure 8. In this altar relief sculpture, probably of the early first century A.D., Aeneas is shown leaving Troy with his son Ascanius and carrying his father, Anchises. Found on the Byrsa Hill in Carthage, this sculpture is in the Bardo Museum.

The Phoenicians and Punic Carthage

The rise of Carthage as mistress of the seas and commerce, land of human sacrifice, and terror of Rome is associated with the Phoenicians.[8] From at least the eighth century B.C., and traditionally earlier (1186 B.C.), port areas such as Utica and Carthage were settled by these Near Eastern navigators and traders from cities such as Tyre. No doubt they were seeking trading centers (*emporia*) and steppingstones to Spain and southern Portugal (the fabled Tartessos). The Semitic Phoenicians had risen to power in the area of Tyre in the eleventh century B.C. when the Hittite empire to the north relaxed its grip on the eastern Mediterranean Canaanite areas. They became master merchants. Through trade, they transmitted their alphabet to the developing Greek world (definitively influencing our own language).

Legend has it that Princess Elissa of Tyre (later Queen Dido) founded Carthage. She had married her uncle Acherbas, high priest of the city god Melqart. Her brother, King Pygmalion, murdered Acherbas for his fortune. Elissa and a group of followers escaped to Cyprus and then went on to found New City (Carthage). Our oldest version of the event is from a history of Sicily by the Sicilian-Greek writer Timaeus early in the third century B.C.[9] He had the advantage of being close to Carthaginian sources, and according to

Figure 9. Plan of ancient
Carthage showing principal
Punic and Roman monuments.

him, Dido settled on land provided by the local king. He allotted her as much land as the hide of an ox could enclose, so she cut the animal's hide into strips. When laid end to end, the strips enclosed an area big enough for a fortress. Then, rather than marry the king, she threw herself on a funeral pyre.

The fortress came to be known as the Byrsa; *Bursa* in Greek means "hide stripped from an ox." The Carthage hill known today as the Byrsa is indeed the site of traces of Punic civilization going back to the eighth century.

According to the Romans and the Augustan poet Virgil in particular, Queen Dido fell in love with Aeneas, who was trying to fulfill his destiny—to found an Italian nation after the Mycenean Greeks had destroyed his native Troy in the twelfth century B.C. Virgil describes Aeneas's first experience with Carthage in the *Aeneid*. (See Figures 8 and 9.) The goddess Venus tells him where he has landed:

You see Carthaginian dominions, the Tyrians and the city of Agenor, but the territories are Libyan [Libyci], a people fierce [intractibile] in war....[The Tyrians] have come to places where now you will see huge walls, and the rising tower of new Carthage.[10]

Aeneas climbs up what is probably the Byrsa Hill:

...which looms largely over the city and faces the towers opposite. Aeneas admires the heaped up buildings where once had stood only cottages; he admires the gates and the bustle about the city streets. The ardent Tyrians press on with their construction, some of them extending the walls and erecting a tower, rolling up the stones with their hands, while others prepare a building site and enclose it with a trench. They are choosing sites for their lawcourts and magistrate offices and of course their sacred senate house. Here some dig harbors and there others lay the deep foundations for theaters as huge columns are cut out from rocks to become lofty decorations for future stage façades.[11]

Virgil's description of the original city of Carthage was written at least seven hundred years after the event and more than a hundred years after the Romans destroyed the city. His description is more in keeping with the layout of a Roman city of his *own* time; the theaters he mentions were not built for hundreds of years after the founding of Dido's alleged city. However, when he describes "a sacred grove in the midst of the city, most pleasant for its shade" where there was "built to the goddess Juno a huge temple," he may be on firmer footing (Figures 10 and 11). Juno/Caelestis was the Romanized name of the Punic Tanit; she became increasingly powerful from the fourth century B.C. on and apparently was firmly fixed in the Roman mind as the patroness of Carthage. Throughout Virgil's epic, she tries to keep him from fulfilling his destiny. Seeking to stop him, Juno encourages him to dally with the Carthaginian queen during a hunting expedition, but Mercury arrives and presses Aeneas onward. And the bereft Dido hurls herself on a funeral pyre.

The story has been retold many times. Dido was a symbol of unrequited love in Chaucer's *Legend of Good Women* in the fourteenth century, and Marlowe wrote a noteworthy *Tragedy of Dido* in the later sixteenth.

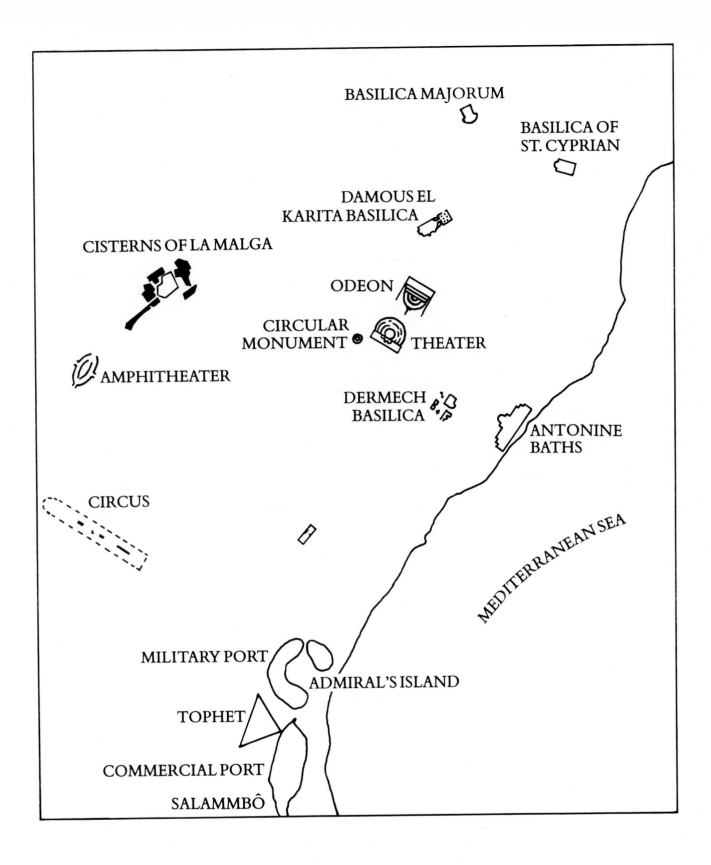

BASILICA MAJORUM

BASILICA OF
ST. CYPRIAN

DAMOUS EL
KARITA BASILICA

CISTERNS OF LA MALGA

ODEON

CIRCULAR
MONUMENT   THEATER

AMPHITHEATER

DERMECH
BASILICA

ANTONINE
BATHS

CIRCUS

MEDITERRANEAN SEA

MILITARY PORT

ADMIRAL'S ISLAND

TOPHET

COMMERCIAL PORT

SALAMMBÔ

Figure 10. View of the Byrsa Hill
in Carthage.

Berlioz and Purcell celebrated her in operas based on Virgil's *Aeneid*.

Carthage expanded in the eighth and seventh centuries B.C. to nearby Sicily and Sardinia and more distant ports in Spain (Gadès, now modern Cadiz), Morocco (Lixus), and the Balearic Islands (Ibiza). Expansion eastward was followed by settlements in Libya (Lpqy, or Lepcis Magna, and Ui, now Tripoli). As Carthage's fortunes increased, so did problems in the mother city of Tyre. With the ninth-century B.C. rise of Assyria, tribute, failed revolts, and prolonged Assyrian blockades crippled Tyre, and Sidon became the more prominent city after 700 B.C. Furthermore, the Greeks and Etruscans continually disrupted Phoenician westward expansion. A thirteen-year siege by the Babylonians (587–574 B.C.) was a prelude to an attack and domination by the Persians. In 334 B.C., Tyre was crushed by the Macedonian general Alexander the Great; many of its people were massacred, and the rest were sold into slavery. No more would Tyre be mistress of the seas.

Meanwhile, the Carthaginians were making alliances. The most important was with the Etruscans of north central Italy against the increasingly dangerous Greeks, particularly the Phocaeans who had founded Massalia (Marseilles) late in the seventh century B.C. Gradually a new force began to

Figure 11. View over the Punic ports of Carthage.

emerge: the Romans. They had grown from a small eighth-century B.C. community of shepherds to become a power to reckon with, able to free themselves from Etruscan rulers who had dominated them throughout the sixth century B.C. But it would be several hundred years before Rome could get a toehold throughout Italy and then look westward and southward for more territory to conquer.

In the sixth century B.C., Carthage was the largest and richest city in the western Mediterranean, but its ruling class was preoccupied: Greek colonies had sprouted all over southern Italy and Sicily. Powerful and independent tyrants such as Gelon of Syracuse posed a great threat. The Carthaginians, trusting in a powerful navy, attacked Sicily in 480 B.C. At the battle of Himera off the Sicilian coast, their fleet suffered disastrous defeat. Carthage was forced to curb its appetite for expansion overseas. Up until this time, Carthaginians had been explorers and traders, plying the western Mediterranean and even the Atlantic and exchanging textiles, Cornish tin, and west African gold and ivory. One of Carthage's greatest sailors and explorers was Hanno the Navigator. His expeditionary voyage—probably in the early fifth century B.C.—along the African west coast took him at least as far as Senegal. Upon his return to Carthage, he erected a stone tablet at the temple to the god Baal; here he described his voyage in the Punic language. The account was translated into Greek; it still survives and is known as the *Periple of Hanno*. (The Greek word *periple* means "sailing around."[12])

Following the defeat at Himera, Carthage adopted an isolationist policy. Carthaginians moved southward, increasing contact with indigenous populations and setting up farms; they spread their form of government and religion all along the Medjerda River valley.

The fourth century B.C. was a time of great expansion throughout Carthage. Two harbors were created. One accommodated the rebuilt Punic fleet; the other was for a renewed commercial program.

In the second century A.D., Appian of Alexandria wrote a history of the Roman Empire. Following an earlier account by Polybius, he gave this account of the port area of Carthage just before its destruction by Rome.

The harbors had communication with each other, and a common entrance from the sea seventy feet wide, which could be closed with iron chains. The first port was for merchant vessels, and here were collected all kinds of ships' tackle. Within the second port was an island, and great quays were set at intervals round both the harbor and the island. These embankments were full of shipyards which had capacity for 220 vessels. In addition to them were magazines for their tackle and furniture. Two Ionic columns stood in front of each dock, giving the appearance of a continuous portico to both the harbor and the island. On the island was built the admiral's house, from which the trumpeter gave signals, the herald delivered orders, and the admiral himself oversaw everything. The island lay near the entrance to the harbor and rose to a considerable height, so that the admiral could observe what was going on at sea, while those who were approaching by water could not get any clear view of what took place within. Not even incoming merchants could see the docks at once, for a double wall enclosed them, and there were gates by which merchant ships could pass from the first port to the city without traversing the dockyards. Such was the appearance of Carthage at that time.[13]

The harbors still exist and—thanks to recent excavations sponsored by Cambridge University and the Chicago Oriental Institute—we know a great deal about the Carthage of this time. Excavations under Henry Hurst's direction have confirmed Appian's description and established that the ports of Carthage were magnificent technical achievements. Some 120,000 cubic meters of earth were moved to make the rectangular merchant harbor and another 115,000 to make the circular harbor. The earth and timber slipways in which ships from the water's edge were brought up to the central island of the military port have been found. Much of the area seems to have suffered from a renewed elevation in sea level—perhaps in the Roman imperial period—and much filling in occurred in the sixth century A.D.

The new ports were a symbol for a resurgent city-empire. The memory of the defeat by the Sicilian Greeks in 480 B.C. did not deter a new generation of Carthaginian leaders from trying again. Carthage had kept a small foothold in western Sicily following the defeat. The Greek city-state Syracuse tolerated this under such leaders as Dionysius I (407–367). But Agathocles (317–289) deemed Carthaginian influence unacceptable. He was a powerful and magnetic figure who had risen from immigrant potter to master of Sicily, and the Carthaginians stood in his way. In 310 B.C., he blockaded and invaded Carthage. The Carthaginians, led by Hamilcar, attacked Syracuse. The assault failed, and Hamilcar was killed. But the Syracusan siege of Carthage was no more successful; it dragged on for month after month.

During the Syracusan blockade, to obtain the favor of the gods, particularly the city's patron gods—Baal Hammon and Tanit—the Carthaginians sacrificed at least five hundred infants in a rite known as Moloch or Molk. The Carthaginians placed the charred bones of children up to four years of age in ceramic urns with small offerings such as bead necklaces and amulets of imported amber, gold, silver, carnelian, and steatite (a reminder of the city's trade connections). The urns were buried in the Tophet, a cemetery near the ports. According to the historian Diodorus Siculus, writing in the first century B.C., five hundred children were sacrificed. Two hundred were from noble families and three hundred from lesser citizens who volunteered their offspring to escape accusation.[14]

The sacrifice of children for religious beliefs was not unknown, of course. For example, the Greek King Agamemnon sacrificed his daughter Iphigenia, and in Hebrew tradition Abraham sought to sacrifice his beloved son Isaac. But the sheer volume of Punic sacrifices staggers visitors.

Carthage had to keep up the pressure on Sicily because it was the vital steppingstone to Italy, an important center for international commerce and a place where enemies could gather within easy striking distance. Syracuse weakened after Agathocles' death, and the Punic fleet sailed into its harbor in 279 B.C. Pyrrhus, the king of Epirus and Agathocles' son-in-law, rushed to the scene, but his hands were already full with the expansionist-minded Romans.

He used his powerful fleet and his land force (which included Indian elephants) to drive out the Carthaginian invaders. Holdouts were the Carthaginian stronghold of Lilybaion on Sicily's western tip and Messana. Pyrrhus won battle after battle but never the war. His ability to win battles but never deal the fatal blow has given rise to our term *Pyrrhic victory.*

Syracuse was caught in the middle. Hiero II (275–216 B.C.) was faced with the menace of Carthage and the threat of Rome. Soon the two rising giants would be locked in the Punic Wars (Figure 12). On the eve of the First Punic War, Messana was the major bone of contention. The Strait of Messana served as the only passageway between Sicily and Italy. Without it, ships would have to detour all around Sicily to get to Greece or Italy.

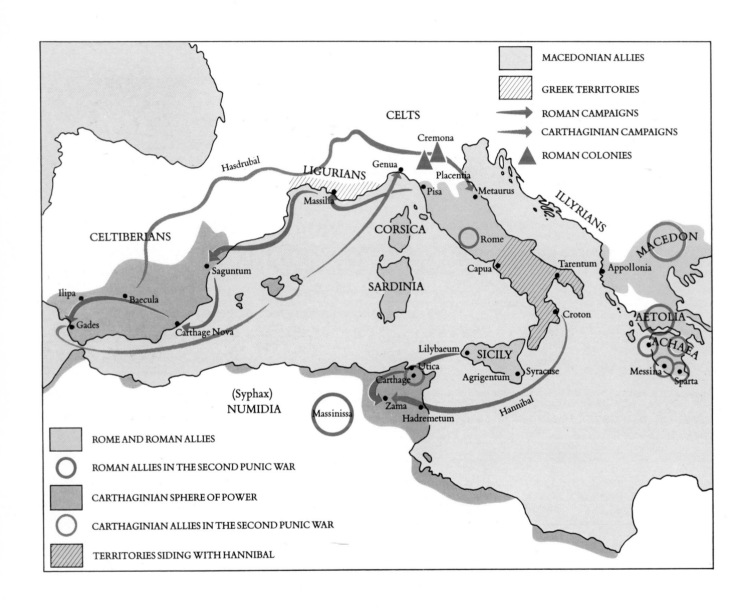

MACEDONIAN ALLIES

GREEK TERRITORIES

ROMAN CAMPAIGNS

CARTHAGINIAN CAMPAIGNS

ROMAN COLONIES

CELTS

Cremona

Genua

Hasdrubal

LIGURIANS

Placentia

Pisa

Metaurus

ILLYRIANS

Massilia

CELTIBERIANS

CORSICA

Rome

MACEDON

Saguntum

SARDINIA

Capua

Tarentum

Appollonia

Ilipa

Baecula

Gades

Croton

AETOLIA

Carthage Nova

ACHAEA

Lilybaeum

SICILY

Messina

Utica

Sparta

Carthage

Agrigentum

Syracuse

(Syphax)
NUMIDIA

Massinissa

Zama

Hadremetum

Hannibal

ROME AND ROMAN ALLIES

ROMAN ALLIES IN THE SECOND PUNIC WAR

CARTHAGINIAN SPHERE OF POWER

CARTHAGINIAN ALLIES IN THE SECOND PUNIC WAR

TERRITORIES SIDING WITH HANNIBAL

Figure 12. Map of the Second
Punic War, 202 B.C.

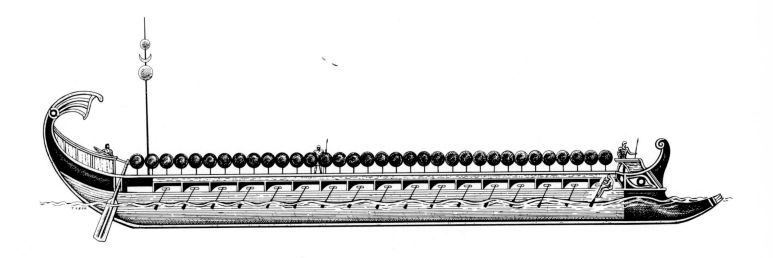

Figure 13. Drawing of Punic
warship of about 241 B.C.

The Carthaginian ruling class at this time was composed of wealthy merchant families. Their government included a senate, an inner council to direct public affairs, a high court, civil magistrates (*suffetes*), and a people's assembly. The great families controlled the military and increasingly used mercenaries and Libyans. Now Messana was caught between its own ruling group of Mamertines (southern Italian mercenaries), Syracusan invaders, and potential invaders such as the Romans. Carthage offered help and drove out the forces of Hiero II.

Hiero then allied with Rome and cut Carthage off from the straits. The Carthaginians then launched a land assault on the south coast and the major city of Agrigentum.

The ancient historians Thucydides and Pliny describe the Punic fleet that brought Carthaginian troops to Sicily. It was the most renowned in the Mediterranean, easily outclassing the primitive Roman fleet—until the Romans found a Carthaginian vessel run aground on a sand bar and hastily copied it. With astonishing speed, they built a similar fleet and won a series of naval engagements that turned the tide of the war. One occurred in 241 B.C.—the Battle of the Egadi Islands, off the coast of Marsala in western Sicily. Some fifty Punic ships went down.

In 1969 a small commercial dredging vessel struck the remains of an ancient ship. English nautical archaeologist Honor Frost was summoned to the scene. She unearthed a remarkably well-preserved Punic warship lying amid fragments of other such vessels (Figure 13).

The ship was 115 feet in length, with a row of seventeen oars on each side, each probably manned by two sailors—a total of more than sixty-eight rowers; including supervisors and fighting men, a Punic warship probably carried over one hundred men. The keel contained a battering ram—for impaling other ships; it was disposable and fit into a breakaway arrangement so that the ship would be safe if the ram broke off. Another important conclusion is that Punic ships probably were constructed from models and prefabricated and thus could be built quickly and simultaneously—according to Frost, "a degree of industrial organization not again recorded until the Industrial Revolution." The sailors lived on a high-protein diet of oxen, sheep, goats, and pigs. The discovery of a bundle of cannabis sticks suggests that their long days at sea may have been made less painful by frequent cups of marijuana tea. Radiocarbon dates of circa 235 B.C. helped to identify the ship, as did Punic inscriptions providing building instructions on its sides.

As the war dragged on, Hamilcar Barca, a young Carthaginian officer, took control as the chief of Punic operations in Sicily. He conducted guerrilla raids on Italy; in response, the Romans built Brundisium (Brindisi) into a port city. Defeat of the Punic fleet forced Carthage to agree to terms in 241 B.C. An indemnity was paid to Rome, and Sicily became a Roman province.

Carthage was far from finished, however. In the wake of the war came civil disaffection. The mercenary soldiers and the loose confederation of Libyan aguellids in the interior rebelled. Overseas, Sardinia broke free from the Punic yoke; by 238 B.C., it was in Roman hands and, along with Corsica, became the second Roman province a year later. (It is this period of time that captured Gustave Flaubert's imagination and led to *Salammbô*.) The Romans could justifiably boast that the Tyrrhenian Sea was theirs (*mare nostrum*). Sicily was by far the plum of the Roman conquests; its agriculture helped to sustain Rome for several centuries. But the Romans had troubles, too—freedom fighters in the newly captured islands and Gallic tribes threatening in the north. Secretly, Carthage was rearming under Hamilcar Barca. He took advantage of Carthage's ties with the Phoenician-settled south coast of Spain and developed a Punic empire by using these coastal footholds to gain access to the interior settled by indigenous Iberians and immigrant Celts.

Copper and silver mines were the attraction—as they had been to the Phoenicians. Their wealth could remedy the depressed postwar Punic economy, and mercenaries were easily obtainable. Hamilcar and his son-in-law Hasdrubal advanced into the area near Gades (Cadiz, near Gibraltar) and continued up the Ebro River. Soon Hamilcar had founded his own new city (Carthago Nova, modern Cartagena).

When Hasdrubal died in 221, Hamilcar's twenty-five-year-old son Hannibal became commander of the Punic forces in Spain. Hannibal's name would soon strike terror into the hearts of Romans, and his military prowess and durability became an international legend that has endured to modern times. A 1954 musical had his life as its subject, with Howard Keel playing

Hannibal; and his biography was filmed in 1960 with Victor Mature in the title role. At least two biographies have been published recently. In 219 B.C., once the Carthaginians felt strong enough to expand in Spain, Hannibal marched on Saguntum on the east coast. The Romans protested and threatened, but the city fell; Rome declared war in 218, and thus began the Second Punic War. Hannibal headed for Italy—by land. With his well-drilled troops and a number of elephants, he headed away from an advancing Roman army and marched directly across the Alps, despite ice, snow, and hostile Ligurian tribes. The route that he took is still a mystery. Attempts to locate it (even using elephants) have not succeeded, although Montgenèvre Pass and the Col de la Traversette have been proposed. The undertaking was so difficult that Hannibal was thought to have magic powers and that he could, with chemicals, dissolve boulders.

The Romans sent out a northern expedition into the Po River valley under Publius Cornelius Scipio, scion of one of Rome's great fighting families; the Roman army was humiliated by Hannibal. (To make matters worse, Rome's Gallic tribes revolted.) Caius Flaminius, from another of Rome's fine families and with a good record against rebellious tribes (the Insubres of northern Italy, for example) was sent to fight. His forces proved no match for Hannibal, and he himself was killed at Lake Trasimene in central Etruria north of Rome. Hannibal had drawn within 150 miles of the Roman capital.[15]

The Romans launched a major offensive at Cannae in southern Italy. Their forces outnumbered Hannibal's by six to one, but Hannibal won again. The Romans were in near panic. By 216, they had lost more than a hundred thousand men. They began to realize that Hannibal was a military genius.

Hannibal's hope was to win a number of battles and then rely on Italian communities to rebel, but few did so. Capua embraced him and fed his weary troops. Lucania and Bruttium in southern Italy gave him consistent support. His dream of defeating the Romans with a people's revolt never caught on. His strongholds of Capua and Tarentum fell—a serious blow, for Capua was the Rome of southern Italy, and Tarentum was critically located. His brother's attempt to send reinforcements failed utterly.

Carthage was forced to ally with its traditional enemy, Syracuse, but Syracuse fell to Rome in 211 B.C. The Roman general Marcellus had invaded the city in 213 and had been repulsed by anti-siege weapons created by Archimedes, a brilliant Syracusan mathematician and inventor; he was murdered by the Romans when the city fell. The Romans formulated a plan to counterattack Carthaginian communities in Spain. The Scipio family, whose monumental tomb adorns Rome's Appian Way, sent two formidable commanders, Publius Cornelius and Gnaeus, to cripple Hannibal's sources of reinforcements. Both died in the effort. In 211, Publius Cornelius Scipio's younger son took over. Bearing his father's name and bent on revenge, young Publius won a series of decisive triumphs in Spain, then courted local Numidian chieftains in eastern Algeria and made plans to invade Carthaginian territory. Publius landed near Utica in 204 B.C. The Punic defenders were short-handed, since Hannibal was in southern Italy and his brother Mago was in northern Italy. Their only hope was the Numidian chieftain Syphax, rival of the fiery Roman supporter Massinissa. Carthage brought in mercenaries from Spain to assist Syphax—to no avail. Syphax lost his capital at Cirta (Constantine in modern Algeria) to Massinissa in 203 B.C., and Carthage recalled Hannibal and Mago.

A year later, the scene was set for a final showdown between Hannibal and the young Publius Scipio. At the Libyan stronghold of Zama, a hundred miles south of modern-day Tunis, the Roman forces completely destroyed the Punic/Libyan alliance. Outmanned and outfinanced, Hannibal almost won anyway. Sixteen years of struggle ended for him and his men.

The End of the Second Punic War in 202 B.C.

In fact, Hannibal survived Zama, and ancient accounts report him next in Syria, where he commanded a Punic fleet for the Seleucid king Antiochus—planning another land invasion of Italy with a Seleucid army from the eastern Mediterranean. In 186 B.C., Hannibal commanded a fleet for King Prusias of Bithynia (in northwest Asia Minor near the Black Sea). The old Roman-hater, now seventy years old, was tracked down by the Roman Senate in 183 B.C. and forced to take poison. But he lingered in the Roman mind for centuries. For sheer tenacity, there had been no one like him. He has inspired paintings by the neoclassicist Poussin, as well as Turner, and every Victorian schoolboy learned about Hannibal leading his elephants across the Alps. What they did not learn is that the elephants' failure to perform well at Zama helped turn the tide of the battle against Carthage.

The Romans never forgot the bitter struggle or loss of life, and there was constant fear that Carthage—with or without Hannibal—would rise again. When Carthage ran into conflict with the pro-Roman Numidian chieftain Massinissa, a new war broke out in the Carthaginian countryside. *Carthago delenda est!* (Carthage must be destroyed!) became a rallying cry led by the censor Cato the Elder.[16] Aemilianus, another member of the Scipio family, led the invasion. Carthage was too feeble to resist effectively but tried; it was destroyed after almost a week of intense fighting in 146 B.C. Traces of ash up to three centimeters in thickness are found all along the harbor area, and there is extensive debris on the Byrsa as well. The survivors were sold into slavery; Utica, another coastal town, replaced Carthage as principal city of the region; and the former lands of Carthage became a new Roman province.

The dreams of the Barca family ended in the ashes of Carthage. A new and perhaps even more beautiful city would rise, but not for almost two hundred years—and that city would be Roman. Still, Carthaginian religion and culture, known as Neo-Punic, would continue to influence the country's interior for centuries to come.

One final episode closed out the story of Punic Carthage as it had begun. Sophonisbe, wife of the last Carthaginian general, Hasdrubal, refused to follow her husband's example and surrender to the Romans on the Byrsa. She, together with her two small sons, threw herself onto a funeral pyre just as Dido had done in the city's first days. The annihilation of Carthage has been described by Professor M'hamed Fantar, Director of the Institut National d'Archéologie et d'Art as the "Hiroshima of antiquity."

David Soren

1. Flaubert, 1963, p.XIII.

2. Ennabli, 1986, pp. 184–190.

3. For Mahdia, see Yacoub, 1978; pp.241–259 with full bibliography.

4. On the Berbers, see Saumagne, 1966, André–Julien, 1972 pp. 9–29; Cornevin, 1967, pp.13–59, 122–141.

5. 30 *Ans 1986* p.136.

6. 30 *Ans 1986* p.137.

7. Poinssot 1983 pp.58–61.

8. For a survey of the Phoenician culture, see Harden, 1965, Moscati, 1965, Herm, 1975.

9. Karl Müller, *Fragmenta Historicorum Graecorum*, I. p. 197, fr.23. (Paris, 1841)

10. Virgil, *Aeneid* 1.335 ff.

11. Virgil, *Aeneid* 1.419 ff.

12. For an English translation and general account of the Periple, see UNESCO Courier 1970, pp. 14–15.

13. Appian, *Libyca 96* quoted in Hurst, 1978, p. 341.

14. Stager, 1980, pp. 1–11.

15. On Hannibal, see Warmington, 1960, pp.164–195; Dorey, 1972 with bibliography; Toynbee, 1965; Picard, 1958.

16. Warmington, 1960, p. 202

The Punic City of Carthage

The Byrsa

The Byrsa Hill overlooks the Punic harbors of the fourth century B.C. as well as the Tophet for human sacrifices to the south.[17] Downtown Tunis can be glimpsed to the west on a clear day. To the southwest are the small mountains (*djebels*) of Zaghouan, a source of remarkably pure water carried long distances by aqueducts in Roman times, and Bou Kornine, a name suggesting that the mountain's double summit was consecrated to Baal Karnine, the two-horned Punic god. A sanctuary area there was, in Roman times, dedicated to Saturn Balcarnensis, showing a fusing of the names of a Roman and a Punic deity. Today Bou Cornine relays a television signal from ancient Tunisia's onetime arch rival—Sicily.

For more than a hundred years, the Byrsa has been excavated by French archaeologists, starting with the White Fathers in the early days of the French Protectorate. In addition to the cathedral erected by Cardinal Lavigerie, there is a chapel to Saint Louis, the pious king who died of plague in Carthage in A.D. 1270 during the Crusades. The Byrsa has long been and continues to be an intellectual and religious center; an important Eucharist congress was held there as recently as 1930. The *scholasticon* became a center for the study of ancient Carthage and, after Tunisian independence, became the site of the Carthage Museum, now headed by Prof. A. Ennabli.

The French excavations have uncovered numerous traces of Punic occupation. Prof. Serge Lancel has carefully documented Punic housing of not long after Hannibal's time that had regular gridded planning. He also uncovered a large Roman terracing operation to completely remodel the top of the Byrsa and obliterate the Punic monuments, including the Temple of Eshmoun, reputedly the most elegant temple in Carthage. There is much we will never know about the Byrsa; it will always be a magic spot, filled with memories—a center of Punic religious and political power.

There is considerable evidence of massive expansion in the fourth century B.C. The ports were built then. An inscription describing a new gate and streets has been found. Professor Rakob of the German Archaeological Institute in Rome has uncovered the remains of Punic housing that seems to be of a rather elegant nature.

Figure 14. View from the Byrsa Hill.

Work near the theater by the Tunisian archaeologist F.Chelbi has led to abundant evidence of entire floors paved with polychrome mosaics, suggesting that the Punic people invented the true mosaic. Previously, pebble mosaics had been used to form decorative patterns in Greek floors—possibly a tradition passed on from the Phrygians. But stones (*tesserae*) cut to fit floor patterns were not commonplace in the Greek world until the third century B.C., when they begin to show up at Morgantina and, in the second century, at Delos. Since Morgantina is in Sicily, we may assume that mosaics were a result of the Punic presence in that country at that time. An example of Carthaginian mosaic features tiny squares of terra cotta tile or reddish-colored ceramic (*opus figlinum*) dotted with white marble cubes. This section of flooring is bordered by a polychrome band in a checkerboard pattern.[18]

Found in a drainage channel that ran through the Punic ports area, seeds—figs, grapes, pomegranates, olives, peaches, plums, melons, Libyan lotus, almonds, pistachios, filberts, and cereals—give an idea of what was grown and consumed. Many were no doubt propagated by grafting, confirming the Carthaginians' reputation in the ancient world as skilled agriculturalists. Mago's twenty-eight books on agriculture, written in the fifth century B.C., were enormously respected by the Roman writers Pliny and Columella.

The Tophet

The Tophet—the place of human sacrifice just to the west of the commercial port—has attracted the most attention (Figure 15). Children up to four years of age were offered to Baal Hammon and/or Tanit to gain favor for wars, for crops, and even for good health. The Tophet was a nightmare to excavate; urns with charred remains were buried in claylike, waterlogged soil that was almost impossible to analyze stratigraphically. Newer offerings had been placed next to older ones. A Tophet urn was usually accompanied by a ritual marker (*cippus* or stele); its form depended on the wishes of the sacrificer and the style of the day. The cippi in the earliest levels were massive blocks with projecting moldings; they featured Egyptian cornices and images of chapels and thrones. By the fifth century, more elaborate scenes and signs of divinity were found on the cippi. Stele that resembled tombstones became popular, at least in part under Greek influence.

The steles are usually slender, more like our own tombstones, and show nonfigural symbols that represent divinities, who cannot be shown. Common images include a bowling-pin shape or stone fetish that archaeologists dubbed "the sign of the bottle." By the later fourth century B.C., the funerary marker shapes derived increasingly from late Classical Greek steles and had triangular pedimental tops such as those found in the Kerameikos cemetery in Athens. Magical signs to bring good luck and ward off evil spirits (apotropaics) are legion. From the fifth century B.C., the sign of Tanit, the mother goddess, is increasingly popular on objects ranging from tombstones to baby bottles.

The urns were often sealed with red or yellow clay or capped with simple inverted bowls or dish-shaped lids. Urn stopples of unbaked clay were also recovered (Figure 16).

The term *Tophet* is known in the Bible as the site of the human sacrifice. Tophet originally referred to the place near Jerusalem in the valley of Hinnom (2 KINGS, XXIII: 10) where those who worshipped Baal sacrificed their children; King Josiah of Judah destroyed it in the seventh century B.C. "so that no man might make his son or his daughter to pass through the fire to Moloch." JEREMIAH VII: 31 calls it "the valley of slaughter."

Recent excavations conducted by Prof. Lawrence Stager have shown that the accounts of the horrors of the Carthage Tophet were scarcely exaggerated. The ancient writer Diodorus Siculus described the state of mind of the Punic people at the Tophet:

They were filled with superstitious dread, for they believed that they had neglected the honors of the gods that had been established by their fathers. In their zeal to make amends for their omission, they selected two hundred of the noblest children and sacrificed them publicly; and others who were under suspicion sacrificed themselves voluntarily, in number not less than three hundred. There was in their city a bronze image of Cronus, extending its hands, palms up and sloping toward the ground, so that each of the children when placed thereon rolled down and fell into a sort of gaping pit filled with fire.[19]

Stager excavated more than four hundred urns containing human and animal bones buried between 700 and 146 B.C. He was also able to determine that the Tophet had extended up to the edge of the port area. The fourth century B.C., by which time the Carthage population may have been more than 200,000, appeared to be the time of the highest density. He believes that some twenty thousand urns, most containing at least one human baby, were interred between 400 and 200 B.C. alone, an average of one hundred sacrifices per year or one every three days. But mass slaughters occurred in times of great peril, throwing the averages off. The bones were analyzed by Dr. Jeffrey Schwartz of the University of Pittsburgh. Small children are so cartilaginous that identification—particularly of sex—is difficult. Normally, only the petrosals (ear area bones), cranium fragments, long bones, phalanges (finger or toe bones), and teeth can be recovered.

Only 30 percent of the bones analyzed from the earliest periods were of sheep or goats; the rest were of extremely young infants. By the fourth century B.C., only 10 percent were animal, and older children were sacrificed at a greater rate. Of the single-child urns, 68 percent contained a child between the ages of one and three years; premature and newborn babies made up 30 percent. But 32 percent of the urns contained two or three children. A surprising number of urns contained the remains of three children; two were premature or newborn, and the third was a two-to four-year-old.

Figure 15. The Tophet of Carthage, site of Punic child sacrifice.

The conclusion may be that a stillborn or premature child was deemed unacceptable to the god, and—since the "dedicant" had vowed the offering and could not back out—an older living child had to be sacrificed as well.

On the stele, the genealogy of the dedicating family frequently appears and the vow (NDR) is cited. Paul Mosca, a leading American authority on the Tophet and the Punic language, has concluded that MULK 'IMMOR* means the sacrifice of a lamb or kid, MULK BA'AL is the sacrifice of a child from a wealthy family, and MULK 'ADAM is the sacrifice of a commoner (although this term is not found at Carthage). Such "labels" may indicate a sort of caste system in which sacrifices are rated or classified in value. (The Latinized term for sacrifices to Punic divinities is *Molchomor*.)

Stager has postulated that the human sacrifices may have had a practical value—limiting the number of claimants for large estates and eliminating subdivision of power within a family. But the practice was so widespread in Punic communities other than Carthage that it seems to have been primarily a way to appease a bloodthirsty deity and ensure the religious health of the community. A tophet at Sousse indicates considerable human sacrifice in the sixth and fifth centuries B.C., less in the fourth century B.C., and virtual cessation of the practice thereafter. Other tophets have been found in Sicily and Sardinia. As was the case in Carthage, nonhuman offerings have been uncovered—bulls, calves, sheep, goats, and lambs.

Figure 16. Punic urns from the Tophet of Carthage, dating to 550 to 500 B.C. Bardo Museum. (Catalogue 16)

A number of tombs at Kerkouane (a Punic community of the late Classical and Hellenistic periods) on Cape Bon contained well-preserved offering plates that date to the third century B.C. The remains included a piglet, a gilt-head fish known today in Tunisia as a *daurade*, and a small bird along with several eggs. Animal rather than human sacrifices became more common in later Punic and Neo-Punic times; ie, times after Roman control. At Kourion on Cyprus (a site with numerous Phoenician/Canaanite connections), tradition had it that any human who touched the altar of Apollo Hylates in his sanctuary must be flung over the cliff into the sea. However, actual practice was to sacrifice a sheep or goat. The substitution of a sheep, goat, or other animal at a site where human sacrifice was practiced gave rise to our "scapegoat."

The Punic Gods

Baal Hammon and Tanit were the supreme deities who ruled the Punic pantheon. The latter gradually became the more popular. Baal appears to relate roughly to the Phoenician deity El, the sun god who sits on a throne and is associated with the bull, the traditional symbol of fertility. Baal is the lord of the Perfumed Altars and may also be connected with the Egyptian deity Seth, a god of thunder, rain, and storm who is also associated with bulls and carries a thunderbolt. Baal has power over seasonal produce and can bring needed rain

Figure 17. Fourth-century A.D. votive stele dedicated to African Saturn. It was found at El Ayaida, in the region of Zahret Mediène not far from the site of ancient Vaga (known today as Beja). Depository of the Institut National d'Archéologie et d'Arts. (Catalogue 83)

Tanit

since he is the god of all creative power. Baal also has a connection with Kronos, the ancient Greek divinity who was the father of gods and men and ate his own children. To the Romans, Baal was assimilated to Saturn in North Africa. Temples of Saturn were often built on hills looking out over fields (as at Thuburbo Maius).

Aniconic, or nonhuman, images (pillars, bottle-shaped stones, etc.) were dedicated as cult statues or icons of veneration in Baal's temples. His image was usually not represented, but his symbols were numerous and could possess magical powers. They included the horns of a ram (as in Bou Cornine, visible from the Byrsa), grapes and pomegranates, a pillar or throne within a chapel (two or three pillars symbolizing the god and his advisers), a spear (power), or an ax (sacrifice). On these rare occasions (such as on a stele from Sousse) when Baal is shown, he may wear a tiara or feather crown of Mesopotamian origin and have a sphinx, Greek and Near Eastern symbol of wisdom, sitting next to him.[20]

During the Roman period, Baal is shown on a stele that reflects the continuation of Punic religion long after the destruction of Carthage. On these Neo-Punic works, Baal/Kronos/Saturn can receive attributes elsewhere reserved for Roman emperors or more traditional classical deities (Figure 17). The imperial eagle, often associated with the supreme Roman god Jupiter and Roman emperors, is a common such attribute. In the Lebanon, Baal became a form of Jupiter; his solar attributes are reflected in the name Baalbek (Baal's city of sun) and then to its Romanization as the city and temple of Jupiter Heliopolis (Jupiter's sun city). In Tunisia, the bull continues to be present as does the sickle, symbol of agrarian toil and the harvest.

Baal's vast influence on Punic society can be observed in the names of its outstanding citizens. Hasdrubal means "salvation in Baal," Hannibal means "favorite of Baal," and Hamilcar means "Baal's servant."

Tanit was Baal's consort. She may have originally been a very ancient Libyan mother goddess who slowly worked her way into Punic religion. Her name does not appear to be Phoenician. Tanit seems to have usurped a good deal of Baal's "thunder" and renown as a goddess of fertility. Her symbol was a stylized image of a human with arms upraised and bent at the elbow, a triangle (point up) with two stick arms and a small circle (head) on its top. The symbol may represent a gesture of blessing from the goddess or a worshipper (*orans* pose) calling the goddess. There are numerous other suggestions as to its meaning. It may have meant many different things (Figure 18).

Other attributes of Tanit include the palm tree, grapes, doves, and the crescent moon, sometimes with the sun above. Tanit is a particularly beloved goddess and even a popular symbol in modern Tunisia. She is the parent of all, mistress of elements, queen of the *Manes* (shades of the dead), and goddess of many names on a Neo-Punic stele from Ghorfa (north-central Tunisia). In

Figure 18. "Biberon," or Punic baby bottle, showing the sign of Tanit. Found in a Punic tomb, this bottle dates from the fourth to the third century B.C. Bardo Museum. (Catalogue 5)

Roman times, she can be seen as the crescent moon with two rosettes, which may stand for the evening star and the morning star (Venus/Aphrodite). The cock and the hare accompany her as fertility symbols, and the second-century-A.D. writer Apuleius says she can ride on a lion like Dionysus.[21] Often she is associated with the Greek Hera, consort of Zeus, or, more often, the Roman Juno, consort of Jupiter. She is often confused with the Greek Demeter, who became increasingly popular in the Hellenistic period as a fertility goddess.

Eshmoun, who was popular in Sidon in the home area of the Phoenicians, had the biggest temple at Carthage and was later assimilated to the healing god Asclepius.

There were rules about worshipping. One Roman account forbids sexual activity immediately before entering the Romanized Eshmoun's sanctuary, and the true worshipper should also abstain from eating beans or pork. Melqart, a powerful city god of Tyre who was later assimilated to Hercules, required celibate beardless priests with shaved heads; women were not permitted to enter his precinct.

Punic Tombs

Not all Punic burials were human sacrifices, of course. Carthaginians were buried in necropolises to the north and east of the Byrsa or on its south slope. We find rectangular ditch (*fossa*) tombs, well-shaped trenches, and elegant un-

Figure 19. Punic glass head pendants from Carthage that were found in Tomb 19 of the necropolis in Kerkouane. The pendants date to 650 to 400 B.C. Bardo Museum. (Catalogue 8)

Figure 20. Punic copper alloy bells from Carthage, Kerkouane, and El Jem. The bells date to the fourth to the third century B.C. Bardo Museum. (Catalogue 11)

derground chambers reached by steps leading to corridors (*dromoi*) that lead past rock-cut façades and into formal burial rooms.French excavations uncovered many objects in these areas. The Bardo storerooms are full of unpublished material—much of it unnumbered with the place of origin unknown. Still, the objects give an idea of the offerings that the Punic people considered important to keep with the dead.

Objects to ward off evil spirits (apotropaics) were of major interest. Masks are found in materials ranging from terra cotta to glass (Figure 19). The images may be demons, women with calm expressions, or satyrs (usually associated with the Greek god Bacchus). They normally are not placed on the deceased but alongside the body or near the door. Their assignment is to "fascinate" an intruding being in the sense of the Latin word *fascino*, which means "to bewitch" or "to give the evil eye." (The ancient Greek word for a sorcerer was *vaskanos*.) Tiny bells were also commonly found in tombs and used to ring away evil spirits (Figure 20). Cymbals, often found with the bells, might also have been intended to frighten them (Figure 21). Mirrors, usually undecorated, are commonly found in women's tombs; examples dating to the sixth century B.C. come from a necropolis near the Roman theater of Carthage (Figure 22). Their popularity has led Tunisian archaeologists to suggest that a dressing ritual went on in the tomb.

Figure 21. Punic copper alloy cymbals found in the necropolis in Kerkouane. They date from the fourth century B.C. Bardo Museum. (Catalogue 12)

Figure 22. Punic copper alloy mirrors found in Tomb III in the necropolis in Kerkouane. They probably date to the fourth century B.C. Bardo Museum. (Catalogue 23)

Another frequently found item is an elegant bronze object that looks like a small ritual hatchet but may actually be a razor (Figure 23). Most Carthaginian men wore beards and thus would not use a razor, but the object is found in both men's and women's tombs. The objects have no trace of a handle; rather, they often feature one end made into the shape of a swan. Common between the sixth and third centuries B.C., they are among the most attractive and original examples of Punic art. Their appearance with the dead may be to bring good luck and keep away evil.

Various toilet articles were also frequently found in the tombs of Carthage and Kerkouane. Small glass vessels for holding perfume or oil (*amphoriskoi*) were popular in the Hellenistic period. Beads, amulets, and necklaces of glass were very common. The amulets feature Egyptian deities most often: a misshapen dwarf Ptah (protector from scorpions and snakes), the eye of Horus, Bastet in the form of a cat, a cow attacking a calf (Isis and Horus).

In real life, the ancients spent a great deal of time on looking and smelling beautiful, and their tombs reflect it. In women's tombs, the great interest in cosmetics is especially evident. Women with ruby red lips, eyebrows and lashes darkened with kohl, blue eye shadow, and fingernails and toenails painted orange with henna are evident in the Tunisian tombs as well as in Egypt. Queen Cleopatra was noted for painting her upper eyelids dark blue-

black and her lower lids Nile green. Egyptian perfume and cosmetic shops were numerous, and even mummies were made up for life after death. Cosmetic jars containing perfumed resins suspended in animal fat were found in King Tut's tomb. In Carthage, glass vials with bone cosmetic applicators and shells with two halves fastened by silver chains to hold rouge were used frequently in real life—and included in the tomb (Figure 24). One such shell contained still-usable Punic rouge: cinnabar.

Coloring the face and anointing oneself with perfumes were associated with partying and lovemaking—in life and in literature. Aristophanes has Praxagora defend herself to her husband,[22] who accuses her of sneaking out to a rendezvous with her lover. Her argument is that she is not wearing any perfume—sufficient evidence she would not be making love. In the first century B.C., a man named Lucius Plotius, fleeing from persecutors in ancient Rome, hid but was given away by his too-fragrant perfume.[23]

The Roman writer Martial[24] refers to a woman named Lycoris, who tried to camouflage her dusky complexion with white lead, and her friend Polla concealed her wrinkles under face powder.

The Roman poet Ovid, writing at about the time of Christ and advising women on how to catch a man, suggests they have rouge on the cheeks, eyes colored with kohl or saffron, penciled eyebrows, beauty patches on the cheek or neck or, to be particularly daring, on the shoulder or arm.[25]

In short, the Punic cosmetic fetish was not Punic alone. Everybody had it back then. The Phoenician perfume-making industry was a big one; perfume was even sold to the Libyans.

Much attention was also paid to the hair. Libyans might have a single braid down the center of a shaved head or, as in Numidia, tightly curled hair that required double combs. This was a popular Punic style for men. The sin-

Figure 24. This oyster shell containing cinnabar was found in the necropolis in Kerkouane and dates to the Punic period. Bardo Museum. (Catalogue 25)

17. Tlatli, 1978; Lancel, 1983, with bibliography.

18. *30 Ans 1986*, p. 57.

19. Diodorus 20.14. 1–7 and following.

20. For Baal, see *De Carthage à Kairouan*, 1982, p. 45; Yacoub, 1982, Fig. 27.

21. On the roles of Tanit, see Picard, 1961, pp. 63–65; for La Ghorfa stele, see Picard, *Catalogue du Musée Alaoui*, pp. 262–273

22. Aristophanes, *Ecclesiazusae* 520–526.

23. Pliny, *Natural History* 13.25.

24. Martial, *Epigrams* 1.72 and 3.42.

25. Ouid, *Ars Amatoria*, Book III; *Medicamina Faciei Femineae*.

26. Wykes-Joyce, 1961 p. 26.

gle hair braid look is still found among certain tribes of Berbers in Morocco. Much tattooing also went on, both for men and, especially, for women—as it does today in Berber communities. In Roman times, prostitutes were generally required by law to wear yellow blonde hair to announce their occupation.[26]

We do not know what the Carthaginians preferred in the way of perfume, but the Romans loved a compound made of bitter almond oil, green olive oil, cardamon, rush juice, reed juice, honey, wine, myrrh, balsam seed, galbanum (the resinous sap of a Syrian plant), and terebinth. This was the Chanel No. 5 of its day. Another luxury compound, known as the Royal Scent in Rome because it came from the kings of Parthia at the eastern fringe of the Roman world, contained spikenard, cinnamon, crocus, cardamon, thyme, marjoram, wine, balm, honey, saffron, rosewood, lotus, and styrax gum. Although we do not know what was in the Carthaginian perfume jars, it must have been something like the above.

With all of this information, we really don't know very well what a typical Punic man or woman looked like under all those accoutrements.

David Soren

Romanization

The Coming of the Romans

After the fall of Carthage in 146 B.C. and the formation of the province of Africa, Romanization began. The Carthaginians had not been completely obliterated; some 2,200 Punic deserters were allowed to settle there.[27] Seven cities (including Utica) that had deserted Carthage were given the privileged status of free and protected communities (*civitates liberae et immunes*), and the Punic language and culture continued to flourish in these areas. Roman administrators sold or leased the remaining land—approximately five thousand square miles—to private investors. Many Romans who bought land sold it back to Carthaginians; others bought up large tracts and had Libyans or Libyo-Phoenician slaves or tenant farmers work the soil on their large estates (*latifundiae*). Merchants moved into the new capital at Utica and began to develop the agrarian resources of the interior, but there was no widespread Roman taming of this area; most people spoke Libyan and/or Punic, not Latin, and accommodations and roads left a lot to be desired. Also, wild, unpredictable tribes, such as the Gaetulians, still threatened the borders, and Africa became a place where Romans who had to leave Italy for some reason might carve out rich estates for themselves—much as in the nineteenth-century Wild West.

Attempts to establish Roman colonies (*coloniae*) were not successful. Rome had an overpopulation of poor farmers and a growing number of discontented city poor. Resettlement in Africa seemed like a good idea to many Roman reformers. Tiberius and Gaius Gracchus, of noble birth but tribunes of the common people, tried to develop a resettlement program in Carthage in the middle of the second century B.C. Although Gaius got so far as to begin the program, both brothers lost their lives as a result of the idea. The Senate and wealthy landowners did not want their burgeoning empire cut up and settled by rabble. In addition, a terrible plague and an invasion of grasshoppers contributed to unrest and hampered settlement.

Utica remained the seat of provincial government, where many bankers and merchants lived in a provincial corporation (*conventus*). Rome did not really begin to take an active role in Tunisia's hinterland and get involved in regional administration until the Jugurthine Wars.

At the end of the second century B.C., Jugurtha became almost as terrifying to the Romans as Hannibal had been a century before. A great Mas

Figure 25. The Capitolium at Dougga.

with an enormous following, he decided to attack and punish the Numidian capital city of Cirta, which had sided with his rivals. Jugurtha massacred the inhabitants.Cirta had been the seat of an important Italian conventus, so the slaughter included innocent Roman citizens.

Jugurtha was difficult for the Romans to defeat. It was only through the treachery of his father-in-law, King Bocchus of Mauretania, that he was captured and handed over to the Romans. After Jugurtha's death, his kingdom was divided; Bocchus got the western portion and his half brother Gauda took eastern Numidia. Many Roman army veterans settled along the Numidian frontier to keep an eye on possible native uprisings; sharply increased Romanization of this region began. The Roman general Marius dominated Roman politics as consul from 104 to 100 B.C. He was a champion of the common man, and his reforms to professionalize the Roman army created a better trained force, but the soldiers were loyal to their leader rather than the state. They came to expect privileged treatment and land bonuses at the end of their sixteen years of military service. This led to the rise of military-based dictators, each with professionally trained supporters. The result was civil wars, which would follow in the next century, involving Africa directly. Marius helped install the Numidian ruler Gauda on the throne. Gauda's son Hiempsal had been a supporter of Marius. Hierbas, Gauda's other son, became a supporter of Sulla, who had been Marius's lieutenant. Sulla rose to power after Marius's death and was at the opposite political pole from Marius. Sulla ordered his military commander and protégé, Pompey, to lead an army to Africa and kill Hiempsal, which Pompey did.

After Sulla retired, a power struggle ensued in Rome. Several major figures began to exert control. Pompey was put in charge of Africa. His rival, Julius Caesar, was rapidly rising in power. Hiempsal and his fellow Africans remained loyal to Pompey, but Caesar and his forces landed at Thapsus (on Tunisia's eastern coast just north of Mahdia). In the battle that followed, Caesar lost but a handful of men; accounts put the Pompeian death toll at over 10,000. Pompey was murdered as he fled to Egypt, leaving his son Sextus to struggle on. Cato the Younger, who had fled to Africa when Caesar took control of Rome, tried to help the pro-Pompey resistance movement. But the citizens, fearing a bloodbath, begged Cato to surrender. Cato gave in and committed suicide, and the grateful citizens of Utica erected a tomb to him by the harbor. Surveys of the area have produced no trace of it. At about the same time, Sittius, Caesar's lieutenant and a soldier of fortune, was destroying the army of Juba I, Hiempsal's son. Juba's young son was packed off to Rome and paraded in triumph. He would later become the Numidian leader of Iol in northern Algeria—Juba II, the most pro-Roman of native chieftains.

So Africa, once under the aegis of the Romans, became a microcosm of Roman internal politics. Chieftains chose sides, hoping that they were investing in the faction that would help them realize their ambitions.

With Caesar's triumph, the Romans began to transform the province completely. Roman traders and moneylenders moved in. The veterans from Marius's time were mingling with, and marrying, local people. Latin was becoming a necessary language. Caesar annexed a much larger area; much of Juba I's kingdom became the additional province of Africa Nova, expanding to the south and west of Africa Vetus (Old Africa). More veterans were given settlements of land. Cities that had not supported Caesar, such as Utica, were given considerable indemnities to pay into the coffers of Rome. Caesar left the administration of the province to a trusted long-time supporter—Gaius Sallustius Crispus, an anti-Senate, anti-Sulla, anti-Pompey politician. For all of his sympathies with the common man, Sallust grew very rich as the governor of Africa Nova, then retired. His writings in retirement provide an account of the Jugurthine Wars and are our major source about that struggle.

Years of confused alliances followed Caesar's death. Mark Antony had seemed to be the heir apparent and briefly held Rome as an absolute dictator. Lepidus, Caesar's aide and Master of Horse, supported Antony and had control of Africa for a short period. But Gaius Octavius, Caesar's grand nephew and legal heir, came from western Greece as a lad of eighteen to claim his inheritance. He charmed the Roman people, paid Caesar's bequests (which Antony had usurped) with his own money, and courted the counsel of statesmen such as Cicero. He became increasingly powerful while Antony dallied in Egypt with Cleopatra—an action that infuriated the Romans and that Gaius used to full advantage. He published a will attributed to Antony by which the Romans' eastern territories would be left to Cleopatra, now his wife, and their heirs. The Roman Senate declared war on Cleopatra. Gaius won the great naval battle at Actium in 31 B.C. and was in total control of Rome and her growing territory. In 27 B.C., he was given the title of Revered One by the Senate. We know him by the Latin version of that title: Augustus.

Although it seemed at the time that he was restoring the Republic, Augustus established a dynastic succession that was the beginning of the Roman Empire. (His family tree included the divine-born Aeneas.) He also began rebuilding Carthage on a grand scale. The task must have taken decades. There is virtually no occupation of the port area until after his reign, which ended in A.D. 14. Carthage had been planned out in a number of gridded blocks (*insulae*), but this regular planning had not been done for the whole city in Punic times. Probably around 122 B.C., during the attempted colonization by Gaius Gracchus, the area around Carthage was measured out, presumably for land distribution. A second-century-B.C. inscription from the La Malga area at the city's northwest limit cites what seems to be a three-man commission (*triumviri*) which controlled land assignments. This "rural cadastration" cannot be definitively attributed to Gaius Gracchus, but in any case, the radical dividing up of the heart of Carthage was clearly done by Augustus, with much of the work still going on after his death. Using the top of the Byrsa as the central point, his surveyors marked out a whole range of east-to-west streets (*decumani*) and north-to-south streets (*cardines*). Each city block (*insula*) measured 480 by 120 Roman feet, four times as long as it was wide. (The Roman foot is a little over 29 centimeters.) From the middle of one cardo to the middle of the next measured just over 42 meters. All of this was most ingeniously figured out by the French scholar Charles Saumagne in the early 1920s.[28]

The focus of the new city was again the Byrsa. An enormous terrace, or platform, of concrete and massive arched piers spanned an area of 160 meters from east to west. (This was a startling technical achievement—not unlike Roman constructions all over the Mediterranean in which the power of concrete architecture was realized.) The platform must have dazzled the eye, standing 56 meters above the lower city and featuring a splendid new forum and apparently a temple of Jupiter recalling the one on the Capitoline in Rome and a symbol of Roman power. The forum area was colonnaded and surrounded by typical attendant buildings, such as a senate house (*curia*), meeting places for the city assembly, public libraries, and lodging for important officials. The Augustan style typically combined Classical Greek façades with dynamic, flamboyant placement of structures for maximum visual effect.

Into this community came veterans, needy urban and agrarian people from Italy, and Punic people who were glad to get their city back and to restore their centers of worship. North of the harbor, the old Punic grid was reused in some cases to construct new buildings on old foundations.

Carthage has a number of insulae, but Augustan planning can be studied more easily at Utica—and without the nuisance of modern construction.[29] Each Utican city block was planned in Augustan times, running right over the destroyed Punic levels; the dimensions were roughly 83 by 42 meters—approximately a two-to-one ratio compared with the four-to-one ratio of Carthage. In Augustan planning, each insula was divided into twelve equal lots with six on either side of a central dividing line. But by the time of Emperor Vespasian (about A.D. 75), the configuration had changed. One person (or a family) had bought up more lots and broken through the dividing walls. Six of the twelve lots had become one house, resembling a small villa (*villa urbana*). It had multiple dining rooms facing in different directions (for more or less breeze—depending on the season), a suite of guest rooms with mosaic pavements, and a huge central courtyard surrounded by columns and porticoes, suitable for after-dinner promenades. It was called the House of the Cascade. It gives us an idea of how the Romans changed the original layouts of their Tunisian cities and expanded according to their means. The House of the Cascade even has a garage for the horses and chariots of dinner guests. At the entry, blocks jut out to prevent chariots from crashing into the doorway.

Little of Augustus's city is visible today. There is evidence of the revitalization of the port area, necessary for developing the new colony. Carthage replaced Utica as the principal city in this period, although both prospered as they shipped off abundant produce from the Medjerda and Miliana areas. Grain and olive oil for Rome was the main purpose for rejuvenating ancient Tunisia. Settlers outside of Carthage received good land allotments in areas such as Uthina (Oudna) and Thuburbo Maius; Djebel Oust with its natural spring and adjacent quarry also attracted settlement.

The Carthage proconsul was the representative of the Senate, which controlled the province. As commander-in-chief, he oversaw—often from afar—such military forces as the Third Augustan Legion, based at Ammaedara (Hydra), which was 150 miles southwest of Carthage. From here, potentially dangerous tribes in the Aures Mountains could be closely watched. The Legion was composed of Roman overseers, foreign recruits mainly from Gaul (France), and locally provided auxiliary troops. With this largely non-Italian army, the Romans defended a 1,500-mile frontier with only 25,000 men.

Roman rule was not without problems. As the legions and settlers pressed farther south into Libyan territories, conflicts sprang up. The seminomadic Berbers needed shelter, favorable climates, and grazing lands. With Romans pressing their borders or building roads right through their traditional homeland, the Libyans organized a frightening resistance movement. Its leader, Tacfarinas had been trained in the Roman African army and knew how the Romans fought. His people lived in the present-day Haidra and Gabès region. The revolt began in the last year of Augustus's rule (A.D. 14) and lasted until A.D. 23. But despite aggravations, the Romans seem to have handled the settling of Africa well, disturbing local traditions as little as possible and making examples of groups that would not knuckle under.

Carthage was a shining example of Romanization. It had been utterly destroyed, but its new beauty displayed the glory of Roman culture and government. For the Libyans—used to being exploited—the Romans were hardly worse than their predecessors. Life went on placidly in most places. The Libyans got new masters, occasionally led temporarily successful revolts, and were gradually assimilated into provincial Roman society or lived in areas rural enough so that they could remain undisturbed. Latin-speaking communities were often plunked down right next to Libyo-Phoenician settlements. Much intermingling occurred within a generation or two. This produced a mixed stock, bilingual inscriptions, Punico-Roman architecture, such as provincial imitations of mainland Roman bath buildings, and a fusing of religious beliefs as the names of Punic and Libyan gods were Latinized and Greco-Roman attributes and cults sprang up in a provincial form.

As the African towns grew and prospered, they advanced in status. A town could hope to become a municipality (*municipium*), with freedom to conduct its own affairs and the right to intermarry with Roman citizens and to enjoy the protection of Roman civil law. Being a municipium brought prestige and status, usually boldly proclaimed on inscriptions. The municipium also enabled the Romans to get auxiliary troops and to have magistrates who were responsible for collecting taxes. The real signal that a community had arrived was its proclamation as a colony; colonies had full Latin rights and even Roman citizenship. Carthage became Colonia Iulia Concordia. The name indicated the city's exalted status, its connection to the family Iulii, which included Julius Caesar, Augustus, and all of the Julio-Claudian emperors who followed (Tiberius, Caligula, Claudius, and Nero), and its association with the goddess Concord, a symbol of the city's newfound harmony.

As the first century progressed, Augustus's African policy bore fruit, and by-and-large peaceful times (*pax Romana*)prevailed. This was an age of growing leisure for the rich and of increasing imperial control. The owners of the latifundia had abundant leisure for pastimes: hunting, boating, fishing, and elegant dining. The wealthy moved into the conquered areas, grabbed up land, and produced agricultural goods for the capital. Augustus took great pains to develop Africa as part of an assembly line for feeding grain to Rome's hungry people through a periodic dole. Trading centers headquartered in Ostia, the port of Rome, were developed and greatly expanded with huge warehouses (*horreae*) and shipping firms in the elegant Piazza of the Corporations, behind the Roman theater. One had a mosaic floor with the name of Carthage and a picture of a merchant ship. Companies from all over the Roman world were represented here, including Alexandria in Egypt and Sabratha in Libya. In the center of the piazza was appropriately enough, a temple to the goddess of grain, Ceres.

Much of the agricultural work was done by tenant farmers and slaves. Even Romans having relatively modest incomes owned one or two slaves. On the latifundia, slaves were sometimes organized in squads of ten. The reasons why a person became a slave were numerous, ranging from being a captive in a war to being in debt. The Carthaginians had developed scientific approaches to farming that were best carried out by large numbers of slaves; the Romans simply continued and expanded this tradition.

Many slaves fared fairly well, especially those with technical skills or special talents in teaching, medicine, and art. Female slaves might look after the mistress of the house in the women's quarter, while another slave might tutor the master's son. Close friendships frequently developed between the masters (*domini*) and slaves (*servi*). Cicero wrote with great affection to his ailing slave Tiro,[30] and the poet Martial in the first century A.D. wrote beautiful epigrams about the death of his little slave girl Erotion.[31] A slave could accumulate a great deal of wealth from gifts or tips from a master who might even be induced one day to grant freedom or an inheritance to a favorite. This happened quite often in North Africa as well as in Rome. Trimalchio (in *The Satyricon*, written by Petronius in the first century A.D.) was a freedman who developed all the affectations of nobility once he inherited his master's estate; in reality, he was still an unrefined bumpkin who picked his teeth in public—but did so with a gold toothpick. In stories like these, we observe the Old Guard's resentment of the slave's rise to power.

On the other hand, a cruel or even an indifferent master could mean a life of endless drudgery and pain for a slave. Whips, stocks, and the arena were always possibilities; slaves were simply property. In imperial times, occasional

Figure 26. This slave collar for a prostitute was found at Bulla Regia and probably dates to the fourth century A.D. Bardo Museum. (Catalogue 93)

legislation, sometimes prompted by massive and terrifying slave revolts, looked out for the rights of the slave class. The city prefect listened to slave complaints of abuse; if the case were proved, the owner might have to give up or sell the slave.

Castration of slaves was quite common, and there were periodic attempts to stop the practice. Cases of slaves being murdered by their masters were not uncommon but illegal by the later second century A.D. But if a slave killed his master, the penalty was death by crucifixion, for the slave and his entire, and probably innocent, family. Occasional revolts were never particularly successful. The most famous one occurred in the first century B.C., led by Spartacus—better known from Kirk Douglas's portrayal in a popular movie based on a Howard Fast novel. Reciting a line from Dalton Trumbo's screenplay, Douglas says accurately: "A free man dies, and he loses the pleasure of life; a slave loses his pain." The solution for many slaves was to run away. Runaway slaves (*fugitivi*) were dealt with most severely, and the equivalent of reward posters were circulated. Bounty hunters (*fugitivarii*) returned captured slaves for crucifixion (as an example to others) or amputation of a foot (a gesture of obvious symbolic and pragmatic value). Often the captured slave was sold to a gladiator trainer (*lanista*) or sent into the arena to fight wild beasts. Some were tied to stakes and torn to bits by attacking leopards as the crowd watched. Branding of the forehead was also common: F or FUG. Less drastic was the use of a metal collar with an inscription identifying the master and promising a reward to the escapee's finder (Figure 26).

Figure 27. View of the second century A.D. Capitolium of Dougga.

Figure 28. The Antonine Baths of Carthage were constructed in the late second century A.D.

The Golden Age

The second and early third centuries A.D. represented the golden age of Roman prosperity in ancient Tunisia. It was generally a peaceful time: and with few exceptions, competent emperors and able administrators brought the blessings of civilization to a wide area. The fortified border (*limes*) reached its greatest extent in the south; magnificent cities featuring beautiful stonework from quarries at Djebel Oust, Thuburbo Maius, Chemtou, and other sites dazzzled the eye. Huge Temples of Jupiter (*Capitolia*) dominated porticoed *fora* (Figure 27). The cities had large market areas with round buildings in the center (probably for selling fish), temples to various divinities (such as Mercury, god of commerce), assembly halls, and baths. Thuburbo Maius had one bath building for every several blocks; some were small and perhaps for a neighborhood, and some were enormous complexes for the public.

In Carthage, as elsewhere in Tunisia, there was a theater and an odeon, or covered hall, for musical performances. On the seafront, the gigantic Antonine Baths looked more like a small town than a simple building (Figure 28). There were at least three different ways to move through the structure. The baths contained numerous cold pools in a large and elegant room (*frigidarium*) decorated with fine statuary. A small room with tepid pools (*tepidarium*) served as a kind of transition to the hot rooms (*caldaria*), where bathers could warm themselves in heated pools as the sun poured in. Patrons could play a game like ninepins, get a good rubdown or scrapedown, work out on an exercise ground surrounded by colonnades (*palaestra*), listen to philosophical discussions, and even wrestle. The bath was a low-cost intellectual and athletic entertainment center for the masses.

By this time, most of the fight had been taken out of the Libyo-Phoenicians, who lived quietly on their "reservations" or tried to survive in the Roman system, hoping to become free men and own great estates. In this increasingly civilized—or at least structured—world, Emperor Hadrian played an important role (A.D. 117–138). Under him, water from Djebel Zaghouan was transported by aqueducts all across Tunisia and especially to Carthage, some fifty miles away. Some of the aqueduct arches reach a height of 38 meters, and stretches of aqueducts were known to have run for over a hundred miles (Figure 29). An extended drought early in Hadrian's reign may have prompted this incredible feat of Roman engineering. Whatever the reason, many Roman cities had an abundance of water for public fountains and plentiful bathing establishments.

At Utica, having water in one's house became a vogue among the wealthy. Water was carried through lead pipes, and sewers were installed in the main streets. Houses had elaborate baroque fountains with alternating semicircular and rectilinear niches that look as if they were pulled from the stage façade of a Roman theater. To install the pipes and drains, whole floors had to be relaid. The second century is, throughout Tunisia, a period of extensive remodeling and trendy decoration.

The amphitheater also became popular; there were all manner of combats, many of a most exotic nature. A major structure was built in Carthage; another was constructed late in the first century at El Jem. A larger, more elaborate amphitheater at El Jem that was started before the middle of the third century A.D. may never have been finished because of economic hard times and military reprisals (Figure 30). Circuses also were enormously popular for chariot racing just as in the Circus Maximus in Rome. The Carthage circus is not well preserved, but it has been the subject of careful study by the Universities of Michigan and Virginia.

The municipia and coloniae were recruiting for the army, and the promise of post-service bonuses gave many something to strive for. Citizens of faraway places could serve in Africa and see the world as they never could afford to on their own. From the tombstone of Marcus Licinius Fidelis at Ammaedara (now Hydra), we learn that he came from Lugdunum in Gaul (now Lyons), that he served time as a soldier and a cavalryman in the Third Augustan Legion, and that he became a ranking officer in the so-called Pannonian wing of the cavalry before his death at the age of thirty-two. He was buried in the military cemetery at Ammaedara.[32]

Another Numidian inscription now in the Louvre dates to the third century A.D. and tells of a man born of an extremely poor family who labored in the fields as a harvester around Cirta "in the plains that dominate the mountain of Jupiter." After working for twelve years, he was put in charge of a gang of harvesters cutting wheat in Numidian fields. He saved enough to own a house with land and to "live a life of ease." He became a respected member of the community, sat on the senate of his city, and as a censor, supervised public morals. He reports watching his children and grandchildren grow up, for he lived to a ripe old age as a happy, honored, and fulfilled man. Stories like this may be documented over and over again.[33]

Roman Tunisia had a thriving pottery industry that began to capture major overseas markets in the second century A.D. Fine glossed red pottery known as African Red Slip Ware was produced at a number of centers including Carthage, Mahdiya, and El-Aouja, not far from El Jem. Though hardly elegant, this attractive and durable ware superseded many of the southern French and Italian wares produced in the later first century A.D.; one can find examples throughout the Roman Empire. Marble from the various quarries was also being shipped abroad in quantity.

Mosaic art also revived. Simple geometric floors in black and white had been the rule in the first century A.D.; the work used small cubes of stone (*tesserae*) and was quite elegant. Second-century work tended to be coarser and used larger cubes, but the designs became quite fanciful; by the later part of the century, it was often figural and featured a brilliant polychromy.

Hunting forays organized by lords of the latifundia—either to stop wild beasts from disturbing the cattle or for the sheer macho glory of the chase—were the subject of depictions on mosaic floors. Images of great hunts have come down to us from all over North Africa, especially from the later second century through the fourth, when it became fashionable to show such figural scenes on mosaics (Figure 31).

From the mosaics, one gets a good idea of how a hunter organized an expedition. A well-trained dog was indispensable. Wolf dogs, mastiffs, and the African greyhound were the mainstays; because they had huge, strong jaws, mastiffs were used against the wild boars. For hare hunts, the streamlined white and sleek greyhound was the champion. Dogs were often kept on leashes at home and were carefully trained to be guards for the house, but they could be protectors and herders of the flock as well as hunting dogs.

Horses and hunting dogs were enormously prized and fetched great sums. Not surprisingly, each horse and dog—and each beast intended for the arena—was given a name. Many names have come down to us through labeling on the mosaics, and they often describe the animal. Among the names of horses, we find Bracatus, which meant "wearing breeches like a Gaul" and may indicate the creature's markings or place of origin; Perdix meant "partridge"—a popular bird both to hunt and to eat; Plumeus meant "downy" and, by extension, "light as a feather"; and Miniatus (an ancient Iberian word for native cinnabar) meant, by extension, "something vermilion colored."[34]

The dogs, too, had wonderful names, especially the greyhounds. Pinnatus was "winged"—and perhaps reached its prey incredibly fast. Polifemus's name derives from the legendary one-eyed Cyclops, possibly indicating odd eye markings or only one good eye. Atalante derives from the name

Figure 29. The Roman aqueduct
of Zaghouan was constructed in
about A.D. 125.

Figure 30. The amphitheater
of El Jem was built in the third
century A.D.

Figure 31. This fragment of a hunting mosaic from the Dermech area of Carthage shows the return from a hunt with a captured wild boar and hunting dog. The dog is wearing a studded red collar and chest protector. The fragment probably dates to the beginning of the fourth century A.D. Carthage Museum. (Catalogue 81)

Figure 32. This fragment of a seasons mosaic is a personification of Summer. It was found at Acholla in the Baths of Trajan, and dates to about A.D. 200. Bardo Museum. (Catalogue 82)

Figure 33. This incense burner in the shape of the head of Demeter was found in the Sanctuary of Demeter in Carthage. It dates to about 150 B.C. Bardo Museum. (Catalogue 6)

of the Greek maiden from Boeotia who was renowned for her incredible running speed. Names indicate that not every dog was a total winner. Spina may have been a problem, for its name meant thorny one, or "full of anxiety"; perhaps this was a problem dog or one with a lot of nervous energy.

After the hunt, the captured prey could be netted and suspended from a pole that was easily carried by a few servants. Women are rarely shown participating in any of this. They are usually seated in their finery watching the farming of the estate grounds and receiving baskets of offerings from the farmers. They are frequently accompanied by dogs. They are often discussing philosophy, for many women of the period did receive an education at specially funded finishing schools.

The fine art of hunting elephants was the specialty of black Africans known to the Romans as *Aithiopes* (Ethiopians). According to Diodorus Siculus,[35] herds of elephants running together were very dangerous indeed, but elephants separated from the group were captured by jumping from a tree alongside of the animal and grabbing its tail. Proceeding quickly, before it turned, the native would hamstring the elephant's leg with a sharp ax while hanging on and planting his feet against its flank. Once the elephant was paralyzed, though still alive, its flesh was stripped off by gangs of hunters. The mortality rate of these professional hamstringers was, by Diodorus Siculus's own account, alarmingly high.

Elephant hunting had been a very popular sport in ancient Egypt, but the Indian elephant was always considered more valuable; it was harder to obtain in the southern Mediterranean and was considered more intelligent and reliable in battle. Not only was the ivory extremely valuable and the meat edible, but the elephant was a good luck figure associated with the goddess Africa, protector of the country. Horses were also considered good luck, and many North African tombs feature horse imagery functioning as a kind of talisman. Fish also had apotropaic properties and were depicted on mosaic floors to keep out evil spirits. Stylized phallus-shaped fish also offered protection from the evil eye. Even today, Carthaginian Tunisians often throw a fish into the foundations of a house construction, and a pleasant gift from a store owner in the Souks of Tunis is an image of a fish to hang on your door for good luck.

The changing of the seasons was seen as proof of a divine order that provided a reliable progression to life. The celestial bodies were widely believed to influence the seasons as well as the eternal life of the universe. Astrology was taken seriously by many. Since the seasons were proof of order and, therefore, symbols of the hope of eternal life, they appeared increasingly on sarcophagi in the second century A.D. and on mosaics. Each was personified as a beautiful woman decked out with the appropriate attributes.

Spring was always young and seductive, lightly clothed, and crowned with flowers. Roses or corn poppies, dogs (an astral sign), rabbits, shepherd's

crooks, and sheep all belong with her. For summer, there are omnipresent symbols of wheat, the sickle, and very light clothing (Figure 32). The zodiac sign of the lion parallels the dogs used for spring. For autumn, there are vine leaves and grapes and the god Dionysus's lovely wine cup, the *kantharos*. Dionysus appears riding his panther or symbolized by his long wand (*thyrsus*) and is surrounded by ivy and vine leaves. Winter is aged and heavily clothed, with her hoe and images of olives, ducks, and the wild boar.

Of course, throughout the period of Romanization, the Greco-Roman gods increasingly held sway, often fusing (syncretizing) with local divinities into fascinating hybrid gods. Baal evolved into Saturn, although there were virtually no human sacrifices by the first century A.D.; and by this time, he could be represented instead of symbolized. He looked a lot like the Roman Jupiter. He might, however, sport an elaborate plumed headdress as he sat bearded on his throne, flanked by winged sphinxes and wearing a full tunic.

The Greek goddess Demeter, who had been so popular during the Hellenistic period in Punic Tunisia, became associated with the Roman Ceres, whose symbols were a torch with snake twining around it and fertility symbols such as wheat and poppies (Figure 33). Hercules was always popular, having developed from Melqart, city god of Tyre in ancient Phoenicia. His muscular image adorned many monuments, and he was a special city patron of Leptis Magna in Libya. Juno Caelestis reigned as Tanit's evolved form and was enormously popular.

Another great mother goddess also gained a strong following: Cybele. Of apparent Anatolian origin, her powers over fertility and cultivation gradually fit in with the African love of mother goddesses in the High Empire. Her cult flourished in Rome during the Second Punic War; she was considered instrumental in defeating Hannibal, and she had a temple on the Palatine hill in Rome. A temple (*metroon*) for her existed in Carthage, where the ceremony of ritually washing her statue (*lavation*) was performed. In about 400 A.D., Saint Augustine took part in the ritual before his Christian conversion.

Dionysus was another of the most popular North African divinities in his guise as protector of vegetation and in his more convivial role as wine god.

The High Empire was a time of general religious toleration and syncretization. Foreign cults gained an increasing foothold, and it is not surprising to see that the Egyptian cults that had been popular from early Punic times retained their grip. The cult of Isis had great support, as did that of the Hellenistic syncretized divinity Serapis.

From the second century A.D. on, another group of worshippers came to prominence: the Christians. By embracing all peoples and walks of life, they were able to develop a large following in a short period of time. As life became increasingly difficult in the third century A.D., when emperors were being crowned and killed every few years if not months, Christianity held out hope of salvation and of a better world beyond this one. But once Christianity became established as the official religion of Africa early in the fourth century A.D. (and even before), things did not go smoothly. Rival sects, intrigues, murders, and assorted tactics of terror almost turned Africa upside down and opened the floodgates to revolt from within and invasion from without.

David Soren

27. For this period, see Broughton 1968; Mommaen, 1974; Abun-Nasr, 1975; Warmington, 1971.

28. Wightman, 1980, with bibliography.

29. Lezine, 1968.

30. Cicero, *Ad Familiares* 16.1, 16.10, 16.13, 16.14, 16.15.

31. Martial, *Epigrams* 5.34, 5.37, 10.61

32. *De Carthage à Kairouan* ,1982, p. 105

33. Picard, Mactas, 1954, p. 14. For an excellent overview of Roman Africa in this period, see Raven, 1984

34. On these names see Enneifer, 1975, pp. 7–16

35. Diodorus Siculus, *Bibliotheca*, III, 26.

Carthaginian Twilight

Figure 34. A Roman street in
Dougga.

Figure 34. A Roman street in
Dougga.

The great peace of the High Empire did not last. The rule of North African–born Emperor Septimius Severus seemed to promise unprecedented prominence for the African communities. When his rule ended, the Pax Romana began to come unglued. There followed a period of soldier emperors, breakdown of international communications, economic instability, and endless warfare. Dissatisfaction with taxation and imperial administration grew in El Jem, the great agricultural center. The last of the great African emperors of the Severan dynasty had been murdered in A.D. 235 in Germany, where he had been forced to defend the Roman frontier against hostile tribes. The Sassanid Persians were a menace in the East. Innumerable pretenders tested their strength in the political arena. Maximinus, the former Roman governor of Mesopotamia and a powerful military leader, was one of them. The African proconsul Gordian I was another. Tired of paying excessive taxes, the citizens of El Jem murdered the procurator and put forth elderly Gordian I for emperor. The Roman Senate accepted the elevation of Gordian and his son and declared Maximinus a public enemy. But Capellianus, the governor of Numidia, supported Maximinus and marched on Carthage. He defeated the troops of Gordian's son—and the eighty-one-year-old emperor killed himself after a twenty-one-day reign. Reprisals at El Jem apparently destroyed elegant houses with attractive mosaic floors and made them part of a large cemetery. The Gordian affair was not an isolated event. The traditional religions were fading away, and new solutions seemed essential. A Persian divinity, Mithras, had a large following.

The Roman response to the rise of Christianity was periodic persecution, beginning in A.D. 180 and continuing intermittently throughout the early part of the third century. Tertullian (Quintus Septimius Florens) was one of of the most important figures. He was a Berber born in about 160 and one of the most intelligent men of his time. He knew both Greek and Latin and had studied medicine, natural science, and jurisprudence. His religious beliefs reflected the confusion of this time over how Christianity should be practiced. He belonged to the Montanist sect that disdained theoretical discussions and tended to trust ecstatic visions, believing that a church existed not where there were bishops but where there were Christians. Tertullian believed strongly in the Last Judgment, and he resented those who were not hard-line supporters of Christianity. He believed that reformed adulterers and fornicators should not be accepted in the Church, nor should anyone who had fled under threat of persecution. His famous *Apologia* (about A.D. 198) attempted to convince the emperor and the provincial governors to discontinue persecution. The *Apologia* notwithstanding, Saints Perpetue and Felicity were martyred in a Carthage amphitheater in 203.

The imperial edict of 250 changed everything.[36] It required all Christians to offer an officially witnessed sacrifice to the gods of the state and the emperor. Cyprian, the Christian bishop of Carthage, fled, thus becoming an apostate in the eyes of many African Christians. They had to figure out for themselves what was selling out to Rome and what was simply prudent.

Cyprian gave terms by which those who had abandoned their faith in time of crisis (*lapsi*) could be readmitted if they had not actually sacrificed before the imperial shrines (*sacrifati*). Even those who bought certificates of civic loyalty from the Roman authorities (*libellatici*) were eventually allowed back into the Church along with those who bought tickets of reconciliation from martyrs about to die. Many North African factions split off from the Catholic core. Cyprian managed to keep the Church from completely falling apart by his moderate position and policies—and his image was enhanced by his final act. During renewed persecutions by the Roman Emperor Valerian, he was picked up by Roman troops while returning to Carthage from Cape Bon. The Romans, knowing his power in Carthage and the fact that putting him to death would endanger peace in the community, offered him the opportunity to escape. Cyprian refused—and was martyred in 258. In Carthage are the ruins of a nine-aisled Christian basilica that stands in the Saint Monique and the Saida district of Carthage; tradition has called it the Basilica of Saint Cyprian.

The third century came to a close with Roman emperors continuing to be made and unmade with frightening rapidity, barbarians closing in on the frontiers of the Empire, and non-Italians playing major roles in the affairs of Rome. One strong leader had finally emerged: Emperor Diocletian. Of Dalmatian (Yugoslavian) peasant origin, he was a statesman who understood how to govern during hard times. Realizing that administering the Empire had become too much for one person, he developed a system in which loyal colleagues would govern disparate areas. The Tetrarchy, as it was called, was strengthened by forced marriages that united the various rulers by blood. Tunisia was subdivided into Proconsular Africa in the north and Byzacenia in the south/southeast, including Ammaedara, Sufetula, Capsa, and Thysdrus.

Christianity continued to grow, despite Roman efforts to suppress it. Arnobius of Sicca (Le Kef) was a respected anti-Christian teacher in Diocletian's time who was converted and wrote influential defenses. Under Diocletian, persecutions occurred between 303 and 305, and the number of lapsi grew. Romans had orders to stop Christian assemblies, dismantle churches, and seize scriptures. Mensurius, the bishop of Carthage, and a moderate in Cyprian's mold, went into hiding, leaving behind heretical scriptures for the Romans to confiscate. After Mensurius's death, his supporters speedily elected and installed Caecilius. The Numidian bishops and religious leaders hated the Carthaginian bishops for their soft line against the Romans, and Christians of the lower classes agreed. Bishop Secundus of Tigisis (Numidia) called the Council of Carthage in 312; over seventy bishops attended. Caecilius was condemned as a lapsus and deemed unacceptable. Majorinus was declared Bishop, but his unexpected death forced new elections; the Council confirmed Donatus in 313.

Thus began the Donatist controversy in Carthage, but it spread throughout Christian North Africa, especially in Numidia. The Donatists believed that the Caecilianists were compromisers and pro-pagan; their movement grew enormously because thousands agreed with them. Meantime, a new emperor appeared on the scene. Out of faith or convenience, Constantine the Great supported Christianity. Hoping to end internal religious bickering, he issued the Edict of Milan in 312. It proclaimed religious toleration throughout the Empire; at the same time, he sided with Caecilius against Donatus, and this provoked a class struggle against the wealthy African Christians and the forces of the emperor.

By 316, it was possible to speak of Roman imperial persecutions of Christians by Christians. The Donatists were made up of disgruntled Berbers, fugitive slaves, tenant farmers, and the poor free classes. Some of them organized into what almost amounted to an anti-rich guerrilla group and became known as Circumcellions (from two Latin words meaning "those who would hang around barns"). Years of overtaxation of the poor, mismanagement, and the falloff of the quality of life—coupled with Diocletian's freezing of opportunities for advancement—all led to this proletarian revolt. Dispossessed and desperate workers formed roving bands and attacked rich landowners. The Donatists may secretly have admired the Robin Hood style Circumcellion forays, but many Donatist bishops condemned the terrorism and violence and occasionally delivered the leaders to the authorities.

Emperor Constantine made another important decision. He centered his rule in Constantinople, the redeveloped Byzantium, and thus continued the trend initiated by Diocletian to make Rome just one of the Roman imperial centers. (As Rome was besieged and sacked in the fifth century, Constantinople became increasingly important.)

By the later fourth century A.D., the Empire was still in a state of confusion. There were invading Goths in the East and mutinies and new emperors being declared in the West. Stability in North Africa had to be purchased rather than demanded, and the most powerful man in all Numidia was the Berber chieftain Gildo, whose control extended over all of North Africa's official Roman troops. Gildo was also in charge of Rome's grain supply. After Emperor Theodosius died, he rebelled and almost caused a severe famine in Rome by withholding all supplies. The Senate of Rome was able to induce Gildo's own brother to attack and defeat him.

Having allied himself with the Donatists, Gildo and many of his supporters only succeeded in helping to bring about a massive retaliation against all of the Donatist movement; it was never again to be a major force in ancient Tunisian religion or politics.

The Catholic Church was enormously strengthened by a Roman of Numidian origin named Aurelius Augustinus (354–430), the son of a Christian mother (Saint Monica) and pagan father. Young Augustine grew up as a non-Christian. He was a good scholar and went off to Carthage in about 371 to study rhetoric. Reflecting the uncertainty of his time, Augustine examined many religious dogmas. In Carthage (between his seventeenth and nineteenth birthdays), he reported in his *Confessions* what a tempting city he was in. He loved the theater but decided that seeing such calamity and suffering on a stage and wishing to avoid it in real life was madness. He moved on to Rome. There Bishop Ambrose aroused his interest in Catholicism; he was baptized in 386. Nine years later, he was made Bishop of Hippo (Bone) in Algeria. The Donatists considered Augustine a lapsus and a promoter of the Roman state against true Christianity. But the Roman Emperor Honorius, the son of Theodosius, labeled Donatists heretics; at a council held in Carthage in 405, he backed this up with violent reprisals.

While this internal dissension continued and Honorius remained at Ravenna, Vandals from the Rhine devastated Gaul, and Rome itself was sacked by Visigoths in 410.

The assembly of Carthage in 411 enabled the Catholics to lock up control of Christian North Africa. But the remnants of the Donatists and other dissatisfied and impoverished citizens and slaves were vehemently against the Church, the upper classes, and the military and not opposed to aiding the Vandals, who had invaded and made a shambles of Rome's once great western Empire; churches were burned and clergy massacred. Occasional resurgences of Donatists occurred in Numidia, but the supremacy of the Catholic Church was maintained—although at a great cost. Laborers were not allowed to leave their jobs in the fields. The working class was against the Church. The latifundia proprietors could and did act like petty potentates. Groups called *honores* made sure that excessive taxes were collected on the basis of a person's productive capacity. The political and economic base of the Empire was coming apart.

What Carthage was like on the eve of the Vandal invasion is difficult to ascertain.[37] An Indian summer of revival is evident in the second half of the fourth century. Mosaic work continued to be of high quality, and churches—indeed, ecclesiastical complexes—proliferated. At Utica and Thuburbo Maius, much rebuilding went on in public and private structures, suggesting revival after a period of neglect in the later third and early fourth century. Recycled materials were used, and the workmanship is not up to earlier standards.

In the rectangular commercial harbor of Carthage, an impressive new warehouse was constructed in about 380, suggesting that trade was still considerable. A flourishing trade of African Red Slip Pottery was continuing, and production of handsome, well-made Christian lamps was beginning.

An elegant peristyle house excavated by the University of Michigan near the supermarket of central Carthage shows the wealth still possible early in the fifth century; clustered, lower-class housing near the circular port gives an idea of the other end of the social spectrum. Street lines were respected, and a bustling industrial quarter north of the ports has been turned up in the German excavations.

Vandals

The name erroneously suggests wild barbarian looters. This powerful group originally came from the Baltic. Attacked by groups such as the Visigoths and pushed from the Rhine into France and Spain, they fled to North Africa seeking food and security. Boniface, a friend of Saint Augustine and a capable general was the Roman military governor at the time. Boniface was not popular with all Catholics because of his marriage to an Arian, a member of a heretical sect. However, he grew in power and gave every indication of turning into another Gildo. Rome's regent, Galla Placidia, daughter of Theodosius and, in effect, empress of Rome until her son Valentinian III came of age, recalled him.

Boniface rebelled and offered to grant the Vandal King Gunderic two-thirds of the land ruled by Rome in North Africa. In 429, under King Gaiseric, the Vandals spread through Tunisia. They introduced many to their newly acquired faith, Arianism, which admitted the greatness of Christ but not His divinity. Boniface, apparently seeing that he had unleashed more than he had bargained for and having reconciled himself with the empress/regent, battled with Gaiseric and was defeated. Quite suddenly, a Vandal king was the ruler of Africa—except for Carthage.

Between 423 and 425 in the reign of Theodosius II (an effective ruler generally headquartered in Constantinople), Carthage fortified itself; the Theodosian Wall was probably built on Boniface's orders. Traces of the wall were examined by Canadian and British teams at Carthage in the late 1970s in such places as the amphitheater district, La Malga, and the circus. Builders' debris levels suggested that its architects drank wine from amphoras imported from the East and awaited doomsday while eating oysters.

The Roman authorities had repeatedly tried to placate the Vandals rather than fight them, conceding large territories in western North Africa. But Gaiseric wanted control of Carthage and seized it easily in 439. This was a disastrous blow, since Carthage had been the great imperial and religious center. Increasingly, Berber aguellids took control over Morocco, and the Roman presence in North Africa began to fade. For the Romans, the invasion of Carthage was the twilight of their golden age in Africa. Constantinople made an attempt to liberate the city in 441, but help never arrived. Instead, a treaty wrote off Tunisia to the Vandals.

Augustine's image of the Carthaginians in immediately pre-Vandal times is one of deceitful, circus-loving hedonists. How accurate this image is we cannot know. We do know that as the fifth century progressed, Gaiseric expanded his area of control into Sicily, Sardinia, and Corsica as well as into the Tunisian hinterland. So powerful had he become that he was able to take advantage of the intrigues and murders in Rome that had left the city a shambles politically. He pillaged the city itself for an extended period, capturing Empress Eudoxia and her two daughters.

Forces from Constantinople tried again to liberate Carthage. Assaults on Tunisia by troops of the Emperors Marcian and Leo in the fifth century accomplished nothing. The Vandals stayed in control.

Life in some of Tunisia actually seems to have improved somewhat, surprising as that may seem; for example, the Bath of the Stars at Thuburbo Maius was patched up, refloored, and restored to use. However, the Vandal leaders were not used to running a community of foreigners with a complicated administrative system, and their constant attempts to force Arian beliefs on everyone created fierce opposition. Vandal King Hilderic, 523 to 530, believed in religious tolerance and allowed the Catholic Church to revive in North Africa. His reign paved the way for eastern Emperor Justinian's new Byzantine incursion led by Belisarius in 533.

Carthage had ups and downs under the Vandal rulers, who apparently were not eager to adorn the city with great Catholic churches. By the time of the Vandal period, signs of deterioration were evident. A circular ecclesiastical monument southwest of the theater, built in the late fourth century, was in bad shape; the Odeon and theater seemed to have suffered; and the harbor areas showed signs of decline that included drainage and sewage problems; the gridded city plan was ignored as houses sprawled, a sure sign of the loss of order and a falloff in the standard of living. Some houses held up fairly well—apparently as the result of individual efforts—but churches and public places were not so lucky. However, people still ate well—sheep or goat, pork, chicken, and fish in quantity.[38]

By the time Belisarius attacked, Hilderic had been deposed. The Vandal nation was in turmoil, and its brief alliance with the Arian Ostrogoths in Italy had been broken. Belisarius landed in southeastern Tunisia. He hoped to arouse local support for returning the formerly Roman provinces to an eastern Roman rule that had much more in common with the African Catholic Christians than did the Vandals of Carthage. The Vandal ruler fled, and the pro-Roman Carthage citizenry welcomed him. (It was one of the last great Roman "hurrahs.") Victorious battles along the northeastern Numidian frontier strengthened Byzantium's hold on Tunisia, a good deal of modern-day Libya, and some of eastern Algeria. The citizens had reason to believe that the Roman Empire had in fact been restored in North Africa.

Solomon replaced Belisarius as commander in 534. He faced serious problems. The Libyans, who had enjoyed the autonomy made possible by

Vandal rule, had no desire to return to enslavement under new Roman leaders. Within two years, a rebellion within the never-too-trustworthy Byzantine army stationed in Carthage forced Solomon to flee for his life; the troops ran amok, looting and destroying. Belisarius had to return to Carthage to straighten out the whole mess.

The Byzantine conquest brought a period of at least limited prosperity in Carthage. The North African bishops' power, which had been gradually reviving under Hilderic, reached a new peak; great attention was given to churches. In Carthage, streets and sewage were improved, extensive renovation occurred in the port area, and the harbor quay walls were fixed up. In provincial areas such as Sufetula (Sbeitla), ecclesiastical complexes entered a real boom period. A Catholic community center in operation by the fifth century was given a huge cathedral decorated with elegant mosaics early in the sixth century. Byzantine input may be seen in Sufetela's sixth-century basilica of Saint Sylvan and Fortunatus, where the suspended cupola (which had been recently used at the church of Hagia Sofia in Constantinople) was introduced.

The University of Michigan's John Humphrey, who—along with stratigrapher Simon Ellis, mosaic specialist Katherine Dunbabin, and ceramics consultants John Hayes and John Riley—has studied the ups and downs of Vandal and Byzantine occupation of Carthage, has provided an amazingly detailed glimpse of this neglected period.[39]

The Byzantine golden age began to fade toward the end of the sixth century. The Vandals were no longer a threat, but the ever-resilient Berber tribes were growing stronger. A fighting force composed of Berbers, Byzantine supporters, and Vandals and led by Stozas, a Byzantine soldier, separated the agricultural area from Carthage. Hadrumetum, the Carthage of eastern Tunisia, was lost as well. Years of warfare weakened Tunisia's new masters irreparably. Doctrinal schisms again divided Catholics.

By the early seventh century, some of the old prosperity returned— thanks to the capable leadership of the Byzantine Emperor Heraclius (610–641), who had come to power in a bloody coup against Emperor Phocas. Heraclius had his own problems with the Persian menace and the start of a well-organized, devout group, the followers of the prophet Mohammed. By the end of his reign, the Arabs were on the move, but internal religious controversies took precedence. Saint Maximus the Confessor came from Constantinople to Carthage to oppose the official imperial doctrine of Monothiletism, the belief that Christ's divine and human natures had one great force. Great debates took place in 645—some of them attended by the provincial Byzantine governor Gregory. The North African bishops found themselves more closely tied to the Pope in Italy than to Constantinople, yet Carthage was Byzantine.

The Arabs, not wasting their time in theological debate, were closing in. Suddenly, Syria, Palestine, and Egypt were lost. Constantinople (which followed hereditary rule) was being governed by a child. Gregory felt closed

Figure 35. This ceramic jug contained the treasure of Rougga. This vessel was found near El Jem in Rougga (ancient Bararus) and dates to A.D. 600 to 650. Museum of El Jem.(Catalogue 96)

Figure 36. The treasure of Rougga, 268 gold coins found in a ceramic vessel at Rougga (ancient Bararus), near El Jem. The coins date to A.D. 600 to 650. Museum of El Jem. (Catalogue 97)

in. With his world crumbling, he rebelled from the Byzantines and took support from Pope Theodorus and the bishops of North Africa. He made his last stand in 647 against Arab raiders from Libya (Tripolitania) and was killed. Sbeitla, like many towns in Byzacenia, was pillaged. A pitcher containing 268 gold coins struck in Constantinople, Carthage, and Alexandria and dated as late as 646–647 and bearing the image of Constans II, was found at Bararus (Rougga). The treasure was excavated from a hastily erected fortress in what had been the forum, doubtless placed there by a citizen fearing invasion (Figures 31 and 32). Sbeitla struggled on after the Arab raids. Crude defenses were erected and sprawled over the devastated town. Houses were converted into forts and fitted out with stables, cisterns, wells, and latrines. In the midst of this, the citizens built a church dedicated to the martyrs of Milan and Saint Tryphon, perhaps sensing that they too would soon be martyrs.

Carthage fell on evil days, too. Buildings deteriorated. The harbor gave out. Burials took place in unusual, once-metropolitan locations. Robbery, hunger, and ruins for housing characterize the last half of the century.

By 670, Byzacenia had been lost to Ugba Biennafi. Kairouan, a Libyan stronghold, was his military base. Hassan Ben al Nu'man captured the debilitated Carthage in 695 but did not hold it. Some of the Byzantine population returned only to witness the city's final fall to Ben al Nu'man in 705.

Tunisia would go on to reach many new heights, and depths of despair, over many centuries. The struggle for freedom has finally succeeded in this century under the Tunisian Combattant Suprême Habib Bourguiba, who has always been enormously conscious of his country's great heritage: "The history of Tunisia, from Carthage to our time, presents to us a great richness ... and we would like our glorious past to inspire our young scholars."[40]

Carthage was like a dream, a great exotic passion, to Flaubert. And yet—as he above all appreciated—it was real. Carthage is equally romantic to the archaeologist who studies its ports today and imagines the lofty ships that once sailed out to meet the Romans. The Byrsa reminds visitors of Dido and Aeneas and Virgil, and of marching Roman troops led by Caesar or Pompey or Marius. Tunisia is the land of Hannibal, Tanit, the Byzantines, and the Berbers. It is the realm of Carthage, a mosaic of ancient Tunisia.

David Soren

36. On Christianity and Carthage, see Frend, 1952; Brown, 1967; Barnes 1971.

37. Courtois, 1955.

38. Wells, 1980, pp.47–65

39. Humphrey 1980 pp.85–120 with full bibliography of his additional monographs and articles; see also Pringle, 1982.

40. *30 Ans, 1986,* dedication.

Carthage
A Tunisian Perspective

Figure 37. Landscape in Tunisia
today.

Carthage: Tunisia in Prehistory

Over the millennia, Tunisia has played its part in human evolution—our environment, technology, and culture. Evidence of the civilizations that spanned the Paleolithic, the Epipaleolithic, the Neolithic and the Protohistoric period preceding the historical period is abundant in Tunisia.

The Paleolithic Age

Acheulean tools from the Early Paleolithic period, dating to at least 250,000 years ago, have been located in the northern, southern, and central parts of the country. The famous Sidi Zin deposit in northwestern Tunisia has yielded some limestone artifacts including hand axes, choppers and chopping tools. A fauna characteristic of the African savanna was found with this material. The three levels associated with the Acheulean industry were sealed by porous rock (*tufa*) containing work of a later period known as the Mousterian. The Acheulean is associated elsewhere in the Mahgreb with *Homo erectus* and early *Homo sapiens*.

The El Guettar Mousterian deposit (in southern Tunisia) revealed objects made from flint and indications that the flora, which had been adapted to a temperate and humid climate, were evolving to suit a colder and drier climate. An important monument at this site was formed by arranging balls of stone and modeled marl and kidney-shaped flints into a pyramidal shape built in the basin of an ancient artesian spring. The center is composed of two slabs: one is triangular, the other is lozenge- or diamond-shaped. The slabs are placed one on top of the other. This extraordinary construction may be one of the most ancient cult structures in the Middle Paleolithic.

The Aterian period (named for Bir el Ater in Algeria), which may coexist with or follow the Mousterian, is characterized by its own objects, such as prepared cores, flake scrapers sometimes designed to be hafted to spears and small haftable bifacial points known as Aterian points. The objects were distributed widely across Tunisia and the Mahgreb. The human remains discovered in Morocco and associated with the Mousterian artifacts (Jebel Irhoud) were originally attributed to Neanderthal man but are different from the Neanderthals of Europe. Aterian man is considered, after recent discoveries in Morocco, as relatively modern *Homo sapiens*.

The Epipaleolithic Period

The Paleolithic period is succeeded by the Epipaleolithic. *Homo sapiens* developed two civilizations in Tunisia, the Ibero-Maurusian and the Capsian. The Ibero-Maurusian owes its name to the now-abandoned theory that this civilization had existed in Spain as well as North Africa. Numerous skeletons discovered in Algeria at Mechta el Arbi associate it with a physical type close to that of early "Cro-Magnon" Europeans.

Ibero-Maurusian deposits span the northern coast of Tunisia. In northwest Tunisia, the Ouchtata deposit characterizes this civilization, as do scattered deposits in the south of the country. Deposits of the Epipaleolithic period have been rich in artifacts. Some objects in the Bir Oum Ali deposit date to 14,000 to 14,370 B.P.

The first Capsian discovery was made at El Mekta, northwest of Gafsa. In antiquity, Gafsa was known as Capsa, and from this derives the name given to the entire civilization. The Capsian deposits are known in southern Tunisia as rammadyat (from *rmed*, meaning ash). The deposits never reach the coast but spread to the west as far as western Algeria and to the south as far as the northern Sahara. While retaining its fundamental unity, the Capsian civilization divides into typical Capsian and superior Capsian. In 8400 B.P., the superior Capsian succeeded the typical Capsian at El Mekta; in 8260 B.P., it is present in Bir Oum Ali in southern Tunisia. The Capsian civilization is associated with the proto-Mediterranean group. Around the eighth millennium, they settled around Gafsa. There an abundance of flint provided raw material. Their artifacts rapidly expanded in number and type. This expansion was accompanied by a territorial expansion as well. In the seventh millennium came a personal, figural art. It includes rock sculptures, figurines, and an engraved plaque from El Mekta; decorated ostrich eggs used as items of adornment; shells etched with fine shallow lines, perforated and decorated with ochre; and ear ornaments. These items supplement the remarkable lithic assemblage, which includes blades which are sometimes coated with red ochre, geometrically-shaped flints (trapezoids, triangles) and objects made from bone.

The rammadyat have preserved abundant traces of the Capsian people that have survived: their kitchen refuse (rich in snail shells), products of their hunt or general gathering, their grinding instruments, the remains of their brushwood fires, the rocks of their hearths, their tools, their weapons, fragments of ostrich eggs, items of adornment, and, finally, their sepulchres.

The Neolithic Period

During this stage of prehistory, descendants of the Capsian Mediterraneans and the proto-Berbers developed settlements from the fifth millennium on. Their artifacts, of Capsian tradition, show new developments: stone polishing, pottery, and the use of grains other than the natural grasses. The Redeyef deposit and the Shelter of Jaatcha in southern Tunisia help illustrate this period of Neolithic civilization. In the south central area, a Neolithic site with laurel-shaped leaves has been observed. All over Tunisia, sites from the period have been identified and studied. The Doukanet el Khoutifa site, with its important cemetery, dates back to 6000 B.P. The presence of sheep has been verified in the Kef-el-Agab grotto in northwest Tunisia. In the coastal deposits, an important new foreign raw material, obsidian, has been discovered; it originates in the Mediterranean islands. At Pantellaria, located 60 kilometers east of Cape Bon (northeastern Tunisia) and occupied during the Neolithic period, all the artifacts are made from obsidian.

Between this period and the founding of the first Phoenician colonies lies the development of the Berber world and of protohistory, whose witnesses are the megalithic (large stone blocks) cemeteries with dolmens (flat stone slabs laid across upright stones) and sepulchral chambers carved into the rock.

Mounira Riahi-Harbi

The Berbers
of the
Pre-Roman Period

In the third and second millennia B.C., new groups of settlers entered northeastern Africa in the area known as the Mahgreb. They mixed with and became assimilated into the indigenous population. The new groups were of different origins, and they followed different paths.

• A Negroid element extended to the encroachment of the desert.

• An Oriental element traveled along the coast across Egypt and Cyrenaica.

• A European element reached the north from Morocco and western Algeria through Iberia.

• Another element arrived by way of islands such as Sicily and Sardinia and settled in the north of present Tunisia and eastern Algeria.

Settlement of these groups was well established by the middle of the second millennium B.C. At that point, it is possible to speak of Berber or Libyan populations: an inscription from Karnak, Egypt, states that Pharaoh Menephtah defeated the Lebou (Libyans) in about 1220 B.C. The names Berber and Libyan may be used interchangeably, although the latter suggests the ancient people of the Mahgreb.

Organization into divisions, tribes, and tribal confederations was the next step following settlement and assimilation; this has been the pattern among the Berbers for centuries, if not millennia. Berbers live in a patriarchal and polygamous society in which the woman plays an important role, especially in the perpetuation of certain magico-religious practices and in such domestic activities as pottery making (Figure 38).

A political organization existed among the Berbers from at least the last centuries of the second millennium. Ramses III won a victory against the Libyans (Mashaouash) led by the prince Kapour. The king of the Maxitani is said to have claimed to marry Elyssa, also known as Elissa or Dido, the founder of Carthage. Several Libyan functions and administrative titles are indicated in Punico-Libyan inscriptions found at Dougga, for example:

GLD: king, prince

MWSNH: leader of the one hundred

GLDMCK: leader of the fifty

The Berbers venerated stones, natural elements, stars, and certain animals. Their astrological beliefs centered on the sun and moon, and their

Figure 38. Berber women.

Figure 39. Village men at
Nabeul livestock market.

zoological superstitions centered on the lion, the bull, and the ram. Climatic conditions helped them to develop a special relationship with water, rain, and springs, which they still have today.

The Berbers revered numerous divinities. Several documents show pantheons of five, seven, and even eight deities. They include steles from Beja and Borj Hellal with eight divinities, a relief from Chemtou, and diverse inscriptions that mention divinities. The Carthaginian and the later Roman influences provoked considerable cultural resistance among the Berbers. References have been made to the Africanization of Roman divinities. These imported divinities were either assimilated into local deities or endowed with new functions that corresponded to African needs.

The Berbers' concern with death was so strong that experts refer to a "cult of the dead among the Berbers." Blood, bright red symbol of life, was generally painted on the dead before burial. The offering which accompanied the burial, though meager, symbolized an afterlife. Various forms of tombs were used for interment: dolmens, tumuli, and chambers carved in rock and today called *hawanets*.

Some 1,200 inscriptions employing Libyan language have been discovered in North Africa. The writing was consonantal and recorded the Berber dialects of the period. The political, economic, and cultural regionalization of the Mahgreb is also reflected in the differences found between inscriptions uncovered in western Algeria and Morocco (referred to in Libyan as the West) and texts discovered in east Algeria and Tunisia (called the East, in Libyan). Bilingual Punico-Libyans and Romanized Libyans allowed the alphabet to be standardized, and this is reflected in the Libyan alphabet of Dougga (24 signs). However, interpretation of texts remains enigmatic; most frequently these are conventional funeral texts that have only limited use. High and Low Libyan was written in ancient Tunisia except in regions that came under Punic influence; at Dougga, for example, where Punic influence was strong, writing was horizontal and read from right to left.

The origin of the Libyans is still debated by experts, many of whom hesitate to claim Semitic influence for it. Libyan writing has spanned centuries and, despite undergoing some transformations, is used today by the Tuaregs, who call the signs *tifinagh*.

Mansour Ghaki

Punic Civilization

The Sources

To learn about Phoenician history and civilization in the Mahgreb, we have abundant literary, archaeological, and epigraphical documentation (Figure 41). Among the ancient classical authors are Homer, Herodotus, Timaeus of Taormina, Sallust, Virgil, Diodorus Siculus, Flavius Josephus, Justin, and Philo of Byblos all giving information relative to the Phoenicians' origins, their maritime adventures, and their contacts with other Mediterranean people, and to their economy, religion, language, writing, and arts. There are many lacunas and much distortion in this information. It is up to the historian to use it with caution. Moreover, if Clio, the Muse of history, is not always a vigilant sovereign, it is because in antiquity the frontier between literature and history is difficult to establish and because among the authors who spoke of the Phoenicians there are Homer, the divine poet, and Virgil, the poet of Augustus. Herodotus presents to us the historical facts:

For Libya, in effect, what is known about it is that it is surrounded by the sea, save the part confined to Asia; it is Necos, King of Egypt, who is the first to our knowledge to have demonstrated it; after he stopped digging the canal going from the Nile to the Arabic Gulf, he sent out some Phoenician men ordering them to go part the Columns of Heracles in the Northern sea and to return by this way to Egypt. These Phoenicians, therefore, leaving from the Erythrean sea, navigated on the Southern sea; when autumn came, they landed and sowed the soil in the place in Libya where they found themselves each year during the course of their navigation, and they awaited the period of the harvest; the wheat harvested, they took to the sea, so well that, at the end of two years, they passed the Columns of Heracles in the third year and arrived in Egypt. And they recounted, things that, as to me, I do not believe, but that others could believe, that during their Libyan voyage they had the sun to their right. Here is how one knows about Libya; following this there are the Carthaginians who confirm it.[1]

The Phoenicians had their main city at Tyre in the early first millennium B.C. The books of Judges and Kings in the Bible consecrate numerous verses to the relations that the Canaanites and the Tyrians had with the Israelite kingdoms of David and Solomon (eleventh and tenth century B.C.); Hiram, king of Tyre, was their contemporary and friend. The great temple of Jerusalem was erected to the glory of God and thanks to Phoenician artisans. King Solomon told Hiram:

Figure 40. Roman mosaics and cut stone flooring (*opus sectile*) at the Carthage Antiquarium.

Figure 41. Map of the
Mediterranean area showing
cities founded by the
Phoenicians.

Thou knowest how that David, my father, could not build an house unto the name of the Lord his God because of the wars which were about him on every side, until the Lord put them under the soles of his feet.

But now the Lord my God hath given me rest on every side, so that there is neither adversary nor evil occurrent.

And, behold, I purpose to build an house unto the name of the Lord my God as the Lord spoke unto David my father, saying, Thy son, whom I will set upon thy throne in thy [stead], he shall build an house unto my name.

Now therefore command thou that they hew me cedar trees out of Lebanon. And my servants shall be with thy servants; and unto thee will I give hire for thy servants according to all that thou shalt appoint. For thou knowest that there is not among us any that has skill to hew timber like unto the Sidonians. (1 KINGS, V: 3-6)

The Sidonians were, of course, Phoenicians; Sidon and Tyre were principal Phoenician cities. Elsewhere, we learn that a certain Hiram of Tyre, son of a widow of the Nephtali tribe, was put at the disposition of King Solomon. He was an artist in bronze working in the king's service. His work is described at length. The description begins as follows:

For he cast two pillars of [bronze] of eighteen cubits high apiece; and a line of twelve cubits did compass either of them about.

And he made two [capitals] of [melted bronze] to set upon the tops of the pillars; the height of the one [capital] was five cubits, and the height of the other [capital] was five cubits;

and nets of checkerwork, and wreaths of chain work, for the [capitals] which were upon the top of the pillars; seven for the one [capital] and seven for the other [capital].
(1 KINGS, VII: 15-17)

For the grandeur of Tyre, its power and the dangers that threatened it, one can listen to the words of Ezekiel.

The word of the Lord came again unto me, saying, Now, thou son of man, take up a lamentation for Tyrus; and say unto Tyrus, O thou that art situate at the entry of the sea, which art a merchant of the people for many isles, thus saith the Lord God; O Tyrus, thou hast said, I am of perfect beauty. (EZEKIEL, XXVII: 1-3)

The lament alludes to the pride of Tyre, to the strength of its navy constructed in cypress from Senir, in cedar from Lebanon, and in oak from Bashan. It evokes the wealth of the great Phoenician city that was the metropolis of all Phoenicia. The other cities of the coast offered the necessary labor: seamen, rowers, and other artisans. The lament of Ezekiel mentions the allies, friends, and partners of Tyre. The importance of Tyrian commerce is strongly underlined here: commerce with Tartessos/Tarshish in southern Spain or Portugal, which furnished metals such as silver, iron, tin, and lead. From other people the Tyrians bought horses, mules, ivory, precious woods such as ebony, crimson dye, rubies, and luxurious fabrics. This lament of Ezekiel presents to

Figure 42. View of Punic
housing taken from the Byrsa
Hill in Carthage.

us the city of Tyre as a great commercial center where diverse merchandise from all over could be found.

Other Biblical verses help the historian to learn about aspects of the Phoenician religion. The prophets of the eighth century B.C. fulminated against the cults of Baal and Astarte. They denounced practices such as sacred prostitution and the sacrifice of Moloch, which involved casting human victims into fire in the Valley of Hinnom in the south of Jerusalem. These practices are attested to in Phoenicia and in the Punic world.

Thus the Old Testament constitutes a choice source for the historian of Phoenicia. The Biblical verses also allow us to the understand certain aspects of the Phoenicians' politics and their relations with people in far-off regions such as Tartessos and Ophir. Phoenician material culture is also highlighted: architecture, metal work, textiles, wood and ebony work, ships, and sculpture.

Tablets of Ugarit

However rich the Biblical material may be, numerous aspects of Phoenician civilization are not represented at all. It is thanks to the library at Ugarit that the historian can have access to the literature in regions frequented by the Canaanites. The excavations at Ras-Shamra (Ugarit) on the Syrian coast, executed under Claude Schaeffer's direction since the discovery of the site in 1929, have uncovered a city destroyed around 1200 B.C. Amongst the discoveries are the famous tablets written in cuneiform and occasionally Akkadian. In these, Ugaritic literature is revealed, and the epic element is shown to be of great importance. It is particularly remarkable in the poems consecrated to the divine struggles and battles such as Koser against Baal and Yam against Baal. Another text records "the birth of the gracious and handsome gods." Apart from these poems dedicated to the divinities, there are tablets dealing with practical problems of a non-religious character such as the Hippiatric texts that deal with problems in veterinary medicine and particularly the ailments of horses. Other tablets constitute administrative letters and documents—even banking statements.

The rich Ugaritic literature, although Syrian, furnishes the historian precious information on the life of areas near to the Canaanites in the second millennium B.C. It permits us to follow the people of Ugarit in their religious, mythological, and poetic life. We can read long texts with diverse themes: religion, economy, accounting, medicine, and politics.

The Correspondence of Tell el-Amarna

For the political situation in 1500 B.C. in the area that would later be Phoenicia, it is a good idea to consult the correspondence of Tell el-Amarna. The Phoenician coast was then under Egyptian domination while also enduring the advances of the Hittite state. The governors or princes placed by Pharaoh at the head of the coastal cities wrote to their suzerain to inform him of the unstable situation and to ask for aid.

The Assyrian Annals

The annals of the Assyrian kings made numerous allusions to the economic and political situation of Phoenician cities at the beginning of the first millennium B.C. There was economic prosperity, but also submission to the tyranny of the great powers, notably the Assyrians. According to King Assurnasirpal II, who reigned from 883 to 859 B.C.:

The tribute of the Kings who are on the seacoast, those of the countries of the Tyrians, the Sidonians, and the Giblites . . . and of the city of Arvan which is found in the middle of the sea, silver, gold, lead, bronze, bronze vases, many-colored clothing, linen tunics, a large and a small pagutu, wood of ushu and of ukarinu, shark teeth, the products from the sea, I have received for their tribute and they embraced my feet. [2]

Epigraphic Data

The rich epigraphical sources are mostly short texts engraved or painted on rock, marble, ivory, metal plates, pottery, or walls. Phoenician epigraphy has long been the special study of Ernest Renan, who founded the *Corpus des Inscriptions Sémitiques*, the first part of which deals with Phoenician, Punic, and Neo-Punic inscriptions which have been found in numerous Mediterranean countries. In Phoenicia proper are those of Byblos, Sidon, and Tyre; the Phoenician inscriptions found at Cyprus were recently the object of a work of Maurice Sznycer and Olivier Masson. [3]

Many epigraphical texts from the western Mediterranean concerning the gods, funeral beliefs, and the construction and restoration of temples or other public buildings are known. Although these deal with brief and often stereotypical formulas, the epigraphist can gather precious information on the society, the institutions, and economic life and general information about the Phoenician language, thus enriching our lexicon through the study of the morphology and the syntax.

The Contributions of Archaeology

The greater part of these inscriptions come from archaeological excavations in the Phoenician and Punic world. We have already cited the excavations of Ras-Shamra (ancient Ugarit), and of Byblos, where Maurice Dunand has brought to light some Phoenician traces and stratigraphy reaching back to the third millennium B.C. Phoenician sites have been unearthed in numerous Mediterranean countries. They include Cyprus, Sicily, Sardinia, Malta, the Balearic Islands, southern Spain, and—above all—the Mahgreb, many of whose main Phoenician sites may go back to the end of the second millennium B.C. Utica[4] in Tunisia and Lixus[5] in Morocco are important sites.

The excavation of Carthage[6] has yielded the most abundant material (Figure 42). Among other Punic excavation sites in Tunisia, however, are Hadrumetum, now the city of Sousse in the Sahel region, and Kerkouane, the best-preserved Punic city of all (Figure 43). Kerkouane seems to have been completely abandoned when the Romans invaded in 146 B.C. Situated on

Figure 43. Aerial view of the city
of Kerkouane.

Cape Bon in Tunisia between Kelibia and El-Haouaria, it is a gold mine of information on domestic architecture and daily life in a Punic city in the time of the Punic leader Hamilcar Barca. For the economy, beliefs, and general history of the Punic civilization, it is the most important archaeological discovery that has been made in the last few years.

The material brought to light in different Phoenician and Punic sites can be divided into three groups: material relating to the gods, the dead, and the living. These remains are found in sanctuaries, cemeteries, fortresses, roads, public monuments, and private buildings such as workshops and houses. The cemeteries are important for their "funeral furniture": ceramics, jewelry, amulets, weapons, money, steles (funerary markers) and the like. In a recently excavated tomb from the Punic cemetery at Kerkouane, for example, we found a wooden sarcophagus with what is known as an anthropoid cover, or cover with a human representation. It was relatively well preserved but filled with water and liable to deteriorate quickly if appropriate care was not provided immediately. Tunisian authorities then called upon international experience. Thanks to the International Center for the Preservation and the Restoration of Cultural Materials (CIERBC), the sarcophagus was saved by treatment at the conservation laboratory of the Swiss National Museum in Zurich. The importance of this sarcophagus lies mainly in its cover, which has a recumbent figure in high relief. (The type is called *gisant* by scholars.) The figure is feminine, possibly Astarte in her role as protector of the dead.[7]

These, then, have been the sources that the historian can use to resolve problems regarding the Phoenicians and their settlements in the western Mediterranean, especially in the Mahgreb, where Carthage was the most important foundation. The cultural impact of this settlement affected the native Berbers (called Libous by the classical sources) and their numerous tribes and federations of tribes such as Numidians, Massyles, Massesyles, Mauretanians, Cetules, and Nasamons.

The Phoenicians and the Phoenician Cities

With these archaeological, epigraphical, and literary sources, the historian tries to reconstruct the Phoenician past of the people who inhabited this coastal region. It was located between the Gulf of Issos to the north and Mount Carmel to the south; the mountainous areas of the Lebanon and the Anti-Lebanon to the east; on the west side is the Mediterranean. Greek and Latin authors named the region Phoenicia. The name seems to be derived from a Greek root word designating a tree or a color, the palm or crimson. Crimson may allude to to the famous crimson dye industry that was highly developed in the Phoenician world. But these "Phoenicians," when they presented themselves, said they were Canaanites and the name is even attested to in the letters of Tell el-Amarna and on coinage struck at Laodicea in the Hellenistic period in the reign of Antiochus IV (176–164 B.C.). Later, we find the term in the words of Saint Augustine. The Bible often talks of Canaan and the Canaanites, two terms that cover geographic and ethnic realities broader than those signaled by terms like "Phoenicia" and "Phoenicians." The territory conquered by Joshua was Canaan. When it talks of Phoenicians, the Old Testament uses the term "Sidonians," evidence of a time when Sidon was the greatest Phoenician metropolis, exercising its political, economic, and cultural empire over other Phoenician cities such as Byblos, Tyre, Avard, and Beryte.

In a classic tradition reported by Justin, Sidon was the first city founded by the Phoenicians:

The Syrian nation was founded by the Phoenicians who, worried by an earthquake, left their native country and settled at first on the shores of the Assyrian lake, then on the coast of the Mediterranean where they built a city that they called Sidon, because of the abundance of fish, for the Phoenicians call fish Sidon. [8]

This text brings up the problem of Phoenician origins. Where did the Phoenicians live before establishing themselves on the Mediterranean coast, in the zone that Greek authors call "Phoenicia"? The Greek writer Herodotus (fifth century B.C.) suggests that they lived on the shores of the Red Sea before going north and settling on the coast. However, this was probably only a small fraction of the group. Current thinking is that the Phoenicians were forged by historical and geographical factors: diverse ethnic groups obliged to live together slowly defined a culture with its own political, social, and economic systems and vision of the world.

Justin gives Sidon the meaning "fish." It may be possible to link the toponym and the Semitic root "sd," whose semantic content concerns the hunt and fishing. In any case, Justin's etymology is not just fantasy; it shows a certain knowledge of the Phoenician language.

Homer qualifies Sidon as a "great bronze market"; and it may be that in the Phoenician language, "sd" also meant copper or bronze. The slave who was able to buy freedom with his own savings bore the name "Ish Sidon" meaning "copper man." According to an interpretation of J.G. Février, he is a man who has freed himself by paying his master. [9]

The Bible, the Assyrian tablets, and the Greco-Roman authors agree with the evidence of Phoenician and Punic epigraphy in underscoring Phoenician wealth in metals: gold, silver, copper, tin, and lead. The Phoenicians clearly dominated the Mediterranean market in metals.

The Phoenician Expansion

As the Cretan and Mycenean empires of the late Bronze Age waned, the Phoenicians could abandon the coastal trade with which they had contented themselves during the preceding centuries and ply the entire Mediterranean in their excellent ships. They dared to cross the entire Mediterranean to reach the kingdom of Arganthonios and the country that the Bible calls Tarshish and that Herodotus calls Tartessos. This fabled kingdom seems to have been situated in the south of the Iberian peninsula, probably in the valley of

Guadalquivir. The Phoenicians were attracted there by the area's incredible wealth of silver, copper, lead, and especially tin. Tin was much sought after by people of both of East and West; they used it to make bronze, an alloy that had strength and malleability. Copper use gave way quickly to bronze. To acquire tin, the purchaser paid any price; the seller was the master.

Through trade and seafaring, the Phoenicians had amassed fabulous fortunes. But let Diodorus Siculus speak:

The country of the Ibers contains the most numerous and the finest silver mines we know . . . the natives don't know the uses of silver. But the Phoenicians who came to do business . . . bought large amounts of silver for small quantities of merchandise. Then carrying it to Greece, Asia, and to other people, they thus acquired great wealth . . . . The commerce they practiced for so long made them grow in power and permitted them to send numerous colonies either to Sicily and the neighboring islands, or to Libya, to Sardinia, and to Spain.[10]

The Phoenicians in North Africa

In the course of their many voyages in the western Mediterranean, the Phoenicians first visited the North African coast. They established small settlements (*emporia*), not for colonization but as friendly ports to shorten trips and improve commerce. These emporia permitted local contact and the opportunity of offering Phoenician goods: weapons, arms, jewels, amulets, etc. In turn, they bought the local products: fruits, skins, ivory, wood, etc. Besides these contacts, the emporia on the North African coast could shelter their ships and permit the Phoenicians to make their voyages in legs, stopping for the night or taking shelter from storms and hostile encounters with the avaricious pirates who infested the Mediterranean. These ports had workshops and could make repairs in case of accidents. And there the sailors could get the rest, diversions, and supplies they needed.

Among the Phoenician establishments founded perhaps as early as the end of the second millennium are Lixus and Utica. For the Phoenician origin of Lixus, the voyage (*periple*) of Scylax can be cited. A text of Pliny the Elder notes a Phoenician sanctuary at Lixus that existed before the temple of Melqart at Gadès. According to classical tradition, Utica was founded in 1101 B.C., although surviving remains are centuries later.

But even if the Phoenicians were on the coasts of North Africa at the end of the second millennium (probably too early a date), they apparently were not trying to establish colonies; all their foundations indicate an intention to simply ensure favorable conditions for navigation and commerce in distant countries. Light constructions must have sufficed: wooden barracks and, for severe weather, buildings of clay or mud brick. At the end of a stay, the merchants, sailors, and workers went home. Burial objects are absent in the emporia; Phoenicians were buried at home, apparently.

Utica and Lixus seem to have been founded when Tyre was the biggest

Phoenician metropolis. The Tyrians directed Phoenician politics and oriented them according to the requirements of maritime traffic and commerce. But other ancient sources suggest different reasons for certain Phoenician foundations in North Africa: they are Hippo Diarrhytus or Hippo Acra (the present city of Bizerte on the northeast coast of Tunisia) and Hippo Regius (the present Annaba in Algeria); Hadrumetum in the Tunisian Sahel; and the two Leptises. The first Leptis is situated on the west coast of Tunisia, thirty kilometers to the south of Sousse; the ancient texts and inscriptions name it Minor or Minus or simply Leptimius. In Roman times, the other Leptis or Lepcis (on the coast of present-day Libya) earned the name "Magna," or "Large."

For Sallust, a Latin historian of the first century B.C., these cities were founded by Phoenicians who had left their country for demographic, economic, political, or social reasons. He speaks of excess populations and of adventurers. On the subject of Leptis, he writes:

The city of Leptis was founded by Tyrians who, they say, having been chased from their country by civil troubles, came by sea to get established in this area. The city is situated between the area known as the two "Syrtas" which owe their name to the very character of these shores. For there are, almost at the end of Africa, two gulfs, of unequal size, but of the same nature: very deep close to the shore, and with their other parts exposed to all chance and storms, with here whirlpools and there shoals. Indeed, when the sea becomes strong and ugly beneath the action of the winds, the waves drag with them mud, sand, and even huge rocks, and the aspect of these places changes with the winds: the name of "Syrtas" comes from a verb meaning "to drag." Only the language of the inhabitants of Leptis has changed as a result of marriages with the local Numidians. The laws and the morals have remained for the most part those of Tyre. To them it was as much the easier to keep them since they lived far from royal authority: between them and the most populated part of Numidia was the great desert.[11]

Sallust's assessment of the causes of the Phoenician exodus seems reasonable, especially since from the ninth century B.C. on, the Phoenicians were threatened by Assyria and Egypt. They lived in the fear of domination or elimination by one or the other; and after a certain time, the politics of balance and compromise wears thin and loses its efficiency. The political and military atmosphere was one of constant crisis in the Phoenician cities. The inhabitants never felt secure, and from this sprang the desire to go elsewhere. The feeling intensified toward the end of the ninth century B.C., the era in which Greco-Roman tradition places the foundation of Carthage.

814 B.C. is the date traditionally accepted for the creation of Qart Hadasht, the Phoenician name for the place that the Latins called Carthada first, then Karthago. In the language of the Beni-Canaan, Qart Hadasht means new city. A recent theory has proposed that the date of the foundation of Carthage be lowered to between 673 and 663 B.C.[12] Presently, the tendency is to retain the earlier date, which agrees perfectly with the situation in the Mediterranian that led to the birth to this great city.

The Foundation of Carthage: Causes and Consequences

Greco-Roman authors relate a tradition: a Tyrian princess Elissa/Dido decided to leave her country after the murder of her husband, Sakerbaal Acherbas, perpetrated by her brother, Pygmalion, king of Tyre. The king-assassin wanted his brother-in-law's money. The widowed princess succeeded in removing her murdered husband's wealth and in fleeing with a group of rich and noble people who must have feared the ferocity of Pygmalion. In the course of the voyage to Cyprus, the princess conceived a plan: she succeeded in gaining an alliance with the priest of Juno (the priest of Astarte) and in finding wives for her companions. She chose them from among the girls who were taking part in the sacred prostitution that was a well-known ritual in Canaan's religion. How can one justify the behavior of Elissa at Cyprus? It was a matter of founding a new city in a foreign country. Two elements were essential for avoiding the dissolution of her community: religion and women. In an authentically Phoenician society, Phoenician traditions were necessary.

Whatever may be the authenticity of this story, we must recognize the sociological legitimacy of princess Elissa/Dido's course. The blessings of the gods and the marriage of her companions with the Phoenician women would ensure the coherence and the continuation of the group; she assured herself that no matter where they landed, they would found a society that was authentic, durable, and able to prosper.

The fleet was outfitted and sailed into African waters, probably the protected waters of the present Gulf of Tunis. After long negotiations with Hiarbas, king of the Maxitani, Elissa and her companions landed and began the construction of the new city on the Byrsa Hill (Figure 44). They were to pay an annual tribute to the local Africans.

Timaeus of Taormina, who lived in the third century B.C., reports the story of Elissa. Carthage had not yet been destroyed; its libraries and its archives still existed. Timaeus could consult Carthaginian sources on the subject of the city's founding. He could even ask the Carthaginians about it. Did he do it? We don't know. But certainly he was the source for numerous historians and poets like Pompeius Troius, Justin, and Virgil. Certainly, too, the story was the object of various reworkings and numerous additions, due to the Greek love of pure fantasy. Nevertheless, the story's basis is authentically Phoenician or the work of an author well informed of Phoenician traditions. Even if the story's historical accuracy is brought into doubt, it is composed of Phoenician elements: the Tyrian presence in Cyprus, sacred prostitution, religion, sailing, etc. If it is a yarn, it is made up of the right ingredients.

Besides, a Tyrian princess might well have contributed to the founding of Carthage on the coast of Tunisia. Could it be that she was among those who established the first base camps of Carthage? Indeed, there is every reason to believe that Carthage was conceived as an official site, under the patronage of the Tyrian authorities. Otherwise, how can one explain the subservience that the new city maintained toward the established metropolis? According to Justin, Carthage paid tribute to the temple of Tyrian Melqart in the sixth cen-

Figure 44. View of Punic
housing on the Byrsa Hill.

tury B.C. The earliest archaeological materials found at Carthage seem in large
measure to be imported from Phoenicia or from a Phoenician satellite. In other
words, the wrath of a princess does not suffice to explain the founding of a city
destined to rule the western Mediterranean. There must have been other more
serious factors, but where can one look to resolve the problem? There is strong
reason to investigate the political, economic, and military atmosphere in the
Mediterranean area between the end of the ninth and the middle of the eighth
century B.C.

We have already alluded to the power of the Assyrians who practiced
their expansionist politics by trying to conquer all of Syria up to the
Mediterranean shores. They took a lively interest in the Phoenician wealth as
well. In the course of the first half of the ninth century, Tyre and Sidon paid
tribute to King Assurnasirpal II (883–856 B.C.). The greedy princes of Assur
tried to seize the Phoenician cities and appropriate all their riches. The
Phoenicians needed a highly sensitive political stance to shelter their wealth
and themselves from Assyrian cupidity.

There was another problem. Between the end of the ninth century B.C. and the middle of the eighth, the Phoenicians felt themselves menaced by the Greek presence in the western Mediterranean. After a long interval of dissolution, the Greek cities were finally awakening with intense activity. Demographic, economic, and political factors were inciting them to send out colonies into the western Mediterranean. This Greek colonization did not always bear an official stamp for private initiative, and the spirit of adventure was at the root of numerous foundations. Thus the Greeks established themselves on the southern coasts of Italy and on the eastern and southern coasts of Sicily. In 757 B.C., the Euboeans founded Naxos, which soon founded Leontini and Catania. The Dorian Greeks soon followed and founded Megara Hyblaia in 750 B.C. Several years later, the Corinthians established Syracuse. By 733 B.C., the many Greek colonies had become a serious threat to Phoenician navigation and commerce. Echoes of this Greek commerce appear in classical literature. Herodotus says:

The Samians . . . who, leaving the island, had gained the open ocean with the intent to reach Egypt, were carried out of their route by the east wind; and since the wind did not stop, they passed beyond the pillars of Heracles, and driven by a god, landed at Tartessos. Here the commerce had been so little exploited at that time that when the Samians returned home, they realized the largest profit of any Greeks of whom we have exact information, with the exception of Sostratos, son of Laodamos of Aegina.[13]

Here is evidence of Greek inroads into the secret of the Phoenician trading empire. Elsewhere he tells us more about the Phoenicians:

It was they who discovered the Adriatic Gulf, Tyrrhenia, Iberia and Tartessos; they did not sail in round-hulled boats, but rather in boats with knife-edged hulls. Upon their arrival at Tartessos, they gained the friendship of the Tartessian king, who ruled Tartessos for eighty years and lived a total of 120 years. The Phoenicians gained this king's friendship to such a point that he invited them to leave Ionia and come live in his country wherever they wanted and then, as they were unable to decide, he gave them the money to build a wall around their city.[14]

In the face of this imposing Greek competition, the Phoenicians had to react quickly to neutralize the Greeks. Their small agencies strung along the North African coast and elsewhere were no longer enough; they needed a large commercial foothold where they could resupply without fear of Assyrian intervention, and they needed military bases capable of opposing the Greeks. Thus they felt a pressing need to establish a city in the western Mediterranean which would be a commercial center and a military and naval base strong enough to oppose any enemy fleet. This situation seems to explain more fully the birth of Carthage. The new city must have permitted the Phoenicians to escape Assyrian tyranny and to oppose Greek enterprises in the western Mediterranean. While preparing to replace Tyre as a commercial center,

Carthage was conceived of as a fortress city and a naval base that would be able to protect Phoenician interests.

Carthage succeeded in stopping Greek advances in Sicily, Spain, Corsica, and especially in North Africa. Outside of Cyrene, founded by the Dorian Greeks of Thera, the present Santorini in the Aegean Sea, the Greeks were unable to push farther into North Africa. An assault by the Spartan prince Dorieus ended in defeat at the end of the sixth century B.C.

The Empire of Carthage

Carthage became the capital of a vast empire that covered almost all of present Tunisia, Tripoli (which included the emporia of Sabrata and Leptis), and other important North African cities like Lixus in Morocco. Tipasa and Hippo in Algeria also seem to have belonged to the Carthaginian empire. Outside of Africa, Carthage dominated a part of western Sicily, Sardinia, the Balearics, Malta, and the southern regions of Spain. The western coasts of Africa were the sites of systematic exploration led by Hanno the Magonid, probably about the middle of the fifth century B.C. A Greek version of this voyage by Hanno has survived. The text begins in these terms:

The story of Hanno, king of the Carthaginians, in the Libyan countries beyond the colonies of Heracles, which story was told in the temple of Kronos, and the text which follows…. It seemed good to the Carthaginians that Hanno sailed outside the pillars of Heracles and founded the cities of the Libyphoenicians.

It would be too long to reproduce the entire text, which includes seventeen paragraphs about different cities founded, descriptions of their locations, and the contacts the Carthaginians had established with the local inhabitants. Hanno's fleet ranged along the western coast of Africa to the Gulf of Guinea dominated by Mount Cameroon. Despite certain doubters of the event, the historic significance of this expedition is widely recognized by modern historians. The voyage of Hanno was conceived as part of the Carthaginian expansion in Africa. Another expedition was directed by Himilco toward Cornwall in England.

Carthaginian Institutions

To administer its vast empire, Carthage established institutions and political, economic, and military frameworks whose efficiency permitted the Punic civilization to expand throughout the Mediterranean.

Using accounts by the Greeks and Latins, some historians emphasize, no doubt wrongly, the existence of a Carthaginian royalty. Herodotus, Polybius, and Diodorus Siculus designate the highest Carthaginian magistrate by the term for king in the Greek language. Speaking of Hannibal, Cornelius Nepos uses the word *rex*. The terms *Basileus* and *rex* attempt to translate the Punic word *sufete*, which is derived from a Semitic root having something of the sense of a judge. The same word appears in the Bible. In the numerous Punic inscriptions discovered in Carthage, there is no trace of royalty or of a Carthaginian king, but judges are often mentioned.

According to Greco-Roman sources and epigraphy, the state was built on three principal institutions: the judicial, the Council of the Ancients (their senate), and the Assembly of the People.

Each year, two judges were elected to ensure that political and administrative affairs ran smoothly. They carried out decisions made by the Ancients or by the Assembly of the People. They convened the Senate and presided over and directed its debates over proposals often introduced by themselves. Therefore their powers rose not only from executive power; but they also played a strong legislative role. There was also not yet a true separation of powers because the judges had very important judicial functions. Justin notes, nevertheless, the existence of a high court of justice formed of 100 members (a tribunal that seems to have been created at the end of the fifth century B.C.) to judge political and military affairs. After their expeditions or campaigns, the generals could be held to account by the tribunal. According to Justin, the tribunal was a way to protect the state against tyranny during the era of the Magonid rulers:

As this powerful family weighed so heavily on the public liberty and took part at the same time in government and justice, the state instituted 100 judges, chosen from among the senators: after each war, the generals had to account for their actions before this tribunal in order that the fear of its laws and its judgements to which they would be submitted in Carthage would inspire in them during their foreign campaigns a respect for the authority of the State. [15]

Numerous questions remain. In order to be a senator, what were the conditions required for age, wealth, and individual status? How did the Assembly deliberate? Who could participate in its deliberations?

Carthaginian Society

Historians recognize different categories of Carthaginian society. There were certainly free men and slaves. Among the former were the citizens of Carthage and numerous foreigners in Carthage. The Etruscan and Greek colonies increasingly played an important role in the city's economy. The citizens of Carthage themselves could be divided according to economic criteria; the rich arms makers and builders, the traders, and the big landowners were the most influential class. The wealthy Carthaginians controlled the political life, orienting it in a direction favorable to themselves, sometimes to the detriment of the state. During the Punic wars, their self-interest drove the state to catastrophe. Their wealth contrasted with the state's financial difficulties. They often failed to recruit and pay soldiers and to equip the fleet.

The lower classes—the artisans, the sailors, stevedores, and farm workers—are met through inscriptions carved on gravestones, but their influence on the city's political life is unclear.

Figure 45. Faience amulets of Ptah, the Oudja, falcon and Horus falcon, and Bastet found in Tomb 225 of the necropolis in Kerkouane. The amulets date to the sixth to fourth century B.C. Bardo Museum. (Catalogue 7)

The Carthaginian Economy

Slaves worked either for the large landowners as farmhands or in the workshops. Those who served in the houses as domestics had a less harsh life. Slave labor was used in the quarries and mines. However, certain slaves in Carthage could save their money and buy their freedom. Punic inscriptions, as we have already mentioned, called them Ish Sidon (men of copper). Slaves had full rights to worship their gods and to perform sacrifices to them, as numerous inscriptions attest.

The three principal resources of the Carthaginian economy were commerce, agriculture, and crafts. We know little about the commercial activities of Carthage because most of the merchandise was perishable. The Carthaginians, like the Phoenicians, often acted as middlemen; what they bought from one source, they sold to another. The lack of truly Punic objects in foreign countries cannot be interpreted as proof of the absence of Carthaginian businessmen in these countries. Carthaginian ships could unload perishable goods or agricultural products or even objects made in Greece or Etruria, for example.

Concerning agriculture, the most eloquent witness is furnished to us by the famous treatise on agriculture by Mago in which grain, fruit trees, and cattle-raising are discussed in detail, based on direct observation. Furthermore, Mago paid attention to the problems of management: how to direct an agricultural enterprise. Along with other pieces of advice, he recommended that the landowner reside on his property in order to keep up on all problems, as Gsell has stated:

Agronomy in Carthage was therefore a true science which had in its aristocracy some very learned masters and skillful adherents. The nobles took a much more active part in the management of their domain than Roman large land holders in the following century.[16]

Artisans were numerous in Carthage: potters, jewelers, wood and metal workers, masons, and glassmakers. They worked to answer the needs of the Carthaginian population, but a good part of the objects made went for export. Items made in profusion include terra cottas, pottery, figurines, and masks. There are all sorts of bronze objects, such as pouring vessels with trefoil spouts and engraved razors. Glass is represented by small vessels (*alabastrons, amphoriskoi*) and masks and amulets. The Bardo Museum owns a collection of rock crystal jewels as well as an onyx jar attributed to the sixth century B.C. Gold and silver jewelry gathered from Punic tombs occupies an important place in the showcases of the Mahgreb museums and elsewhere, notably at Cagliari in Sardinia. Bone and ivory combs and perfume boxes, and faience amulets were also popular (Figure 45). The most remarkable object discovered in the Punic world is the coffin from Kerkouane with the carving of Astarte on the lid. A collection of marble coffins is presently on display at the Carthage Museum. The lids are sometimes decorated with divine or human figures, goddesses or priests.

The World of the Gods

The tophet is considered the principal sanctuary of every Punic city. The Tophet of Salammbô was discovered in 1921, thanks to a stone collector who appeared one day in the market with an engraved stele bearing the image of a priest holding in his arms a child destined to be sacrificed to Baal. The Tophet is indeed the sanctuary of Baal Hammon and his consort Tanit, and the faithful came there to present a sacrifice (known as Molk) to this divine couple. At first a human was required, but at times substitutions were allowed. The human victim was replaced by an animal, usually a ram or a bull. Other cultures knew human sacrifices as well. Abraham received a divine order to sacrifice his son until the angel Gabriel offered the ram as a substitute. In the Bible, it was Isaac that God demanded in sacrifice; the Koran designates Ishmael as victim.

When the human or animal victim's throat had been cut and the body was burned according to the ritual, the ashes were put in an urn that was placed in the tophet. Very often a stele was placed above the urn. The form differed from one period to another.

Besides rich decor, these steles often have a Punic text with an invocation of the gods, mention of the one who is offering the sacrifice, and a prayer addressed to Baal Hammon, Lord of the Tophet. We know the other members of the Carthaginian pantheon, thanks to texts like the oath of Hannibal[17] and to Carthaginian epigraphy. Besides Tanit and Baal Hammon, the Carthaginians worshipped Astarte, Cid, Melqart, Eshmoun, and Hoter Miskar. Egyptian divinities were abundantly present in Carthage, including

Horus, Isis, Osiris, and Râa. Around 396 B.C., Carthage seems to have introduced the official cult of Demeter and Kore, as Diodorus Siculus tells us:

The Carthaginians, against whom the gods were infuriated, gathered together, at first in small groups in a great confusion and pleaded with the gods to put an end to their anger. Then the entire city was seized with superstitious fright, for each imagined that the city would be reduced to slavery, in consequence, they resolved to make themselves favorable by every means to the gods against whom they had sinned. Not having introduced either Demeter or Kore into their rites, they designated the most illustrious of their citizens to be priests of these goddesses and established them in the city with a great solemnity.[18]

The Punic Temples

Numerous tophets have been found. in areas such as Hadrumetum in Tunisia, in Sardinia, and in Sicily, but there were also temples built conforming to the principles of religious architecture of the Semitic world. In addition to Carthaginian temples, like the temples of Eshmoun on the hill of Byrsa, cited by the authors of antiquity, archaeological excavations have exposed other traces of sacred buildings.

The Carton Sanctuary

The Carton Sanctuary was discovered near the present Salammbô railway station in Carthage and published after the death of its discoverer, Louis Carton, who had described it:

The part of it that I have been able to explore is composed of a rectangular room whose walls have been razed to a uniform height of 0.60m, the interior length of the room is 4.80m and the width is 4.0m . . . the floor is made of a mortar of crushed tiles measuring 1mm to 1cm along which small angular fragments of irregular white limestone have been scattered.[19]

These facts allow us to imagine the inside of a Punic chapel or sanctuary or sacred room (*cella*) on the eve of the destruction of Carthage. During the excavation of the cella, rich cultic material was found.

The Sanctuary of Sidi Bou Saïd

This sanctuary was discovered in 1917 in the immediate area of Sidi Bou Saïd. The modest remains seem to have belonged to a vast religious ensemble. The small shrine area uncovered is probably the cella known as a *qodesh qodeshim* or Holy of Holies.[20]

The Sanctuary of Kerkouane

At Kerkouane is an entire temple, including a courtyard, a chapel in the interior of the courtyard, and in front of the chapel, almost perfectly on axis, an altar for sacrifices and offerings.[21] Thus it conforms to the designs of the Semitic temples of the West, recalling two large sanctuaries, the temple of Solomon in Jerusalem and the temple of Abraham la Kaaba in Mecca. The temple of Kerkouane is the largest Semitic temple in the western Mediterranean, comparable to the large Phoenician temple of Kition.

Punic Cemeteries

Numerous Punic cemeteries have been found in Tunisia and elsewhere in the Punic world. Thousands of tombs were excavated in Carthage,[22] as well as Utica, Sousse, Thapsus, Cape Bon, (notably Menzel Temine at the Ta Feke site), Kelibia (Aspis or Acimer), and Kerkouane (Tamezrat).

Punic tombs take diverse forms. Often they are are pits, sometimes 5 to 6 meters deep. They may have three chambers: access stairway, passageway (*dromos*), and burial chamber. There are variations: the hollowed-out stone chamber, the constructed stone chamber, the tomb cut into the side of a hill. Some cavern tombs in the Sahel, notably at Thapsus, recall the troglodyte dwellings of Matmata or the subterranean Roman houses of Bulla Regia.[23]

On the walls of the burial chambers were red ochre paintings of the sign of Tanit, birds, roosters, plants, and even structures such as mausoleums, and altars. In one of the tombs of Arg el Ghazouani—Kerkouane's cemetery—was found the painting of a fortified city thought to be the City of Souls (*Rephaïm*), the subject of a tablet of Ugarit. Let us note that the Rephaïm are also mentioned on a Neo-Punic inscription that belonged to the mausoleum of el-Hamrouni in the middle of the desert, next to Remada. On the same stone stele, there is a Latin translation which shows that the term corresponds to the term *Manes* (souls of the dead).[24]

Domestic Architecture

Before the discovery of Kerkouane, Punic architecture and city life were poorly understood. Some remains of Punic dwellings were found in Carthage, but they were not well studied until the Byrsa Hill excavations in Carthage by J. Ferron and M. Pinard and the French archaeological mission directed by S. Lancel. German excavations have also enriched our knowledge of the area.

For domestic architecture, Kerkouane's contribution remains the most important. Huge sectors have been uncovered and examined, revealing the diversity of the dwellings in opulence and form. The most popular house type is organized around a courtyard and a patio, either with portico or without. Visitors note an anteroom or vestibule before a bathroom and a bathtub (hip bath) which is in the shape of a slipper with a built-in seat for the bather.

The Contributions of Punic Civilization

With the arrival of the Phoenicians and the founding of Carthage, North Africa came out of the shadows to become the scene of intense economic, political, and cultural activity. And it was Carthage that created this new resurgence. The disappearance of the library, with its Punic works, of which Herodotus, Sallust, Pliny the Elder, and Saint Augustine spoke, prevents us from appreciating certain contributions of Carthaginian civilization. "According to the learned men, there were many good things in the Punic books," said Augustine. For the Mahgreb, the Phoenicians' arrival and founding of Carthage resulted in the opening of the Libyan world to the economic and cultural currents of the Mediterranean.

Important discoveries in geography and agriculture should be mentioned among other Carthaginian contributions. Hanno and Himilco, the two great Carthaginian explorers and discoverers, must have profited by the acquisitions and experiences of the old Phoenician navy. In agriculture, Mago's agronomic treatise was certainly important. Roman senators recommended translations for their own use. During all of antiquity, Mago was the revered master of agriculture.

For the Africans, the arrival of the Phoenicians in North Africa meant great changes in their society, economy, political organization, and religion. In Numidia and Mauritania, the cult of Tanit exerted its influence.

The work of Carthage was so profound and persuasive that some incontestably Libyan peasants carried the inner conviction of belonging to the race of Canaan. It is curious to state that through these Punicized Libyans whom we call Libyo-Phoenicians, the civilization of Carthage survived in the Mahgreb up to the present day.

M'Hamed Hassine Fantar

1. Herodotus, *Histories*, IV, 42.

2. E. Dhorme, *Revue Biblique*, 1910, pp.60–61.

3. Sznycer and Masson, 1972.

4. Lézine, 1968.

5. Chatelain, 1968.

6. Moscati, 1966; Picard, 1970; Carthage, 1970.

7. Fantar, "Un Sarcophage en bois à couvercle *anthropoidal* découvert dans la nécropole Punique de Kerkouane," *Comptes Rendus de l'Académie des Inscriptions et Belles Lettres,* 1972, pp. 340–354.

8. Justin, XVIII, 2, 3, 4.

9. Février, 1951–1952 pp. 13–18.

10. Diodorus Siculus, V, 35.

11. Sallust, *Jugurthine War,* LXXVIII, 1–5.

12. Edmond Frézoul, 1955, pp. 153–176; Cintas, 1970, pp. 473–485.

13. Herodotus, *History* IV, 152

14. Herodotus, *History* IV, 163.

15. Justin, XIX, 2, 5, 6

16. Gsell, 1920, p. 8.

17. Polybius, VII, 9, 2, 3.

18. Diodorus Siculus, XIV, 77, 4, 5.

19. Carton, 1920, p. 3.

20. Merlin, 1919, pp. 177–196.

21. Fantar, Vol. III, 1986.

22. Benichou-Safar, 1982.

23. Beschaouch, 1977.

24. Fantar, 1970.

Kerkouane:
A Punic City
at Cape Bon

The First Excavations

The Kerkouane site was discovered in 1952, and French archaeologist Pierre Cintas undertook the first excavation in 1953. The greater part of the excavations carried out at Kerkouane was the work of the National Institute of Archeology and Art of Tunisia (INAA).[1] Tamezrat seems to have been the ancient name of the city.

The city was built on a steep cliff oriented north–south; to the east is the sea. Facing the sea are great expanses of cultivated earth—garden plots, fruit trees, and pastures—all dominated by green hills.

The cliff is flanked to the north and south by two sandy beaches that could have served as shelters for the small boats of fishermen. The Kerkouane site has also suffered undercutting by wave action; thus the greater part of the structures that were located at the edge of the cliff have disappeared.

The Buildings

Although the city was encircled by double walls, provided here and there with towers, doors, posterns and staircases leading to a principal street, the greater part of the monuments uncovered up to this point have been houses. One luxurious house had a peristyle of carved columns, but the capitals have not been found. The most prevalent type of house was built according to a plan still familiar in Tunisia: the house with adjoining storerooms. The entrance is marked by a doorsill, then a long corridor is traversed. It ends in a small courtyard that generally contains a well. To get rid of waste water, a small drain was installed; it leads from the courtyard to the street. The system still exists in Tunisian villages of the Sahel, such as Moknine, to the south of Sousse.

Around the courtyard are the rooms, often paved in a red mortar that is dotted with particles of crushed bricks or broken pots and a sprinkling of small pieces of cut white marble. One could almost call this a mosaic pavement. Decorative motifs are found —the sign of Tanit, for example. In Kerkouane houses, particular attention was given to the bathroom, which features a changing room and a hip bath (Figure 48).

In the courtyard was a staircase (of which there are usually three steps remaining). Through ancient authors, we know that the streets of Carthage leading from the port to Byrsa were bordered by six-storied houses. Here, the staircase could have led to only one upper floor and access to terraces.

Figure 46. View of second-century B.C. Punic houses as seen from the Byrsa Hill.

Figure 47. Hip bath from a Punic house at Kerkouane.

The Sanctuary

Two sanctuaries have been recognized and brought to light at Kerkouane. One appears to be the largest sanctuary yet recovered in the Punic world. This discovery is all the more important since so little is known about the religious architecture. After two short excavation campaigns in July and August of 1976 and 1977, the Kerkouane sanctuary was mostly uncovered. Its plan seems to resemble that of a Semitic sanctuary: a monumental entrance with two frontal pilasters, a vestibule provided with a room filled with seats and a chapel or tabernacle preceded by an altar in the middle of the courtyard. Among its dependencies was a sculpture workshop.

Materials and Techniques

Punic architecture used modest materials: small building stones, mud bricks, baked bricks, beaten or pressed earth, cut stones, and columns. To hide the poor quality of the material, the walls were often covered with a layer of hard stucco and then painted; the colors encountered are white, red, and gray.

Different materials are sometimes used together; in the foundations of a wall, we have uncovered small building stones and baked bricks covered with a thick and solid layer of stucco. Some are built entirely of mud brick.

The architectural techniques attested to at Kerkouane are numerous; for example, there is contruction using regularly set stones and large, vertically set ashlar blocks linked by curtains of rubble stone walling.

Town Planning

The urban plan shows a well-designed checkerboard pattern with regular crossing streets, but the city blocks (*insulae*) have varying dimensions and adjacent components: the large town squares and smaller squares.

Artisanal Activities

Phoenicians were masters in the production and the commerce of purple dye, which they are said to have invented. Kerkouane was certainly one of the production centers of purple dye during the Punic epoch; a layer of broken murex shells bears witness to this.

Besides fishermen, dye makers, and sailors, there were at Kerkouane potters, sculptors, glass makers, stone cutters, people who applied stucco, weavers, jewelers — all represented through vestigial remains of their work.

Chronology

The city of Kerkouane has yielded a great quantity of pottery imported from Magna Graeca (southern Italy). This pottery, whose chronology is relatively well known, leads us to believe that the city was abandoned around 200 B.C.

As to the city's foundation, the current state of documentation shows that the oldest datable vestiges, found immediately above virgin earth, include Ionian and Attic pottery, which sets the date at the sixth century B.C.

Concerning the ethnic background of the population, the funeral practices and the family names recovered suggest a relatively important Libyan presence in the city. One is tempted to speak of the Punicizing of a Libyan embryo rather than a Phoenician or Carthaginian colony.

M'Hamed Hassine Fantar

1. P. Cintas, 1953, pp.256–260; M. Fantar, 1984–1986.

From the Fall of Carthage to the Arrival of the Moslems

The three Punic Wars, from 246 to 146 B.C., involved the two superpowers of antiquity—Carthage and Rome—in a conflict that spread across the entire Mediterranean world. They were truly the world wars of the third to second centuries B.C. They ended in the defeat and obliteration of Carthage.

Carthage and her territory became a Roman province. This region, which had played a major role on the political, economic, and cultural scene, went into eclipse. The era of Carthaginian competition for political and military hegemony was indeed past. Rome had become the master of the ancient Mediterranean. For Tunisia nothing henceforth could free it from the role of a simple province integrated into the vast empire of which Rome was the center. (Egypt and Greece, other historical entities with particularly prestigious pasts, were forced to contribute to this same empire.)

Roman Organization of the Province

The Punic territory that the Romans annexed was not large. Massinissa, a neighboring Berber king and strong ally of the Romans, had been gnawing away at Punic territory for years. His often-repeated motto was "Africa for the Africans," and his goal was unifying all of North Africa under his own aegis. As a result, only the northeast section of Tunisia and a narrow coastal strip from the Gulf of Tunis to the Gulf of Gabès was left to Carthage. Annexed by the Romans in 146, this territory was immediately divided into "centuries" of around 50 hectares each. All of the good real estate, whether Punic or Berber, became public property. The natives lived on and worked the land for Roman owners. Rome tried several times to establish Italian settlers in the new province. Caius Gracchus, a famous Roman reformer, was the unhappy author of one of these attempts. It failed. Gracchus's political enemies succeeded in ruining him with the accusation that he was provoking the gods' anger by settling a colony on the cursed Carthaginian soil. Utica replaced Carthage as Africa's capital, and a Roman proconsular official administered the province and was responsible for defending the provincial frontiers and for maintaining order in the entire area.

Nothing could stop the progression of Roman expansion and influence in Africa. Jugurtha, an important Berber prince, tried to assert his sovereignty

Figure 48. View of the Capitolium of Dougga.

over the central Mahgreb and put up a fierce and heroic seven-year struggle (112–105 B.C.) against the Roman legions, only to be put down by his Rome-backed stormy rival, Marius. Rome was determined to safeguard her recent conquests and expand her domination over all the Mahgreb.

Africa did not again assume a leading place in Rome's list of concerns until the bloody civil wars in Italy. The traditional republicans throughout the Empire backed Pompey; the partisans of power to the people backed Julius Caesar. Cato, leader of the republicans in Africa, rallied the Berber king Juba I to his cause. Juba secretly hoped to reconquer the former Carthaginian territory and unite the Mahgreb under his own leadership. Caesar's troops routed those of Cato and Juba in 46 B.C., near Thapsus in the Sahel area. From then on, Caesar met no serious resistance. Utica opened its doors to him, and Cato killed himself there. Juba, too, was pursued—and committed suicide. Rome annexed Juba's territory and named the new province Africa Nova to distinguish it from Africa Vetus. Under Emperor Augustus, the two provinces were melded together into Africa Proconsularis; the province included all of present-day Tunisia, a part of Libya, and a part of eastern Algeria. Carthage, rebuilt by Augustus in accordance with Caesar's wish, became the capital.

The occupation of the country, its pacification, and its Romanization were not without difficulties. The Romans came up against sometimes tenacious native resistance. Indeed, Rome herself provoked some of the troubles. Efforts to increase control of the land were sometimes detrimental to the local tribes. In creating their regional defenses and expanding their influence, the Romans failed to take into account certain profound geographical and climatic realities of the semi-nomadic natives' lives: they transformed "wandering lands" into agricultural areas and closed seasonal migration paths by building and improving roads and generally disrupted the equilibrium of regions in which the nomadic way of life prevailed. A result was the revolt of Berber tribes led by Tacfarinas. After serving in the Roman auxiliary corps, he used against the Romans the lessons he had learned from them. Starting in A.D. 17, the war lasted for seven years. This was the most prominent of a series of Berber uprisings that shook the country during almost the entire first century. The public triumphs in Rome that were accorded the victorious generals is an indication of the importance of these native rebellions. Rome was unable to eliminate resistance and only succeeded in confining it to marginal zones, away from the most usable land. Gradually, the alerts became localized and episodic, but the threat was real in the vulnerable border zones; Roman troops there remained constantly on the lookout.

From the end of the first century A.D. on, peace was rarely disturbed in the interior of Proconsular Africa. This peace and security encouraged tremendous economic development; for the country and for many, ancient Tunisia became a land of unprecedented prosperity.

Romanization

In agriculture, Tunisia had a reputation for excellence due to the age-old work of the Carthaginians. The conquering Romans made the province a colony for exploitation much more than one for habitation. They continued the development of agriculture but gave it a new orientation. The vineyards and olive groves that had been destroyed at the end of the Punic period were left abandoned to avoid competition with Italy, which then dominated the wine and oil markets.

Rome's economy and political requirements made Tunisia a one-crop province, and that crop was wheat. Rome had 200,000 citizens on the dole. They were getting free distributions of wheat, and Italy and the whole Empire were suffering from a shortage. Tunisia had to provide 1,260,000 quintals (over 200 pounds per quintal) of wheat annually. This covered two-thirds of Rome's needs and nourished the Roman plebiscite for eight months out of twelve. (The final one-third was taken care of by Egypt.) This contribution permitted Rome to avoid riots and famine—dangerous to the stability of the regime. The major part played by Africa Proconsularis in supplying Rome earned it a reputation of enormous prosperity. Ancient Tunisia was considered the granary of Rome, and Latin writers never ran out of praises for the fertility of the Tunisian soil. They said the sowings gave 150 to 1 and that one could see the tufts of nearly 400 stems coming from the same seed.

Rome's requirements changed for a number of reasons. The conquest of a number of new wheat-producing lands lightened the load on the Proconsulary. An economic and social crisis in Italy led to lower Italian production of wine and oil. More liberal emperors of provincial origin promoted respect for non-Italian regions. Concerns about reclamation of land unsatisfactory for wheat growing led to planting of trees and exploitation of previously unproductive areas. All of this led to the cultivation of grapes and olives from the second century A.D. on.

The olive is particularly well suited to the land conformation and climatic conditions in many parts of the country. The extraordinary expansion of olive groves contributed for centuries to Tunisia's economic and social evolution. From the beginning, the production was impressive. Oil was distributed free—as wheat had been—and the African oil succeeded in conquering many markets at a time when this material was the only lamp fuel, the main food oil, and the only base for perfumes. The olive groves continued to prosper until the end of antiquity. At the moment of Islamic conquest, Arabic authors continually sang the praises of the expanse of this "continual grove from one end of the country to the other." Traces of Roman oil factories remain today and denote a massive level of production.

Linked to this development of the agricultural industries, another industry expanded during Roman times: ceramics. Ceramics had great importance; many household utensils were made of pottery. During the Punic era, production had been extensive, but it seems to have stopped after the fall of Carthage. But around the end of the first century A.D. and the beginning of

the second came an increase in production of jars for transporting grain, oil,
and wine as well as lamps. A type of attractive red pottery that soon conquered
all of the markets of the Roman world appeared (Figures 49, 51, 52).

The production centers were established on the steppes of central
Tunisia around Kairouan, Hajeb-Al Aioun, El Aouja, and El Jem. These areas
are not very fertile but are rich in clay. Some pottery was appreciated for fine
decorations and was very much in vogue: from the third century A.D., vases
bearing appliqués in relief with designs often inspired by the amphitheater
games; from the fourth century, small round cups with stamped decoration;
from the fifth, great rectangular plates whose form and decoration were inspired by models in silver. In addition to quality dishware, lamps, and ordinary
ceramics, the potters made all sorts of terra cotta statues. These are often classical in style and are found in abundance in the Thysdrus and Hadrumetum
cemeteries. Baked earth tiles or plaques done in relief covered the ceilings and
walls of fifth and sixth century Christian basilicas (Figure 50).

Another flourishing industry was producing *garum* (fish and seafood
dried and reduced to powder or mashed with salt and herbs to produce a sauce,
or *liquamen*). The Romans frequently used this product as a condiment or
drank it as an aperitif or digestive. Factories outfitted for producing this sub-
stance have been found at Neapolis, Sullectum, and Kelibia.

Figure 50. This Paleo-Christian plaque of the sacrifice of Abraham was found at Kasserine and dates to the sixth century A.D. Bardo Museum. (Catalogue 84)

Figure 51. This ceramic lamp with the image of a camel was found at Ksar-es Zit (ancient Siagu). It dates to A.D. 50 to 100. Bardo Museum. (Catologue 60)

Figure 52. Roman North African red slip dishes and bowl found at Sidi El Hani (in the Sousse area), Dougga, and La Skhira. The objects date to A.D. 150 to 425. Bardo Museum. (Catalogue 53)

Other fabrications of the period were bone knife handles, needles, pins for the hair, make-up spoons, gaming dice, and statuettes. An important workshop for this activity was recently discovered at El Jem, as were others that produced sculpture and/or casts. The most important workshops were those where mosaics were made to satisfy the demand that was increasing as the wealth and a taste for luxury developed in the cities.

Agricultural, industrial, and craft and art production and Carthage's commercial and maritime traditions gave African shipowners a place envied by competitors in the other provinces. The African shipping companies were strongly linked with Ostia, where they had their head offices. Traces of them have been found in the famous Piazza of the Corporations. Merchants and seafarers placed themselves under the protection of Neptune, lord of the seas, who is abundantly represented on African mosaics.

The Province: Political, Artistic, and Intellectual Center

The Roman conquest marked a rupture with the past that is expressed in important economic changes. The same thing did not occur in sociocultural circles, where a remarkable continuity of the Punico-Numidian heritage could be observed. However, if this pre-Roman legacy cannot be ignored, the Italo-Roman contributions should not be overlooked either. Carthage was rebuilt just one century after its destruction by the same Romans who had destroyed her. The city quickly regained its prosperity (*iterum opulenta*) due to its traditional mastery of sea and commerce, its rich artisanal excellence, hardy agricultural system, and new conditions that were instituted by the Romans. Carthage quickly found her place, providing complementary resources within an immense empire.

Carthage was able to bloom again largely because of the peace and security brought by Rome. New works increased the value of the countryside and cities. Besides an impressive network of roads, all of Tunisia has traces of remarkable Roman development: bridges, dams, irrigation works, aqueducts, cisterns, farms, and oil factories.

Urbanization took on an exceptional magnitude during the imperial epoch. For the Romans even more than for the Greeks, the city became a center of attraction for the whole population. The ancient centers quickly overflowed, and even the outlying districts became populous. All Africa's political, economic, and social organizations were planned in accordance with the city. At the peak of the Empire, Tunisia had no fewer than 200 closely placed cities, as shown on the ancient maps and itineraries. Ten cities crowded in on each other in a 10-square-kilometer radius around Dougga. Aerial photographs show that there was one inhabited center in each centuriated area of 50 hectares. Urban life was characterized by leisure and based in large part on going to the Roman thermal baths, amphitheaters, theaters, and arenas. An estimated one-quarter to one-third of the population lived in the towns, a considerable proportion for a Mediterranean world whose economy was essentially rural.

Historians have noted that this urban density differentiates Africa from other Roman provinces (such as Gaul) that were just as rich but remained deeply rural. To them, this explains the remarkable success of Romanization and the province's strong political and spiritual role in the Empire. Besides offering a luxurious lifestyle, the cities also offered surprising promotional possibilities to an elite African class that performed the highest administrative and political functions in the Empire. Around the end of the second and the beginning of the third centuries, about 15 percent of the Roman senators and knights (*equites*) were of African origin.

Among those who rose to the top were Fronto, a consul, lawyer, and man of letters so influential that he became the tutor of the future Emperor Marcus Aurelius; Salvius Julianus, a senator and jurist under Emperor Hadrian and the first compiler of Roman legal documents; Antistius Adventus, a top general of Marcus Aurelius; and Asinius Rufus, consul in A.D. 184. The part played by Africans in managing imperial affairs reached its peak at the end of the second century. Controlling the highest military posts and holding key administrative positions, Africans made and unmade emperors.

In A.D. 192, Aemilius Laetus, a praetorian prefect (a type of military "prime minister") from Thaenae (near Sfax), created a crisis in shipping supplies to Italy. By allowing this to become a political crisis, he opened the road to power to Septimius Severus, a fellow countryman. Severus came from a wealthy family of Leptis Magna (Libya). He had succeeded in becoming, with Clodius Albinus from Hadrumetum (Sousse), joint ruler of the Empire. Severus would later eliminate Albinus in order to be the sole master of Rome. This man of Punic ancestry was the head of an African dynasty that would dictate the destiny of the Roman world for almost half a century. (In Rome, certain people did not hesitate to say that Severus's ascension was Hannibal's revenge.) Roman civilization attained its peak under the Severans; one of them, Caracalla, extended citizenship to all the inhabitants of the Empire in 212.

The considerable role played by the Proconsulary in the political arena was underlined by the events which shook the Roman world in 238. Thysdrus (El Jem), famous today for its magnificent amphitheater, headed up a rebellion against the reigning emperor, Maximinus Thrax, who had become widely hated due to his fiscal abuses. In the course of this insurrection, the procurator for gathering taxes (*fiscus*) was massacred there, and the proconsul, Gordian, a Roman senator of high birth, was proclaimed emperor. Carthage and the other African cities enthusiastically followed this movement, and Thysdrus's choice was quickly confirmed by the Roman Senate.

Africa's role in the Empire's artistic and intellectual life was just as important as the political and economic role. Tunisia's collection of mosaics is so rich that the country may be said to be paved with them. They can be admired in the Bardo, Carthage, Sousse, and El Jem museums and in the ruins of Carthage, Utica, Dougga, Thuburbo Maius, Bulla Regia, Thysdrus, and Sullectum. In the beginning, they had classic themes, but at the end of the second century A.D., artists in local schools and workshops began to give free rein to their inspiration. The golden age of the African mosaic had been born. The idyllic and mythological scenes were increasingly eclipsed by scenes inspired by social and economic life. They were dealt with in an alert and captivating manner that reflects fantasy, humor, or passion—all part of the African temperament. Barely a century later, the style became characterized by frontality and abstraction and the quest for spirituality, symbolism, and irrationality. Around the middle of the fourth century, this popular current gave birth to the African Christian mosaic with its two tendencies: the one monumental and aristocratic in a classical tradition and the other completely popular. During the course of this century, African mosaic art still exerted an influence that went well beyond its borders. For example, Sicilian and Spanish work gives clear evidence of the African influence throughout the Mediterranean.

The history of ceramics is similar; the African production established itself throughout the Empire because of both its quantity and its quality.

In the area of sculpture, there was an "official" Roman art, often of a political character, imported by urban and bourgeois purchasers of art from the Greco-Roman world and produced by foreign masters living in Africa. However, as Gilbert Charles Picard noted: "Local sculptors were able to withstand the foreign competition from the middle of the second century on." This art was not only of Greco-Roman inspiration; it often drew from eastern sources as well. However, the most interesting phenomenon is the triumph of an authentically popular artistic current fed by deeply rooted pre-Roman traditions. Thousands of funerary and votive steles provide evidence of this. (The most famous are those from Ghorfa.) The characteristics that distinguish these steles from the Roman models and techniques are numerous: division into registers, flat relief, frontality, stylized energy, and disregard of proportions. The Roman influence is weak and superficial, affecting only certain exterior details in scenes and clothing. Mistakes in perspective, inaccuracies in representing the anatomy, and lack of equilibrium between the figures and the scenery give a rather gauche appearance to some of these representations. This naive figural style has incurred some fairly severe judgments from certain scholars, but the attention of many others has been caught more and more by this exacerbated realism and the freshness and vigorous originality that lack neither beauty nor strength when compared with the bourgeois official art, which was often conformist and cold.

The splendors of Tunisia's Roman past are best appreciated in walking through the ruins of the cities. If Carthage, despite its beautiful remains, offers but a pale reflection of antique grandeur, numerous other less prestigious cities have well-preserved attractions. Among them are Dougga, attached to cliffs dominating the Oued Khalled valley, an old Berber citadel and one of the most beautiful Roman towns with its temples, theaters, Roman baths, Libyo-Punic mausoleum, mazelike roads, and collection of monuments in almost perfect condition; Maktar, a village situated in the mountainous heart of

Tunisia, overlooked by history but having important monuments in which Numido-Punic traditions have been well maintained; Bulla Regia, with almost unique storied underground houses; Thuburbo Maius, with its monuments, vast esplanades, and numerous porticoes; El Jem, with its grandiose amphitheater; Sbeitla with its original architecture, its famous Capitolia and Paleo-Christian basilicas.

If there is an area in which Tunisia is most indebted to the Roman Empire, it is that of the mind. Teaching was diffused, thanks largely to the zeal of the municipalities and the help of rich citizens. In the humblest townships, a reader taught the children reading, writing, and arithmetic. In schools similar to the American one-room schoolhouse, these humble African instructors used methods that were criticized by Saint Augustine but that nevertheless resulted in the invention of the graphics called "primitive lower case" from which our present-day handwriting originated. On the next level up and still in a small town, grammarians taught grammar, explained Cicero and Virgil, and introduced the sciences. Teaching at higher levels was provided in the cities by rhetoricians who taught eloquence (indispensable for politics and law), literature, philosophy, history, and science. Carthage, the intellectual capital, had the most prestigious university.

Carthage had no reason to envy Rome, Athens, or Alexandria. In her, the humanist tradition shone with lively brilliance. In Juvenal's eyes, Tunisia was "the nourishing land of lawyers." Some of the most illustrious African intellectuals are Fronto, "master of two emperors"; Salvius Julianus; Cornutus, famous rhetorician and stoic philosopher in the time of Claudius and Nero (middle of the first century A.D.); Florus, poet, historian, and panegyrist of the second century; and Septimius Severus, grandfather of the emperor of the same name and a rhetorician revered for his intellect. The master of the Carthaginian school was incontestably Apuleius, proud of his Berber origins and author of a brilliant speech for his own defense against charges of using magic, the *Apology*. He also wrote the *Florides* and the *Metamorphoses* (also known as *The Golden Ass*), in which he displays a pronounced taste for the fantastic, for exalted mysticism, and for humor and a profound knowledge of the social and human problems of his time. His sensitive observation enchants the reader and gives precious information to the historian.

Christianity in the Province

The meeting of African literary genius and Christianity was a happy one. African life has always been marked by strong religious feelings. The sense of the sacred was always present in even the most backward rural populations, and the Punic civilization asserted itself most vigorously and originally through religion. In the Roman period, next to the official cult of the emperor and the gods of Rome (to which one belonged mostly for political reasons), the province remained loyal to its religious traditions. Syncretization facilitated the assimilation of the Punic deities with their Greco-Roman equivalents; the popular cults of Juno-Caelestis and of Saturn developed from the worship of Tanit and Baal Hammon. The latter remained the great omnipotent and transcendent god. The followers of Baal and Tanit, ever ready to admit to divine transcendence and the dogma of their gods' intervention or mediation between the heavenly and the earthly, were attracted to Christianity. In the last years of the second century, when the Catholic Church had had only limited success in the West, the African peasants were converted en masse. Persecuted under Commodus, twelve among them became the first African martyrs.

Repression only increased the numbers and ardor of the faithful. During the first ten years of the third century, Tertullian declared—not without exaggeration—that the Christians outnumbered the pagans. Many Africans sought martyrdom, following the example of Saint Perpetue, Saint Felicity, Saint Monica, and Saint Cyprian. Once deeply Christianized, the country was filled with basilicas. The Church may have suffered from the Donatist schism, but its vigor was not diminished. The first literary Christian primary school in the Latin language was created around the end of the second century and produced Tertullian, one of the greatest Christian apologists and influential throughout the West. In his *Apologia*, he defends the Christians with eloquence and attacks the enemies of the Church with vehemence: the pagans, the Jews, and the heretical sects. Very different from Tertullian, Ninucius Felix is the author of *Octavius*, a scholarly apology for Christianity. Saint Cyprian has a choice place in third-century Church history. Born around A.D. 210 in Carthage and converted at the age of thirty-five, he turned away from classical culture and devoted himself to the Scriptures. He became the Bishop of Carthage in 249. He reacted against the lessening of zeal and discipline in the Church and was in conflict with the Bishop of Rome—an indication of the autonomy of the African Church, which had been assertively independent since Tertullian's time. A victim of Valerian's persecutions, he died a martyr in 258. His prestige remained immense in Carthage, where three basilicas were consecrated to him and the people honored his memory until the end of antiquity with a popular festival. The works about him had a considerable influence on Latin Christianity.

African Christianity reached its peak in the fifth century, thanks to the exceptional personality of Saint Augustine. Born in 354 in Thagaste, Augustine was a Berber; his father was a pagan, and his mother, Saint Monica, was one of the noblest figures of Christian Africa. His youth was as studious as it was troubled. He received a good classical education but at the same time gave free rein to a fiery temperament that pushed him toward a life of pleasure and spectacles. From 374 to 383 he taught rhetoric in Carthage, but was depressed by the tumultuous lifestyle of the city and especially the students. He left the African capital, the "boiling pot of shameful passions," for refuge in Milan, where he converted to Christianity under the influence of Bishop Ambrose, and where he was influenced by Neo-Platonic philosophy. Upon his return to Africa, he was ordained Bishop of Hippo and remained there until 430. Ardent defender of Christianity, founder of a social Christian order, theologian and philosopher, he wrote more than a hundred works, the most famous of which are *The Confessions* and *The City of God*. Saint Augustine was incontestably the greatest mind of his time.

The Roman Period: A Summary

This was the end of a great epoch. In this epoch, pre-Roman traditions were considerably enriched by Italo-Roman contributions, opportunities for expansion of the country's creative vitality, and spectacular changes in economic, social, political, artistic, and intellectual life. Importers in the beginning, the Africans often became exporters. From a people being governed, they transformed themselves into those who governed. From being disciples, they often became masters. Picard summed up this remarkably rapid ascension: "Africa therefore gave as much to Rome as it received and showed itself capable of bringing to fruition the borrowings from Rome in a spirit that is not Greek nor of the Hellenized Orient."

Thanks to this harmonious development, the province could put up some resistance to the tremors that began to shake the Empire around the middle of the third century. In the beginning of the fifth, Tunisia was a refuge for the senatorial aristocracy fleeing Rome before Alaric and a promised land for the Germanic invaders. Tunisia had the resources required for supporting itself but began to suffer when commercial exchanges were disrupted and general insecurity prevailed. The collapse of the Empire and internal disorders weakened the country and prepared it for the Vandal invasion.

The Vandal Period

Domination by the Vandals, conquerors of Germanic origin who were little adapted to the reality of the country, appears as an isolated episode in Tunisia's history. A population destabilized by Berber uprisings, religious conflicts, and social discontent favored the newcomers. Led by Gaiseric, the Vandals founded a new state that would last a century. They put Vandal families at the head of great expanses of the country. Ruling Corsica, Sicily, Sardinia, and the Balearic Islands, they could control a part of Mediterranean commerce and make pillaging raids in Italy. Witnesses attest to the Vandal brutality—vandalism became synonomous with destruction. Today we know, thanks to archaeological documents and a critical spirit, that the Vandals' reputation was exaggerated and that they sinned much more through incompetence than intention. They hardly concerned themselves with Tunisia's problems during their time. The Vandal state disintegrated in its turn in 534. Its decay was due to disorder born of religious quarrels concerning the Arianism that they professed and ongoing peasant revolts and repeated assaults by Berbers from Aures and the camel-riding nomads of Tripolitania. The final blow was delivered by the Byzantines.

Carthage as a Byzantine Satellite

The Vandals' persecutions and despoilings led the African bourgeoisie, still loyal to the Empire, to request intervention by Justinian, the emperor of Constantinople, just when he was seeking to reconquer the western provinces. So, beginning in 533, Tunisia became Byzantine for more than a century. The new masters established an annual tax payable in wheat (*annona*). They confiscated the royal Vandal domains and gave them back to the families of their former owners. Commercial routes and trade developed, and a certain economic prosperity returned. Once again, Carthage and its territory took on a reputation of great wealth. However, the tax system, the corruption of officials, the repression of religious beliefs perceived as social dissent, and the continuing uprisings of mountain tribes and desert nomads produced an atmosphere of almost continual insecurity. The Byzantines covered the country with a network of fortified works often built with materials from ancient monuments. Nothing helped. Collapse was inevitable.

In this period, the country renewed its ties with its pre-Vandal past. Numerous churches such as the one at Kelibia were restored and embellished. In this period, too, fortresses that would mark Tunisia's countryside were constructed.

In 647, the Moslems launched their first victorious raids against the Byzantines. Running up against the Berber resistance in their turn, they did not definitively subjugate the country until 698.

Carthage: Melting Pot of the Mediterranean World

Ancient Tunisia was deeply marked by the superimposing of several civilizations: Berber, Punic, Hellenistic, Roman, Vandal, and Byzantine. It was a great crossroads of civilization. The country's geographic position makes it, in fact, a place of passage between Africa and Europe and a privileged link between the East and the West. Tunisia's population has been constantly renewed by the continuing mixing common to all residents of the Mediterranean area. Favorable topography has always facilitated cultural exchange, which has continually enriched and not destroyed the country. Conquerors attempting to dominate have had to renounce imposing their values. The natives accepted from foreign civilizations only traits that had become universal or those that could be assimilated into their own traditions. Ancient Tunisia's unity remained deep, despite the country's apparent diversities.

Hédi Slim

Tunisia After Classical Antiquity: A Personal View

The Conquests of Ifriqiya

In the waning days of Byzantine control of ancient Tunisia, the force of Islam became increasingly stronger. There were raiding expeditions from Egypt. One led by Abdellah Ibn Saad in A.D. 647–648, humbled the Byzantine forces at Sbeitla (Sufetula) and took the life of their leader, Gregory. With the Byzantine forces laid low, the forces of Islam still faced the Berber nomads, the unseizable enemy.

According to Arabic chroniclers, the Berber resistance crystallized around two intrepid chiefs, Kassila and Kahena, who dominated North Africa during the heroic epoch of the conquest, but information about these two is rare and often contradictory. Abou el-Mohajir (successor of Okba, the founder of Kairouan) wanted to undertake a spectacular march across the Mahgreb. Kassila rallied the Berber tribes and, aided by the Byzantine forces, surrounded him near Tahouda at the exit of Oued el-Abiod, where he was killed. The invaders retreated to Barqua, beyond Tripoli.

As to Kahena, it is said she was the queen of the Aures, but what do we know of her? She galvanized the Berbers to oppose the Arabic leaders and once again the Arabic army was thrown back to Tripoli. The powerful queen of the nomads was then able to extend her power to Tunisia. However, the Orientals took up the offensive again. After having put up a desperate fight near Tarfa, Kahena perished. From then on, the Tunisia of ancient Africa became Ifriqiya of the Arab-Muslim world.

The Arabic language and the Moslem religion spread across the country. The old Carthaginian culture that had resisted Romanization seems to have facilitated the task. With peace and security, confidence was reborn; the civilization bloomed under the protection of the Arabic princes. Vassal of the Abassids with their capital at Baghdad, a dynasty founded by Ibrahim Ibn Aghlab governed Tunisia, but the distance and mediocre means of communication must have encouraged the emirs (Arab rulers) to set themselves on the path of independence.

The Aghlabid Emirat

At the time of the Aghlabids (A.D. 800–910), Ifriqiya was prosperous. Agriculture, cottage industries, and commerce developed. Kairouan was then the center of wealth and knowledge.

To defend themselves, the emirs provided the villages with walls and fortified monasteries such as the ribats of Monastir and Sousse, where soldier monks gave themselves over to their devotions, yet all the while watching for infidels. The Sousse ribat was surrounded by a retaining wall squared with bastions at the angles and the extremities of the axes; a high watchtower dominated the horizon and allowed the surveying of broad expanses of the surrounding countryside. A single entry gave access onto a court bordered by a gallery that sheltered the cells. On the second floor are more cells and a vast oratory that attests to the citadel's religious character. The plan of the structure seems to have been inspired by Syrian castles of the Umayyad epoch.

The Fatimids, the Zirids, and the Hafcids

As the Fatimids succeeded the Aghlabids (A.D. 910–973), a Shiite dynasty came to power—thanks to the Kotama, a Berber tribe hostile to orthodoxy and to the external power. The Fatimids first settled themselves into the former Aghlabid residence, Raqqada, near Kairouan. However, a new capital was necessary for political reasons. Sitting on a plain, Raqqada was too vulnerable—not what a dynasty installed by violence needed. The Fatimids had always dreamed of conquering all of the Moslem world. Egypt was the second stage in this great march, and a port was necessary. These factors seem to have determined their plan to develop Mahdia on the east coast as a palace site. They created there an almost islandlike fortress surrounded by a wall with only two doors providing access to their village. On the southern coast of the near-island, a port that could shelter thirty ships was prepared. One can still admire the monumental entrance to the city, the "Squifa Kahla," and also see some traces of fortifications, the port, and foundations of the minaret of the Grand Mosque. Mahdia was, however, a utilitarian city. Far from being a capital of luxury, it had strategic value as a base for the expedition against Egypt. Sabra, Mahdia's opposite, was luxurious and destined to compete with Baghdad.

The reign of the Fatimids was marked by great economic prosperity, and it favored intellectual life. Learned men like Ishaq Ibn Soulayman and his student Ibn Al Jazar were part of this period of Tunisian history.

In A.D. 973, Caliph Fatimid installed himself in Egypt, leaving to the Zirids the administration of Ifriqiya and the right to found a new dynasty (A.D. 973–1050). To punish their vassals who dared recognize Baghdad to the detriment of Cairo, the Fatimids opened the door to the turbulent and nomadic tribes of Ben Hilal and Beni Soulim, who, like an invasion of locusts, ravaged Ifriqiya. The country descended into anarchy.

Not until the Hafcids was Tunis—old as the Libyan civilization—promoted to the rank of capital in A.D. 1236. The Hafcid kingdom gave birth to little principalities, and the ports became small republics organized for carrying out commerce. Tunis, Bizerte, Algiers, Oran, and other areas sent their galleys against the Christians, touching off the African Crusade.

The Regency of Tunis

On August 18, 1534, Tunis fell into the hands of the Turkish corsair Khair ed-Dine. The city was pillaged and the dynasty declared fallen. Charles V, championing Christianity against the barbarous corsairs, hesitated between Tunis and Algiers. On July 15, 1535, the Spanish fleet won La Goulette, near Carthage. Six days later, Tunis fell. Not wanting to conquer all of Barbary (the name now given to the Moslem region of North Africa west of Egypt), the Spanish limited themselves to building a fortress at the Strait of Gibraltar and restoring Sultan Moulay Hassen. However, Sinan-Pacha succeeded in conquering Tunisia and turned it into an Ottoman Turkish province in 1574. The regency of Tunis was conferred upon a pasha seconded by a militia commanded by an agha. A military revolution brought a dey to power.

The seventeenth century was marked by revolutions and battles that led to the victory of Bey Mourad (1612–1631). He obtained the title of pasha with the right to pass this title down to his descendants and thus to his son Hamouda. The Mouradite dynasty sank in a military plot.

The eclectic architecture of this time shows Turkish, Andalusian, Hispano-Moorish, and Italian influences. However, these foreign contributions were so well assimilated that they do not clash with the Hafcid heritage. Among the edifices of the century are numerous mosques: for example, the mosque of Youssef Dey, erected in 1616 not far from Dar El Bey, the current president's residence in Tunis; the mosque of Hamouda Pasha on Sidi Ben Arous road with its octagonal minaret. The quarter of Bab Souika in Tunis is dominated by the Sidi Mehrez mosque, whose construction goes back to 1675. The Ezzitouna mosque was notably enriched by the construction of its current double gallery. For the interior villages, there is the great mosque of Testour.

Also worth mentioning in the area of civil architecture are the enlarged and refurbished palace of Bardo and the markets (*souks*) such as the Ettrok Souk, Souk el Berka, Souk el Bechmaq, and Souk of the Chechias.

One cannot speak of the architecture without mentioning military and public works structures: for example, ramparts such as those of Kairouan, defenses and barracks in Tunis, the Tebourban bridges of Medjez-el Bab, and fountains in Tunis and elsewhere— an expression of hospitality and welcome.

Hussein Ben Ali proclaimed himself bey in 1705 and assured the regular succession of this throne to his descendants. Hussein was known for his prudence, energy, and intelligence. Under his reign, Tunis prospered. He maintained excellent relations with the European countries, and treaties were concluded with France, England, Spain, Holland, and Austria. In the interior, he maintained peace, necessary for prosperity; it was said that a girl wearing a diamond crown could go without danger from Tunis to Tozeur.

The French Protectorate

The Chamber of Deputies in France voted funds for a Tunisian expedition in April of 1881. On May 12th, the ruling bey signed the Treaty of Bardo, which allowed for a provisory occupation of Tunisia. According to this treaty, France would be represented by a resident minister general who would have control of external relations and affairs. At the convention of La Marsa (near Carthage) on June 8, 1883, Tunisia was declared a French protectorate.

Tunisia lost the greater part of its sovereignty; the protectorate concerned itself more with protecting the interests of the French in Tunisia than watching out for the Tunisian state. Paul Cambon was named resident general on February 18, 1882. Tunisia had to react.

The Khaldounia was founded in 1896, and Bechir Sfar was one of the founders. Its goals included spreading culture and modern science and providing a meeting place to discuss the political, social, and economic situation of Tunisia and all the Arabic countries. Through a very normal evolution, the Khaldounia became a hotbed of opposition to the colonial regime, giving rise to the Association of Former Students of the Sadiki College, founded in 1905 by Ali Bach Hamba. The objective was to protect the personality of Tunisia and create links between the intellectuals of the traditional culture and those educated in Western schools.

President Wilson's declaration concerning the right of people to self-determination, made on the eve of World War I, was greeted with enthusiasm by the colonized peoples. The successors of Bechir Sfar and Ali Bach Hamba decided to assemble under the banner of the Tunisian Party. This was the nucleus of the Tunisian Constitutional Liberal Party, which was created in 1920. The party's first doctrinal publication was *The Martyred Tunisia*. Writing in French, Cheikh Thallbi and his companions exposed the situation of the Tunisian state and proposed solutions. The Tunisian Constitutional Party endured longer than preceding movements, but it too was destined to fail due to its inability to draw on the masses and to asssemble the national organizations around itself. It alienated intellectuals such as Tahar Haddad (1899–1935) as well as men of action such as Mohammed Ali, the founder of Tunisian syndicalism in 1924. Organized as a syndicate, Tunisian workers organized, demonstrated, and carried out strikes in Tunis, Hammam-Lif, and Bizerte. The colonial authorities reacted violently; the syndicate was dissolved and its leaders arrested and exiled.

The year 1930 marked the triumph of French colonization in North Africa; it was the year of the centennial in Algeria and the Eucharistic Congress in Carthage. Reduced to misery and frustrated in their religious feelings, the Tunisian people got ready to fight. The youth of the Tunisian elite thought it was time to rejuvenate the Constitutionalist Party. Some intellectuals, directed by Habib Bourguiba, a young lawyer who had been educated for the most part in Western schools, knew the necessity of going into the streets, meeting the people, and making speeches in public places. This new approach of Habib Bourguiba took definite form at Ksar Hella on March 2, 1934. However, a long path, not without danger, still remained.

After having fought hard to liberate Tunisia, Habib Bourguiba next engaged in a fight against the forces of obscurity and misery. With his leadership, the Tunisian people have mobilized to fight underdevelopment. There has been concern for the liberation of women, mental health, and the growth of hospitals. Reforestation is another key program, along with the modernization of agriculture and development of industry.

Thanks to his policy of cooperation, mutual respect, and friendship, Bourguiba maintains Tunisia as a place where one can live a good life in an atmosphere of social peace, security for all, confidence, equality, and stability—all founded on love of nation and devotion to national unity, which creates prosperity and encourages progress.

Without neglecting its heritage, Tunisia links itself to the Arabic-Moslem world while retaining its links to the heartland of Africa and developing connections with the West and the East as well.

Tunisia has always supported international occasions where sovereign nations are invited to cooperate and override narrow interests and solve conflicting situations through sincere negotiations and dialogue. Whether it deals with the OAU, the United Nations, or the Arab League, Tunisia has always worked for the triumph of peace, liberty, fraternity, friendship, solidarity, and reciprocal esteem. Tunisia believes in the productiveness of dialogue. Land of civilization and international meeting place, Tunisia is also a land where one can appreciate the openness, the tolerance, and the love of one's fellow man.

M'Hamed Hassine Fantar

The African Mosaic in Antiquity

Tunisia has the world's richest collection of mosaics. Thousands of mosaic pavements and cut marble floors have been unearthed in the last century, and the search for new examples continues. It is a rare excavation that does not result in the discovery of one or more mosaic pavements having simple, geometric, floral, figural, monochrome, bichrome, or polychrome design. The discoveries have greatly aided archaeologists and historians to gain knowledge of Roman civilization—especially its provincial aspects.

Excavations have been made in Carthage by Tunisian, German, French, American, and other teams under the aegis of the UNESCO Program for the Preservation of Carthage. These have forced mosaic experts to reexamine the record concerning the beginning of mosaic work and, more precisely, *opus tessellatum* (the juxtaposition and insertion in mortar of small, more or less equally sized cut stones to form a smooth surface).[1] Until recently, scholars agreed that *opus tessellatum* originated at Morgantina, Sicily, in about the middle of the third century B.C.[2] But several years ago, archaeologists discovered a small mosaic piece in a fifth-century B.C. layer.[3] More recently, F. Chelbi uncovered a pavement in Carthage of *opus figlinum* (square ceramic pieces laid flat, comprising a band of *tessellatum* in a checkerboard pattern). Excavation beneath this revealed fourth-century B.C. Attic ceramic pieces, which establishes a *terminus post quem* for the pavement.[4] In addition, German and French teams working on the seafront of Carthage's Magon quarter and Byrsa Hill have uncovered apparently utilitarian pavement fragments in layers of earth fill dating between the fourth and second centuries. In light of these discoveries, it appears that *opus tessellatum* originated in Carthage probably in the fifth or fourth century. This should not be surprising, since the Carthaginians were already familiar with *pavimenta punica*, or pavements in *signinum* (mortar with a base of lime, sand, and bits of crushed tile) which were inlaid with small pieces of limestone, marble, and sometimes even glass, were usually white and were either plain or patterned in design and featured plants, the symbol of Tanit, the crescent on a staff, and so on. These pavements are found at sites outside Africa that were under Carthaginian hegemony; for example, Motya and Selinus in Sicily[5] and Nora Tharros and Cagliari in Sardinia.[6] The production of these pavements continued in the Carthaginian world at least until the first century A.D. while that of *tessellatum* apparently experienced an eclipse between the second and first centuries B.C.

Opus tessellatum reappeared in Carthage in the first half of the first century A.D. Then it was seen in Utica in simple monochrome or bichrome (black and white) pavements with geometric designs. Sometimes the mosaic copied the decoration of the *opus signinum*. Toward the end of the first and the beginning of the second century, African mosaic production began. Artisans in such areas as Carthage, Utica, Pupput, Hergla, and Acholla created black and white geometric mosaic pavements with very simple patterns, recalling mosaics produced in Italy during the same period. Artisans in Africa proceeded as if they were relearning the mosaic techniques from Rome and relegating their own traditions to secondary importance.

Only toward the end of the first half of the second century A.D. did African mosaicists begin to free themselves from Rome's influence. Their first innovations consisted of the gradual introduction of polychrome in the borders of floors and the integration of plant elements and geometric patterns. During the second half of the century and the first half of the third, the now-Romanized African cities began to experience economic prosperity and social tranquility. At the same time, the African ateliers disassociated themselves from the Italian mosaic canons and established their own style. It was distinguished, essentially, by the permanent adoption of polychromy and a fondness for very sophisticated vegetal decoration. Within this convention, each region had its own style and each city its own characteristics. The Carthaginian craftsmen perfected their well-known florid style, which became very popular in and outside of Africa, especially in Sicily, Sardinia, southern Gaul, and Spain in the third and fourth centuries.[7] Except for some exceptional mosaics (in the House of the Laberii at Oudna[8] and some pavements at Carthage[9]), the ProconsularProconsular ateliers apparently did not produce great quantities of figural mosaics during the second and third centuries. On the other hand, the Byzacene cities, especially El Jem and Acholla,[10] produced large figural groups: for example, the mosaics from the so-called Baths of Trajan and the House of Neptune at Acholla, the pavements from the House of the Dionysiac Procession[11] and the Domus Sollertiana at El Jem,[12] and the magnificent pavement of the triumph of Neptune from La Chebba.[13] These figural mosaics adhere to the Hellenistic tradition in their classical style.

From the middle of the third century—even if the depression did not affect Africa as much as it did the other provinces in the Empire—African mosaic production slackened because of decreasing construction activity. Pavements from the second half of the century are rare. But the fourth century and a good part of the fifth was the golden age of African mosaic production. Until a few years ago, mosaic experts hesitated to date certain key works to the fourth century, since historians considered this period as the decline in all fields. However, for more than a decade and following several archaeological excavations and rereading certain texts, the scholarly world has been discovering an African fourth century full of life and creativity, relatively insulated from the crises that severely afflicted other Roman provinces. Several years ago, C. Lepelley showed that the fourth and fifth century municipal bourgeoisie was very prosperous and continued to build luxurious houses richly decorated with mosaics.[14] Since then, several archaeological excavations have confirmed this new view. At Thuburbo Maius, some 60 kilometers from Carthage, recent excavations have shown that new quarters (in the east and west areas of the city) constructed in the fourth century were devoted to houses that were the equal of the most beautiful in Carthage.[15] The same was true at Bulla Regia and Dougga. The African bourgeoisie had an undisputed taste for grandeur and beauty, and commissions encouraged mosaicists to express their creativity; this resulted in great masterpieces at Carthage, Sidi Ghrib, Nabeul, Kelibia, Thuburbo Maius, Bulla Regia, Dougga, and elsewhere.

The mosaics, particularly the figural mosaics, are of great beauty and craftsmanship and were designed and carried out by well-established African ateliers. These ateliers also produced a great number of polychrome, geometric, and floral mosaics with increasingly sophisticated designs and considerable use of garlands and laurel wreaths. The African style, which had developed since the second century, had at this point reached its maturity and was widely disseminated in great strength and splendor throughout other Roman provinces. The discovery, about twenty years ago, of the mosaics at the villa of Piazza Armerina in Sicily has done much to further the argument of this African influence on mosaic work in other areas.[16] Some scholars even believe that the pavements in the Piazza Armerina are the work of African ateliers. More recently, the discovery of another great villa in Sicily confirms African influence on the great Sicilian creations. The influence of the African school is also found in the mosaic production of Sardinia and Spain. It is seen even in Rome, where the mosaic ceiling of Santa Costanza wonderfully recalls the scattered vegetation in the House of the Aviary in Carthage.[17]

The African ateliers continued to produce original work all through the fifth century under Vandal rule. The mosaic of Lord Julius and the crane hunt from Carthage and the magnificent hunt scenes from Kelibia are especially noteworthy. In the field of geometric and floral mosaics, African mosaicists continued to create new compositions like the plant pyramids, which were tremendously popular, especially in Gaul and Spain.[18]

We should also note the rich collection of grave mosaics, highly characteristic of Africa, whose influence is found especially on the Adriatic coast and in Spain.

With the Byzantine reconquest in the seventh century, mosaics in the Christian basilicas developed rapidly. Parallel to the traditional African style, a very similar new style appeared during the same period in northern Italy, particularly at Ravenna. Mosaics on non-Christian and mythological themes continued to be produced. Discoveries at Kelibia and elsewhere that date from the sixth and seventh centuries are evidence of this.

After the eighth century and with the Moslem conquest of Africa, mosaic production seems to have ceased, at least according to the present state of our knowledge. Henceforth, the centers of mosaic production moved from the western basin of the Mediterranean to the east. Africa, which had monopolized mosaic art for ten centuries, turned from it to other artistic fields.

Aïcha Ben Abed Ben Khader

1. Since 1973, the international UNESCO campaign to save Carthage has been carried out. Summary reports of the work appear in the Bulletin of Centre d'Etudes et du Documentation Archéologique de la Cónservation de Carthage (CEDACE).

2. Stern, 1976, p.12; Darmon, 1976, p. 28.

3. J.P. Morel, 1971, p.473–518.

4. Chelbi, 1983, p.79–88; 30 Ans, 1986, p. 57.

5. Fantar, 1978, p.6–11.

6. Angilillo, 1981, nos. 52, 53, 91, 68, 61, etc.

7. Several days of Franco-Tunisian discussions were held at Tunis in October 1985 on the topic: the floral style of Africa. The results will soon be published.

8. Gauckler, 1896, p. 177–229.

9. Let us note particularly the circus scene of Carthage: Yacoub, 1982, p. 55, A. 341.

10. Gozlan, 1974, p. 94–135.

11. Foucher, 1963.

12. Foucher, 1961, p. 15–25, pl. XV-XXVI.

13. Yacoub, 1982, p. 62, A. 292.

14. Lepelley, 1979.

15. Ben Abed, 1983, p.291–298.

16. Carandini, 1982.

17. Ennabli, 1983, p. 147, Pl. LXXXV, LXXXVII.

18. Ben Abed, 1983, p.61.

Carthage
A Mosaic of Ancient Tunisia
Catalogue

Catalogue

1. Herm Featuring the Head of a Libyan

Height: 80 cm; *Height of head:* 23 cm; *Width of head:* 16 cm
Material: Black schist with a white vein running diagonally through the head
Provenance: Carthage in the 1946 excavations of the Antonine Baths. Found with Catalogue 46.
Location: Bardo Museum
Date: Circa A.D. 150
Number: Inv. 3109

One of a pair of sculptures found in the Antonine Baths at Carthage, this carved head was the top of a stone pillar, or herm. The head is slightly asymmetric, and a "natte," or single plait of hair, is axially placed on the elongated shaved skull. A cross-shaped amulet hangs from the front of the hair. The eyebrows are very fine, and the eyes are almond-shaped. The nose is damaged. The mouth is slightly open, and the large ears extend to the sides.

The head appears to be that of a Libyan/Berber; the attribution is suggested by the hair style. The plait with crescent at its end frequently characterizes an infant god; examples have been recovered in Punic sanctuaries in Africa. They are sometimes the emblem of initiates in the cult of the Egyptian divinity Isis. This sculpture probably has no religious connection, but rather is an expressive portrait of an indigenous individual, probably executed in an African workshop. The tress coiffure is often worn today by Libyans in Egypt.

Bibliography: *De Carthage à Kairouan*, 1982, p. 119, with full bibliography.
NAO

2. Mold of the Face of a Man

Height: 29 cm; *Width:* 22 cm; *Thickness:* 8 cm
Material: Plaster
Provenance: El Jem in 1970 in a Roman house.
Location: Museum of El Jem
Date: First half of the third century A.D.
Number: None

This mold, from which a modern plaster cast has been made, was found in the workshop of a modestly proportioned house in the artisanal quarter of ancient Thysdrus. Broken into pieces since antiquity, it has been reconstituted by joining the six principal fragments; a few fragments from the left side of the face are missing. The mold bears no noticeable traces of heavy use.

Apparently the mask was applied in antiquity over the face of a dead man. It was then allowed to harden. It preserves the impression of the chin, mouth, nose, eyes, hair, and even

traces of facial hair. The plaster cast made from this mold reveals the individual's face with veracity. The characteristics of the face are those of a dead man: sunken eyes, closed tight-lipped mouth, uncut, untrimmed facial hair that gives the impression of a short beard and a slight mustache. (This may also simply be a stylistic vogue of the time.) It is a remarkable countenance: the forehead is large and slightly wrinkled; the eyelids are closed and the lashes clearly defined. The hair is short but tends to curl and carries down slightly over the forehead. The nose is flattened, apparently broken; and the left side of the face is also indented, perhaps the result of trauma and suggesting premature and violent death. The deceased must have been about forty years old.

Study of the features shows that this reproduces as faithfully as possible the image of an individual of Berber stock who died at Thysdrus about the middle of the third century A.D. Molds from other sites, such as Pompeii or Herculaneum, were often damaged and thus alter the individual's image. The El Jem mold is an important indicator of family life and funerary and religious practices of this period. Families kept galleries of casts (*imagines majorum*), and on the occasion of an important family event, such as a funeral, these ancestral portraits would be brought out to participate in the ceremonies. Such practices were codified and presided over by a *ius imaginum* originally limited to the nobility but gradually extended to the public at large.

Although they were made in great numbers, these *imagines* are almost never found. They are extremely fragile, and were normally destroyed once the cast had been made.

Bibliography: *De Carthage à Kairouan*, 1982, p. 127, with full bibliography.

HS

3. Relief of the Seven Berber Gods

Height: 98 cm *Width:* 1.01 m
Material: Limestone
Provenance: Beja, the ancient Vaga
Location: Bardo Museum
Date: Third century A.D.
Number: 3195

This votive relief shows seven individuals facing the viewer, each flanked by a lance. They are in front of a curtain facing the viewer. Behind the curtain is a grove with the tops of date palm trees

discernible; their branches are bent under the weight of the fruit, and the curtain is attached to three of the trees. The heads and shoulders of two people are visible—observers or harvesters. This two-line text appears at the base of the relief.

MARCURTAM, MACURGUM, VIHINA, BONCHOR, VARSISSIMA, MATILAM, IUNAM

M(ARCUS) AEMILIUS IANUARIUS ET Q(UINTUS) AELIUS FELIX DE SUO FECERUN(T) ET

DEDIC(AVE)RU(NT)

The last syllable RUNT of the Latin verb *dedicaverunt* is wedged in between the lines. The first line names the seven divinities represented, each shown with a characteristic attribute. The second tells us that Marcus Aemilius Ianuarius and Quintus Aelius Felix paid for and dedicated this monument. They are no doubt local African divinities.

The faces of all the figures are mutilated: in the center, in the place of honor, sits Bonchor, the master of this pantheon, holding a staff. To the viewer's left sits the goddess Vihina, wearing a plumed shoulder wrap and holding a forceps. The infant at her feet suggests that she may preside over childbirth. Next to the left is Macurgum, holding a scroll (*volumen*) in his right hand and a serpent-entwined staff in his left; he may be a god of health like Asclepius. To the viewer's right of Bonchor is Varsissima, without attributes. Next to the right is Matilam, who presides over the sacrifice of a boar and is advancing his right hand over an altar in a sacrificial gesture and holding a small pot in his left hand. At the ends of the relief are the horsemen and their steeds: Macurtam to the left and Iunam to the right, looking like the Greek divinities, The Dioscouroi. Each wears a short tunic that covers his left side and is fastened on the right shoulder with a brooch (*fibula*). Macurtam holds a bucketlike receptacle (*situla*) at shoulder height. Iunam might derive from the word *lunam*, suggesting the moon.

Although the gods' names are probably indigenous, their attributes may be at least partially those of the Greco-Roman pantheon—particularly since the text is in Latin and the dedicants are Roman or Romanized. It has become customary to refer to the African pantheon as the *Dii Mauri*, which literally means Mauretanian (northwest African) gods but by extension refers to the gods of Africa and/or Carthage. The Latin dedication to indigenous divinities gives strong evidence of Romano-African syncretism.

Bibliography: *De Carthage à Kairouan*, 1982, pp. 113–114, with full bibliography.

ZBA

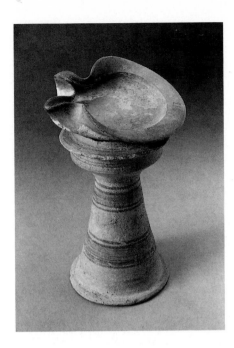

4. Punic Lamp and Support

Lamp

Dimensions: 13.2 cm x 13.1 cm
Material: Terra cotta
Provenance: Carthage, in the Dermech necropolis
Location: Bardo Museum
Date: Sixth to fifth century B.C.
Number: None

The typical Punic lamp form is a bowl, pinched in three places to form two spouts for wicks. They were important for tomb furnishings and are often found in a niche with a supporting stand or saucer.

Bibliography: Cintas, 1950, plate XL, No. 5; Deneauve, 1969, p. 24.

ZC

Support

Height: 17.7 cm
Material: Terra cotta
Provenance: Carthage, in the Dermech necropolis
Location: Bardo Museum
Date: Seventh to sixth century B.C.
Number: 81/43

This support has a bell-shaped shaft with a roundel at the base, while its upper part terminates in a bowl with carinated walls. The rim is surrounded by a molding inclined outward. The shaft carries a painted decoration of red bands limited by double black fillets separated by surfaces left in reserve. This lamp support was probably destined to carry a shell lamp of Punic type such as was just described above. It was sometimes used in place of a saucer or patera.

Bibliography: *30 Ans 1986,* p. 109, for the general type.

ZC

5. "Biberon" or Baby Feeding Bottle

Height: 11 cm
Material: Terra cotta
Provenance: Carthage, from a Punic tomb
Location: Bardo Museum
Date: Fourth to third century B.C.
Number: Inv. 82/1

This vase is a baby's bottle (*biberon*) and may indeed have been used for children. Thousands have been found at Carthage in the early Hellenistic period, and they are mostly associated with infant burials. The neck features a chamfered orifice; paint strokes of brown decorate this and the strap handle. The sucking spout is made as a nose or nose/mouth combination and is flanked by a pair of eyes and eyebrows. On either side of the eyes along the sides of the vessel are a leafy (palm?) branch and a sign of the great goddess Tanit, who had become the chief Carthaginian divinity by the early Hellenistic period. The biberon rests uneasily on its ring foot. Some of

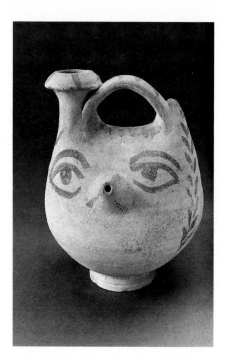 

these bottles may have been wrapped in soft coverings so as not to irritate a child while others may simply be ornamental or symbolic to protect the child after death. The vase is often said to intentionally resemble a female breast.

Bibliography: Cintas, 1950, plate XXXV; *De Carthage à Kairouan,* p. 67; *30 Ans 1986,* p. 109.

ZC

6. Head of Demeter/Incense Burner

Height: 25.3 cm
Material: Terra cotta
Provenance: Carthage, in the Sanctuary of Demeter
Location: Bardo Museum
Date: Circa 150 B.C.
Number: Inv. 1693

This elegant female head features almond eyes, a straight nose, petite mouth, and delicate lips. The earrings are composed of a globular pearl from which is suspended a spindle-shaped member. The hair is parted in the center; two masses of hair are arranged in locks and form graceful curves on the forehead. The sides of a veil, festooned at the ends, flank the neck; the veil is held in place by a crown decorated with stalks of wheat that almost look like rays. The crown, which resembles a *polos*, is flanked by projecting oreillettes.

The upper part of the crown ends in a bowl, which is pierced by a hole in the middle. The area at the base of the exterior is perhaps intended to indicate drapery with a clasp in the center of it, or the pattern may be a band with leaf decoration. A vent hole appears on the reverse. The wheat stalks help to identify the figure as Demeter, the Greek goddess of agriculture, who became extremely popular in Carthage during the Hellenistic period. The find spot also confirms the identification.

Bibliography: Delattre, 1923, p. 361; *30 Ans 1986,* p. 70.

ZC

7. Faience Amulets

Height range: 1 – 1.8 cm (Ptah) 1.2 – 2.5 cm (Horus) 0.9 – 1.5 cm (Oudja) 1.7 cm (Bastet)
Material: Faience
Provenance: Kerkouane (Cape Bon in northeastern Tunisia), in Tomb 225 of the city necropolis
Location: Bardo Museum
Date: End of the sixth century B.C. to the fourth century B.C.
Number: Inv. 2854

These twenty amulets represent Ptah (eight), the Oudja (six), Horus (five), and Bastet (one).

Ptah

These eight amulets reveal different aspects of Ptah. The simplest shows the god as a nude dwarf with a large head, a ballooning belly, short arms, and bowed legs. Five amulets are double-faced and present him on two crocodiles, with his hands over his chest and two falcons on his shoulders. Three of them show the scarab beetle on his head with a simple cross pattern. On three amulets, Ptah seems to be flanked by the goddesses Isis and Nephthys. On the base of three amulets, a geometric motif composed of two diagonals cut by an arrow at their intersection can be seen.

The two largest amulets show Ptah standing on two crocodiles, with his hands across his chest and holding two serpents. He has two falcons on his shoulders and a scarab on his head; Isis and Nephthys apppear on the lateral faces. On the back of these amulets is found Isis Pteroforos (winged) with the solar disk; she holds the ostrich feather of the goddess Maat. This type of amulet is very common throughout the Punic world.

The idea of a dwarf divinity associated with Carthage or Phoenicia came to be termed Pataikos by the Greeks, so that a dwarf Ptah would be Ptah Pataikos. Pataic images were used as figureheads on Phoenician ships. In Egypt, Ptah was traditionally the master craftsman of the gods who brought forth everything.

The Oudja

Known in Tunisia as the Oudja, this amulet represents an eye and an eyebrow above it; a vertical feature and a sort of volute are below. Egyptian in origin, this symbol appears very frequently in

143

the Punic world—often used in jewelry and on funerary steles and the hatchets or razors found in Carthage tombs. It is the symbol of the god Horus, possessor of great magic powers. The eye helps the dead ascend to the solar disk. Horus's left eye signified the moon. He was wounded in battle by Seth, god of darkness, but the eye was healed by Thoth. Sometimes both eyes are shown on opposite sides of an object, as in the case of Catalogue 31.

Falcon and Horus Falcon

The falcon is an attribute of Horus and is especially used to represent Horus without a crown or wearing a double crown. Horus Ra, crowned, was very popular in the Punic world—appearing on scarabs, rings, and hatchets/razors. Horus was a sky god whose symbol was a falcon or hawk; both were sacred to the Egyptians. Anyone killing one of these birds would also be put to death.

Bastet

The amulet showing the cat attributed to the goddess Bastet was somewhat less popular in the Punic world than the preceding types. Bastet or Bast was a protector of pregnant women and an apotropaic against disease and evil spirits. At Bubastis, Egypt, cats were mummified and buried.

Summary

The success of these various types of amulets was due to their role as powerful protectors. Ptah Pataikos was famous for his prophylactic role against snakes, scorpions, and evil-doing animals. The falcons suggest syncretization to or assimilation with Horus, the deliverer from crocodiles, who is also invoked against dangerous animals. The scarab may suggest resurrection and reincarnation; in Egypt, scarabs often symbolized creation and were associated with spontaneous creation and regeneration, and thousands of scarab amulets are known. Oudja stands for "the eye bringing good fortune" and symbolizes the triumph of good over evil as well as new life. The dating of these amulets is not certain.

Bibliography: *30 Ans 1986,* pp. 92–95; Acquaro, 1977, Plates LI–LII.
HBY

8. Rod-Formed Glass Head Pendants

Height: 2.0 cm
Material: Brown and white glass
Provenance: Kerkouane, in Tomb 19 of the necropolis
Location: Bardo Museum
Date: 650 to 450 B.C.
Number: Inv. 2157

These almost comical glass head pendants are common in Punic tombs. The brown-and-white example features enormous eyes, a white popeyed pellet surrounded by a white circle. The iris of the left eye is brown. The nose is bulbous, the lips are thick, and the chin is pointed. The ears are asymmetrical with the ear to the viewer's left shaped like a macaroni and the right is a scooped-out disc. The smooth skull is topped with a ring for suspending the mask, perhaps from a string. A horizontal groove passes just above the level of the ears on the forehead; at its two ends are traces of a white band. Since the forehead is very narrow, the artisan had to abandon applying the headband all around the forehead due to lack of space—an example of mediocre workmanship. This example and its scarcely more elegant companion are typical on many Pu-

nic sites, especially in the Carthage area. The second example uses yellow to highlight a beard, brows, and nostrils.

The two glass head pendants in the Catalogue are part of a far larger series of similar pendants and cylindrical beads produced between the sixth and third century B.C. and commonly found on Phoenician or Punic sites in the eastern and western Mediterranean. Although found in Egypt, Cyprus, and Greek lands as well, they are often considered to be the products of Phoenician or Carthaginian glassmakers who fabricated several recognizable classes of such pendants in two or three distinct phases. These pendants were formed from a large blob of hot glass applied over the tip of a metal rod. Facial features and suspension rings were added in the form of trails and tiny blobs of colored glass. The pendants, found singly or strung in groups with beads to form necklaces, served either as jewelry or amulets.

Among the earliest are a class of representations of male heads, or demonic masks, dated to the sixth to fourth centuries B.C., and widely disseminated throughout the eastern Mediterranean and Punic areas of the western Mediterranean. A more outstanding and elaborate class depicts male heads with spiraling ringlets for hair and beards and large gold rings in their ears. These are mostly known from Carthaginian centers in Sicily, Sardinia, Spain, and the Balearic Islands. They date to the fourth century B.C. and are possibly the products of a glass industry located at Carthage or elsewhere in the western Mediterranean.

Bibliography: Seefried, 1982, pp. 6, 26, Plate I; *De Carthage à Kairouan,* 1983, pp. 61–62, with bibliography.
ABYK

9. Gold Pendant for Carrying an Amulet

Height: 4.1 cm; *Width:* 1 cm; *Thickness:* 0.6 to 0.8 cm
Material: Gold; *Weight:* 4.69 g
Provenance: Kerkouane, in Tomb 210 of the Necropolis
Location: Bardo Museum
Date: Fifth to fourth century B.C.
Number: Inv. 2840

This pendant represents the goddess Sekhmet with a lion head surmounted by a divine snake (*uraeus*) with disk mounted on a solar disk surrounded by a thread of beads. The goddess is standing on a little podium, cubical in shape and decorated on three sides with two triangles that are pointed toward the base and filled with green glass. She is clothed in a long-sleeved robe, the lower part of which is made up of a bird's wings. A belt, visible primarily on the back, surrounds the garment, and a necklace adorns her chest. Above the elbows on each arm are three bracelets. The hair consists of a series of channels that fit together in the manner of an Egyptian wig.

The goddess's left hand rests on her chest and holds a green ivy leaf, and her right hand seems to be dropping a thin stem that terminates in a large ivy leaf; the leaf totally hides her knees. The green color of the large leaf has largely vanished. The overall quality of workmanship is good despite some imperfections. The body of the goddess was molded in two parts that were soldered together; there is a slight asymmetry as a result of the joining. The podium, the solar disk carrying the handle on the reverse, and the ivy leaves were added later. The interior of the pendant is hollow.

This unpublished piece seems to have functioned as an amulet carrier; if this hypothesis is correct, this is the only example that has been found. Punic sites around the Mediterranean have yielded a number of amulet carriers or holders; usually, they are boxes or cylindrical cases surmounted by a protome of Sekhmet. But this example reveals the entire goddess.

The robe of the goddess is found on some of the hatchets/razors found in Carthage, and it also occurs on Carthaginian sarcophagi. A winged bust of the goddess has been found in the sanctuary of Es-Cuiram on Ibiza, but the lion-headed goddess of Thinissut in Tunisia is the closest parallel. In this example, the goddess Sekhmet differs from her image on many amulets. Particularly difficult to explain is the double presence of the ivy leaf, since her typical attribute, shared with Bastet, is the sceptre illustrating her relationship with birth and rebirth. The ivy leaf is a motif more at home in the Hellenistic or Classical world, and its use here may be a borrowing from the Dionysiac repertoire as a symbol evoking eternal life.

This amulet carrier reflects the tendency of Punic art to transform motifs inherited from other cultures. The choice of motifs shows a knowledge of magic and religious beliefs of cultures in the periphery of the Punic world. The name of the goddess Sekhmet is invoked on Punic flasks along with Ptah and Nefertoum. She plays a role that is both apotropaic and medicinal, and her iconography appears frequently on magic bands placed inside the amulet carriers. The ivy leaf probably represents a Greek attribute that the Punic artist added to the goddess's repertoire to extend her powers of goodness.

This is a protective case for a magic band or amulet—a kind of talisman produced in metropolitan Carthage; roughly similar work was produced by Punic craftsmen in Sardinia. The Sardinian examples are generally more carefully made. The date of the piece, difficult to establish, is suggested by the location in which it was found.

Sekhmet is traditionally a lion goddess who symbolizes solar force, a powerful ally in battle and a consort of Ptah, so popular in Carthage. Their son was Nefertoum/Nefertem. The uraeus was often employed as a warning to keep people away from a sacred area, and it had strong apotropaic powers.

Bibliography: Quillard, 1970–1971, p. 10.

HBY

10. Incense Burner in the Shape of an Altar

Height: 16 cm
Material: Soft limestone
Provenance: Carthage, in the Dermech necropolis
Location: Bardo Museum
Date: Seventh to sixth century B.C.
Number: CMA 625

This altar is generally pyramidal in form, but its upper part contains three superposed moldings, the top and bottom of which are painted red. The moldings recall a prototype found throughout Egypt and used on many Punic monuments. Egyptian influence in the seventh through fifth centuries B.C. was particularly pervasive in Carthage. The top is designed for burning incense. This example is one of the best preserved of this "small altar" series with the paint surviving extraordinarily well. Similar but larger altars were used as votive stone markers (*cippi*) in the sixth and fifth centuries B.C.

Bibliography: Picard (no date), pp. 129–130; 19–20 for the general form.
ZC

11. Three Bronze Bells

Bell (left)

Height: 4 cm
Material: Copper alloy
Provenance: Carthage, in a Punic tomb
Location: Bardo Museum
Date: Circa fourth to third century B.C.
Number: None

Bell (center)

Height: 5.5 cm
Material: Copper alloy
Provenance: Kerkouane, in Tomb 222 in the necropolis
Location: Bardo Museum
Date: Circa fourth to third century B.C.
Number: Inv. 2933

Bell (lower right)

Height: 4.5 cm
Material: Copper alloy
Provenance: El Jem
Location: Bardo Museum
Date: Circa second century B.C.
Number: None

The left bell is in the shape of a truncated cone and has a small ring for hanging. There is usually a small clapper of the same material fastened inside through the use of two tiny perforations near the summit of the bell and on opposite sides. Only one example (lower right) still has its clapper. These bells were enormously popular in Punic tombs between the fourth and third centuries B.C., while the El Jem example may date to the second century B.C. They cannot be dated stylistically but rather from the contexts in which they were found.

Bibliography: Benichou, 1982, p. 267; *30 Ans 1986,* p. 83, with bibliography.
ZC/ABYK

12. Bronze Cymbals

Diameter range: 9.5 cm
Material: Copper alloy
Provenance: Kerkouane, in the necropolis
Location: Bardo Museum
Date: Fourth century B.C.
Number: None

Along with bells, cymbals of small size were also extremely popular in the Punic tombs, notably in the Carthage and Cape Bon areas. They must have had a magic quality, serving as talismans and, through their musical sounds or noise, could keep evil spirits away from the tomb.

Like the bells, the cymbals are found commonly in Punic tombs and remind one of the importance of music in ancient Carthage and around the Mediterranean at this time:

In entering into the city, you will meet some prophets descending from the high place, preceded by the lute, tambourine, flute and harp and they are prophesying. (I SAMUEL, X:5)

David and all the house of Israel played before the Eternal One all sorts of instruments of wood, including cypress, lutes, tambourines, sistra [rattles] and cymbals.(II SAMUEL, VI:5)

And David said to the chiefs of the Levites to make their brothers singers with musical instruments such as lyres, harps and cymbals so that they would make with their noise sounds of rejoicing. (I CHRONICLES, XV:6)

For the music of Carthage, evidence comes from ancient writers, steles with Punic or Neo-Punic inscriptions, and terra cotta and ivory figurines. Among the instruments are the flute, harp, and other stringed instruments (cithara, chelys perhaps); the remains of numerous ivory bridges appear in quantity in the Punic tombs of ancient Carthage. For percussion, rhythm, and meter, tambourines and cymbals were used.

From remote antiquity in the Semitic East and in the Mediterranean, music occupied an important place in both profane and religious activities. Music was used at social festivals; it was also important for temple and sanctuary ceremonies, performed by singers and musicians who were slaves for the divinity. Plutarch, a Greek writer living in the Roman Empire in the early second century A.D., tells us that when child sacrifices were made in the Punic Tophet, "some flute and tambourine players were placed before the statue of the god and they drowned out with their musical uproar the cries and lamentations of those being sacrificed."

Bibliography: Gauckler, 1915, pp. 8,20; Fantar, 1970, Plates CLXIII–CLXIV; Fantar, 1970–1972, Plate XI; Picard, 1982, pp. 168–169. For a female tambourine player engraved on a razor found at Punic Ibiza and now in Madrid, see Moscati, 1966, Figure 126.
MF

13–15. Three Steles from the Salammbô Tophet in Carthage

As very often happens in Punic archaeology, a great discovery is accidental. The Salammbô Tophet, the greatest sanctuary of Carthage, was found by a rock hunter, and subsequently identified by archaeologists in 1921.

Since the discovery of the Tophet, several excavation campaigns have followed one another on the site, although the precise limits of the sanctuary remain difficult to define.

In 1923, L. Poinssot and R. Lantier presented a report on the whole zone which had been excavated up to that point. Two years later came the American excavation under the direction of Kelsey and Chabot. The third excavation campaign at Salammbô was the work of P. Lapeyre. Excavation by P. Cintas took place just after the Second World War. One of the last excavations of the Salammbô Tophet was conducted by a team from the American School of Oriental Research (ASOR) directed by Professor L.E. Stager from the Chicago Oriental Institute. It was carried out within the framework of the International Campaign for the Protection of Carthage, overseen by UNESCO with the collaboration of the National Institute of Archeology and Art (Tunisia).

In the light of these different excavations, the Salammbô Tophet appears to be an open-air sacred area in the middle of which rise funerary steles, and votive or funeral chapels.

The sacred area of the Tophet could, moreover, shelter some cult buildings. An architectural fragment with an Egyptian molding seems to belong to either a cult edifice or to a monumental entrance to the Tophet itself. In support of the hypothesis of the cult edifice, one could cite the example of Mount Sirai in southern Sardinia, where the Tophet is equipped with a well-built temple reached by a staircase cut into the rock.

Besides these few architectural fragments, the excavation campaigns, which have allowed the partial uncovering of the Salammbô Tophet, have given archaeologists an enormous amount of material: amulets, jewelry, masks, and terra cotta statuettes. However, it is the sacrificial urns and the votive steles that are most common and offer invaluable typological, iconographical, and epigraphical evidence. The excavators were able to certify that the sacrificial urns, which differ in their form and dimensions over time, were buried in the soil in superimposed but nonhorizontal layers. They overlap like fish scales. The Salammbô Tophet must have appeared to living Carthaginians like a vast area strewn with artificial mounds of earth, sand, and cinders: these mounds were urns and steles crowded in upon each other to the point of interpenetration, which has confounded archaeological statigraphy.

In Roman times, the sacred area of the Tophet was completely turned upside down to install new structures, including probably a sanctuary, docks, and warehouses.

The decor of the funerary steles is sometimes reduced to simple symbols expressed in a "language" that could seem mysterious and esoteric to us but was certainly accessible to those for whom it was destined. Here are the principal elements of this abstract decor: the sign of Tanit, the crescent and the disk, the sign of the bottle (or cylinder), the diamond (or lozenge), and the baetyl, or stone, as an idol.

This iconographic repertoire seems to derive from Semitic sources—excluding the sign of Tanit. The sign was probably created at Carthage and may have served as an emblem of the city (P. Cintas). Perhaps it served as a divine hypostasis; it also had a prophylactic value on a Punic pavement in the city of Kerkouane. Sabatino Moscati attributes the sign of Tanit to a stylization of a female image such as those often represented on the steles of Motya.

The other symbols, such as the so-called sign of the bottle, the astral group of the crescent and disk, the bottle and the diamond (lozenge) also bring up difficulties of interpretation; presented here are three collected by the American team directed by L.E. Stager in 1975–1977, half a century after the excavation carried out by F.W. Kelsey, of which the results were published in 1926 in New York.

Bibliography: L.E. Stager, 1978, pp. 151–189; L.E. Stager 1982, pp. 155–173; L.E. Stager, 1984, pp. 31–51 with full bibliography of earlier excavations.
MF

13. Stele from the Tophet of Carthage

Stele: Length: 24 cm; *Width:* 10 cm; *Thickness:* 8.5 cm;
Base projection: Length: 6.9 cm; *Width:* 6.7 cm; *Breadth:* 3.6 cm;
Material: Gray, fine-grained limestone
Provenance: Carthage, in the Tophet
Location: Tophet of Carthage
Date: Fourth century B.C.
Number: None

This stele has a rough base projection that probably fits into some sort of support. The stele proper is well cut and polished and contains a three-line inscription in Punic characters and language; it deals with a gift that was probably offered for the Tophet divinities.
Transcription of the epigraphy:

(M) TNT ʿ Z R B
(ʿ) L BN BD ʿSTR
(T) BN MHRBʾL

The missing first letter of each of the three lines of the inscription can be easily restored with an M at the beginning of the text, where it must be read (M) TNT which means offering, gift. For the second line, the letter that was removed is certainly an aïn; it is the next in line of the name of the dedicator ʿZRBʾL (Azrabaal), a very frequently used name in Carthage and which the Latins pronounced Asdrubal.

As to line three, the lost letter is the end of an equally frequently used name BDʿSTRT (Bodashtart).

Taking into account these restorations, the translation of the Punic text could be:
Gift of Azrabaal
Son of Bodashtart
Son of Mahr baal

At the end of this presentation, it is important to note the absence of much of the dedicatory and propitiary formulae.

Contrary to what is ordinarily found, the divinities to whom the gift MTNT is addressed are not mentioned. As to why there was this silence, we can only put forth conjectures: the stele being destined for the Tophet, the destined divinities were therefore already known; the benedictory request is also not expressed. It would be implicit.
MF

14. Stele from the Tophet of Carthage

Length: 24 cm; *Width:* 11.5 cm; *Breadth:* 4 cm
Material: Gray, fine-grained limestone
Provenance: Carthage, in the Tophet
Location: Tophet of Carthage
Date: Fourth century B.C.
Number: None

This funerary stele is in the form of an obelisk with a triangular summit; only the anterior face was decorated and polished, while the other faces were roughed out with a chisel and left. The symbol called the bottle or cylinder is shown on a support—maybe a pedestal or an altar—with small concave sides. It would deal with the hypostasis of the divinity: Tanit, Astarte, or maybe even Baal Hammon. It would be a representation of the presence of divine power.

Underneath the bottle sign, which occupies the upper part of the stele, there is an inscription in Punic characters and language of which only three lines remain. It is a dedication to the Tophet's divinities: the Lady Tanit and the Lord Baal Hammon.
Transcription of the epigraphy:

L RBT L TNT PN B (C)

L W L'DW L B 'L H

'(M) N 'S N D R H

The stele lacks a good part of the bottom portion; moreover, certain letters have vanished: an aïn at the end of the first line, a W near the beginning of line two as well as the shaft of the M at the beginning of line three. The context allows the proposed restoration and the reading and translation of the text present no difficulty.

To the lady Tanit Face of Baa-

l and to the Lord Baal Ha-

Moun to whom has dedicated H

It is a typical dedication. The text begins with the dedicatory formula with the evocation of the lady Tanit, Face of Baal, and of the Lord Baal Hammon. After that, there is the dedicator who presents himself. His name starts with an H. There are numerous possibilities: Himilk, Himilkat, Hannon, Hannibal.

We cannot know if the inscription ends with the propitiary formula very frequently used on the steles of this type, but it probably was a contractual sacrifice.
MF

15. Stele from the Tophet of Carthage

Length: 39 cm; *Width:* 14.3 cm; *Breadth:* 10.5cm
Material: Gray, fine-grained limestone
Provenance: Carthage, in the Tophet
Location: Tophet of Carthage
Date: Fourth century B.C.
Number: None

This fragmentary stele is in obelisk form with a triangular summit. Only the anterior face is well polished; the other faces were roughed out with a chisel and left. At the level of the base of the triangular pediment, the stele offers an image frequently found in Carthaginian iconography, the crescent turning back onto the disk. It deals with two primary luminaries, the coupled moon and sun; the interpretation of this remains controversial. It may be a symbol that underlines the universal character of the Tophet divinities or a request for protection and for benediction. The crescent symbol in particular has carried through as a religious and national symbol for Muslims.
MF

151

16. The Urns of the Tophet of Carthage

Urn

Height: 24.5 cm; *Maximum diameter:* 19.5 cm
Material: Ceramic
Provenance: The Tophet of Carthage
Location: Bardo Museum
Date: 550 to 500 B.C.
Number: Carthage 1899

This urn of reddish fabric and gray-green surface (in the first illustration, left)comes from one of the middle strata in the Tophet of Carthage. When it was found, it contained sacrificial ashes. The puffed-out form and elevated handles close to the line of the rim determine the date.

Bibliography: Cintas, 1950, Plate XX, Number 251; Chelbi, 1985, pp. 79 – 80; Harden, 1937, Figure 5.

Urn

Height: 21.5 cm; *Diameter:* 15.5 cm
Date: 450 to 400 B.C.
Number: Inv. 475, Carthage 1.904

This urn of brownish fabric with lime inclusions and a pale green surface (in the first illustration,right)is sandy and rough to the touch—like most Punic ceramics. The handles are elliptical in section and present a triangular form. The belly is thinner when compared to earlier examples of the same type. This is a vessel of the so-called Tanit II type.

Bibliography: Harden, 1937, Figure 5.

Urn

Height: 21 cm; *Diameter:* 15.6 cm
Date: Circa 450 B.C.
Number: Inv. CT76-1.034-226

This urn of Cintas Form 251 (second illustration, right) has handles a bit lower than those of earlier urns. In section, this urn is more flattened out and tends to be slightly more elliptical than its predecessors.

Bibliography: Cintas, 1950, Plate XX, NumberM6251; Harden, 1937, Class Fa,C of Tanit II; Chelbi, 1985, pp. 79-80.

Urn

Height: 22.5 cm; *Diameter:* 14.8 cm
Date: 450 to 400 B.C.
Number: CT76-1.034-220

The section of the handles of this type of urn (second illustration,center) is nicely elliptical, and the handle is low with respect to the rim. The belly of the urn is thinner and gives the vase an elegant and slender shape. The shoulder is characterized by a carination.

Bibliography; Harden, 1937, Figure 5.

Urn

Height: 17.5 cm; *Diameter:* 14 cm
Date: 500 to 450 B.C.
Number: CT77-2.088-5531

This urn of micaceous rose fabric (second illustration, left) is quite small and comes from the intermediate strata of the Tophet of Carthage. The placement of the handles and the swollen form allow for dating the piece.

The Tophet of Carthage was the place of human sacrifice where infants and children occasionally up to ten years of age were offered to the Punic gods Baal Hammon and Tanit. Their cremated remains were placed in urns, which were buried and usually marked with a stele, or gravestone such as has been shown (Catalogue 13–15). The complex stratigraphy of the muddy strata of the Tophet and the fact that it was mostly excavated so long ago make chronological understanding of the area difficult and classifying the various urn types by date often hazardous.

Despite the research undertaken by D.B. Harden and the results his excavation produced, the typological and chronological story of the urns of the Tophet is not yet complete and rests on stylistic conclusions about Punic pottery in general. The publication of the recent Stager excavations by the Chicago Oriental Institute will help to fill the lacuna. Some help has also come from excavations at Motya in Sicily. There have also been discoveries of the Tophet urn types in Punic tombs, where they may occasionally serve as little amphoras.

Bibliography: Harden, 1937, Figure 5.
FC

17. Dea Nutrix (The Nurturing Goddess)

Height: 35 cm
Material: Terra cotta
Provenance: Area of the Village of Soliman (Cape Bon), in a Roman cistern
Location: Bardo Museum
Date: Late second or first century B.C.
Number: 3471

One of the most beautiful pieces in the Bardo, this statuette brings to mind traditional imagery of the Madonna and Christ child. It was found along with sixteen other terra cotta statuettes and statuette fragments. They may have all come from a rural sanctuary of Punic type during the early period of Roman domination. The term Neo-Punic is used to describe such works, and this statuette may have been dedicated to the cult of the goddesses of fertility and fecundity.

The statuette shows a young woman seated on a bench and holding a nude infant on her knees. She wears a tunic and a rigid veil over her head. She is supporting the child's back with her left hand and bringing the child to her breast with her right hand. Commonly, statuettes such as these are identified with the Greek goddess Demeter, known to have enjoyed a certain vogue in Hellenistic Carthage. The infant on her knee would then be Damophon, whom Demeter tended in infancy to comfort herself over the loss of her own Persephone. Demeter was the great earth goddess and patroness of agriculture, as well as the being who causes the changes of the seasons. But this may not be Demeter, and it is possible to think of the statuette as the *Dea Nutrix*, the nourishing goddess whose cult was widespread in Africa in the Punic epoch and during the Roman period. Images of Isis holding baby Horus were also widespread. This statuette brings to mind traditional imagery of the Madonna and Christ child.

Bibliography: Yacoub, 1978, pp. 23-24; Picard, 1956, p. 56.
MK

18. Lamp in the Form of a Bearded Human Head and Frog

Height: 15 cm; *Width:* 8 cm
Material: Brownish limestone
Provenance: Kerkouane, in the Punic necropolis
Location: Bardo Museum
Date: Third century B.C.

The oldest lamps found at the Punic sites of Carthage and Utica date to the eighth century B.C. Late in that century, they probably began to appear in tombs. During the Punic period, local and imported lamps, especially from the Greek world, were popular. The basins of the Punic lamp

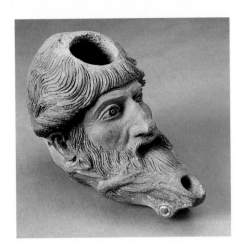

examples retain the form of a simple bowl, or coquille Saint Jacques form, with spouts for wicks made by pinching the clay. (See Catalogue 4.) The double-spouted lamps easily contained the necessary oil. Wicks were made of a material such as low-grade flax (oakum). Lamps of this type continued up until the time of the Punic Wars with Rome in the third and second centuries B.C.

The lamps were usually made of clay, but various materials were used. Beginning in the second century B.C., Punic lamps have a more closed form and may have more than two pinched spouts. Without forgetting tubular lamps or lamps in the form of a chalice, which were used a great deal in the Carthage area and locally made, the Punic people appreciated Greek lamps also, both from a practical and an aesthetic viewpoint, and local imitations were produced.

This imported lamp, which might have been made in Alexandria, is one of the most extraordinary ever found in Tunisia. On the upper part of the body or reservoir is the head of a bearded personage with eyes of dark blue glass inlaid with gold. It makes a strong impression, and the figure may be a divinity. But a surprise awaits, for when the lamp is turned over, a frog is on the lower side. The frog may be intended to refer to the Nile and to the idea of resurrection.

Bibliography: *30 Ans 1986*, p. 71, with full bibliography.

MF

19. Vase in the Shape of a Bird

Height: 15 cm
Material: Terra cotta
Provenance: Carthage, in the Odeon area necropolis
Location Bardo Museum
Date: Fourth to third century B.C.
Number: 170

One of the most elegant of the zoomorphic vases in the Bardo Museum is this pouring vessel in the shape of a bird, probably that of a dove. The neck and filling opening are placed at the summit of the back, and a strap handle is fitted between the neck and the fanlike tail; the pouring spout is at the tip of the cylindrical beak. Traces of red paint are found on the sides of the body and were probably intended to indicate the wings and feathers. The vessel's general form compares to an askos or bag-shaped container for liquid (usually wine) made from animal hide but also produced in ceramic form.

Birds were popular tomb offerings, since they could be thought of as the winged soul of the deceased or at least as an intermediary between the faithful and the divine. On Cyprus, for example, they often appear as cultic accoutrements hovering atop sacred trees or on representations of sanctuaries, although this example shows the influence of southern Italy. Dr. Arielle Kozloff notes close parallels between this dove and those on Canosan urns of the fourth to third century B.C.

Bibliography: *De Carthage à Kairouan,* 1982, p. 68, with full bibliography.
ZC

20. Askos in the Form of a Black African

Height: 8.9 cm; *Length:* 9.5 cm
Material: Black glazed pottery
Provenance: Kerkouane, in the public necropolis of Arg el Ghazouani
Location: Bardo Museum
Date: Fourth to third century B.C.
Number: None

A surprising number of objects representing blacks have been found in Punic Tunisia; the black remained popular as a striking figure for sculpture in the Roman period as well. Here a young and muscular black has been rendered by using the lustrous Greek black glaze technique; this vessel must have been an import.

The figure is down on all fours but seated rather than truly kneeling. He seems to be pouring a drink from an amphora that has been tipped down onto its side. The pouring spout emerges from the lower back of the boy and behind his neck, and the spout is a handle that gives the impression of being a rope knotted in the center. Such an object could have been an elegant novelty gift containing sweet-smelling fragrance or oil.

The askos has two known parallels. One from south Italy or Sicily is described thus:

an Ethiopian slave...is crouching on an oval base, dressed in a donkey skin and holding an indistinct object in its hand.

Jean-Paul Morel hints to a production in Magna-Grecia or it might even be Punic; he cites a similar vessel from Spain, which he dates to the fourth or third century B.C.

The second parallel, from southern Italy, is currently in The Metropolitan Museum of Art in New York. The askos is in the form of a boy seizing a goose and is dated to the fourth century B.C. It has the same double handle and the same knot as this piece.

Bibliography: *30 Ans 1986,* p. 124; Picard, 1956, p. 53; Morel, 1981, No. 9471a; Snowden, 1970, Figure 38, Plates XV–XVI.
ZC

21. Pouring Vessel in the Form of a Mouse

Height: 7.3 cm; *Length:* 13 cm
Material: Terra cotta
Provenance: Thapsus, in the Punic necropolis
Location: Bardo Museum
Date: Third century B.C.
Number: C.M.A. 322

This vessel in the form of a mouse bears a striking resemblance to a modern-day piggy bank but is really a pouring vessel with a spout on top flanked by projections for hanging. It has amusing, dumpy proportions and a tiny triangular head with pulled-up ears. The eyes are indicated by two black dots flanked by two short lines. The feet are shaped like truncated cones.

The light orange surface is highlighted by black glaze, including the ears, neck area, mouth, hanging handles, and spout. A decoration of ivy leaves on a thin branch occupies much of the upper body. An elongated palmette appears between the ears and above and on the forehead. Whether the piece is of local manufacture or a Hellenic import is unclear, but it represents the sense of humor that existed in Punic Tunisia and clearly shows the considerable Greek influence in the Hellenistic period. A very close parallel from Sicily with grapevine decoration on the back has been dated 450–400 B.C. and is identified as a shrew.

Bibliography: Gauckler, 1915, p. 70; Bloesch, 1974, No. 292.
ZC

22. Cast Gold-Band Alabastron

Height: 6 cm; *Diameter:* 2 cm
Material: Glass, with a bone applicator
Provenance: Carthage, in a Punic necropolis
Location: Bardo Museum
Date: First century B.C. (Neo-Punic)
Number: None

Among the finest examples of glassmaking in the late Hellenistic period (second to first century B.C.) are a score of gold-band alabastra with detachable stoppers. They were made to hold scented oils, cosmetics, or other substances. These vessels, cast from pre-formed canes of dark green, purple, royal blue, turquoise blue, and gold-yellow glass, also incorporate one or more long canes of sandwich gold-glass—that is, a strip of gold leaf laminated between two thin

layers of colorless glass. Although the stopper of this alabastron is missing, a simple bone applicator with a carved conical tip was found with the object in a grave at Carthage. Similar alabastra are known from Greece, Cyprus, Turkey, Etruria, and southern Italy.

ZC

23. Punic Mirrors

Diameter: 16.2 and 17.4 cm; *Thickness:* 0.4 and 0.3 cm
Material: Copper alloy
Provenance: Kerkouane, in Tombs 111 and 140 in the necropolis
Location: Bardo Museum
Date: Probably fourth century B.C.
Number: None

Makeup boxes, polychrome glass perfume bottles, jewelry, and jewelry boxes, and even—at Kerkouane—molds for making jewelry have been recovered in excavations of tombs. French archaeologists working in Carthage earlier in this century and at the end of the last (Paul Gauckler, R.P. Delattre, A. Merlin, and others) have discovered in tombs of Punic date skeletons still wearing their favorite ornaments—hairpins, headbands, finger rings, pearl and gold necklaces. In 1899, Paul Gauckler wrote about one of his extraordinary finds in an excavation of a Punic tomb on the Bordj Djedid in Carthage:

Her left wrist disappears under a bracelet of pearls, scarabs, and diverse figurines. On the right arm are strung many rings of silver and ivory. The fingers bear rings of silver and one of gold. On the left ear a gold pendant with a tau cross, on the neck a great gold necklace formed by forty elements of various forms disposed symmetrically around a central brooch, forming a crescent in turquoise falling on a disc of hyacinth. Another necklace of silver completes the finery.

  The mirror is almost always round, made of copper alloy, and silvered on one side. Most examples are undecorated—not incised as in the Etruscan tradition. One example found in a tomb in Carthage was wrapped in flax. Mirrors are common in tombs at Kerkouane as well. Occasionally, they have bone or ivory handles in the form of statuettes. One found in Douimes in Carthage ends in a bird or serpent form. Mirrors are often found lying on the body inside the sarcophagus—conveniently placed for the deceased to fix her face for another life.

Bibliography: Fantar, Vol. III, 1986, pp. 526–528, with full bibliography.

MF

24. Lead Makeup Box

Height: 4.3 cm; *Diameter:* 6.6 cm; *Cover:* 1.2 cm x 6.9 cm
Material: Lead
Provenance: Carthage, in a Punic tomb
Location: Bardo Museum
Date: Punic period
Number: None

This cylindrical compartmentalized makeup box is complete with its original cover. Inside, strips of lead have been soldered in place to form three compartments. The original contents have been preserved—powder of a chalky nature and pale color which proved to be calcium carbonate and contain silicate with traces of magnesium, aluminum, sodium, and potassium. These traces are common in certain clays. Similar compartmentalized terra cotta boxes are known to have been used for jewelry in Carthage. Lead boxes have also been found in Kerkouane; many have their original contents. Production of such goods was a small but important industry.

Bibliography: Delattre, 1905, p. 17; Delattre, 1906, pp. 15 and 41; Delattre, 1898, p. 9.

ABYK

25. Oyster Shell Containing Cinnabar

Dimensions: .06 m x .05 m
Material: Oyster shell containing rouge of cinnabar
Provenance: Kerkouane, in the Punic necropolis
Location: Bardo Museum
Date: Punic period
Number: Inv. 2978

This oyster shell was reused as a makeup case. Its interior contains traces of a rose-colored powder, which appears to be rouge and in laboratory analysis proved to be cinnabar. Shells were commonly used as makeup cases in the Punic world. In this case, an object that had been used in daily life found reuse for funerary purposes. Sometimes both halves of the shell were used and linked with a chain.

Bibliography: Delattre, 1897, p. 24; Delattre, 1899, pp. 15–16; Gsell, p. 106.

ABYK

26. Copper Alloy Hatchets or Razors

Hatchet or Razor (top left)

Length: 16.1 cm; *Width:* 2.6 cm; *Thickness:* 0.2 cm
Provenance: Kerkouane, in Tomb 97 of the necropolis
Location: Bardo Museum
Date: Third century B.C.
Number: None

Hatchets and razors are among the most typically Carthaginian objects of art found frequently in tombs. This engraved example has an almost rectangular shape, but the curved blade end flares out. The opposite end forms a handle consisting of a swan's neck and carefully detailed head with a slightly curved beak. On one side of the swan's neck are three parallel slashes.

On the principal side, the wings are summarily indicated; under them—at the intersection of the neck and the body—is a ring lacking the customary half-palmette decoration. When the object is held with the swan at the top, two superposed rows of decoration are seen. In the very full upper register and to the right, a woman clothed in a transparent garment and seated on a footstool is shown in profile, her elevated left hand holding a distaff and her right manipulating a spindle. Facing her is a crescent with points reversed surrounding a disk and the rough outline of the half-palmette decoration. In the lower register is the image of an empty throne or funeral bed. Below is an altar with straight feet (often found in Punic iconography) or a footstool. On the left is a candelabrum with a three-footed support, a stem terminating in a reversed V and topped with a rectangular plate. The opposite side features the swan's feathers beneath an arc decorated with dots. Under the wings, the hanging ring appears and is supported by a half palmette. The single register is bordered in the same way, as is the opposite side. A crescent with reversed points encloses a disk; under it and on an altar is an ovoid-shaped pouring vessel (*oinochoe*) with flaring neck and lip, high arching handle, and crown of (probably) laurel. The altar is a large table; its straight feet rest on the handles of a water-carrying jar (*hydria*) that has a biconic form, flaring neck and lip, and two huge handles. Laurel garlands surround its body and neck, and more laurel appears at the base.

A representation similar to that of the upper-register seated woman found here is on another hatchet/razor from a Punic tomb in Carthage. In this example, the woman is seated on a throne; apart from that, the two are identical. This piece has only one new detail: the crescent and disk, celestial symbols.

The scene might show the deceased in her daily role while preparing for the empty throne or funeral bed. Empty thrones (signaling the presence of a divinity) are known in the Near East in general and in the Phoenician world in particular, the image is more likely that of a bed—empty because of the resurrection of the deceased into another world, where she can return to her domestic activities. Numerous Punic votive steles from Carthage have representations of the funeral bed, the altar, and candelabra.

On the other side, the oinochoe (also noted in Etruscan tombs) would contain a revivifying liquid. The concept of the scene suggests that it is a Punic work and the oinochoe and hydria are types known in the Hellenistic world. The laurel is significant; it symbolizes rebirth—the resurrection of the deceased.

This hatchet/razor is representative of Punic art and provides a glimpse into the Punic attitude toward death and the afterlife. The piece is unpublished.

Hatchet or Razor (bottom left)

Length: 18.2 cm; *Width at the center:* 3.4 cm; *Thickness:* 0.3 cm
Provenance: Kerkouane, in Tomb 190 of the Punic necropolis
Location: Bardo Museum
Date: 350 to 300 B.C.
Number: Inv. 2945

This hatchet/razor features a swan's head; its eyes (only one preserved) are glass pearls with blue pupils on a white field. Against the hanging ring are placed incisions indicating wings. Above the two rows of feathers is a crosshatched band with a row of dots; another small necking band appears above that. The half-palmette decoration by the hanging ring appears only on one side and was added after the rest of the decoration was completed. If the swan's head is taken as the top, the decorative field is bordered at the far, or lower, side by a row of rectangles marked with crosses.

The principal side consists of a falconlike bird with outstretched wings and six feathers forming a fanlike pattern. The neck and plumage are rendered in a dotted imbrication pattern. The right talons of the bird (which is rendered in awkward profile) clutch an unidentified globe-shaped object. The bird is surrounded by four palms or plumes. The representation suffers from inadequate rendering.

On the other side and in front of a palm background is the realistic and detailed image of a bull, apparently sniffing a bell-shaped lotus flower on a thin stem.

Falcon-type birds of prey usually indicate an association with Horus. But the hatchets/razors published from Punic sites in the western Mediterranean have never used this type of bird with outstretched wings. We may hypothesize that this is the vulture of the goddess Mout or Mut (or the goddess herself), who personifies the sky and acts as a protector with outstretched wings. (Mut is often shown enfolding an ankh, the Egyptian sign of life.) If this image relates to the goddess, it is her first appearance in such an art work—apart from scarabs.

The bull appears on three hatchets/razors from Carthage—never the principal motif and never shown with much realism. The bull in Semitic religions evokes the generative force of the gods; on the ex-votos of Carthage, he appears at the end of the third century B.C. and represents Baal Hammon's revivifying powers. But the representations on the steles differ from the image on the hatchet/razor. This animal may also be the Egyptian god Apis, god of fertility before becoming linked with the solar deity. On a Louvre bronze dating to the sixth century B.C., Apis is shown with a vulture. The lotus flower and the palm may be seen as symbols of resurrection and life.

The hatchets/razors are truly original Punic funeral accoutrements; their decoration is a blend of Near Eastern, Egyptian, and Hellenistic ideas. Their function was to protect the deceased and provide the strength to revive in the hereafter. Here, the Egyptian influence is dominant. The work was probably produced in a Carthaginian atelier. It has the typical feather collar and half-palmette, but the four palms, the lotus flower's thin stem, and the glass eyes are unique. This work, because of both its technical characteristics and its message, occupies a place apart from all other Punic hatchets/razors. It is published here for the first time.

Hatchet or Razor (right)

Length: 9.1 cm; *Width in the center:* 1.85 cm; *Thickness:* 0.15 cm
Provenance: Kerkouane, in Tomb 68 of the necropolis
Location: Bardo Museum
Date: Late fifth to early fourth century B.C.
Number: Inv. 2951

This small hatchet/razor is of traditional form. It has a stylized handle representing the head of a swan or a duck. The bifid beak is quite long. The hanging ring is worked into the body of the piece near the bird's shoulder. There is no interior decoration. The small dimensions suggest that the piece should be placed among the more ancient examples of this group, despite the fact that the swan's neck is convincingly rendered. It may be a transitional piece produced between the early examples of the sixth and fifth centuries B.C. and those of the fourth and third.

These objects are unpublished.

Bibliography: Picard, 1966, pp. 61–62; Acquaro, 1971; Benichou-Safar, 1982, p. 266; *De Carthage à Kairouan*, 1983, p. 78; *30 Ans 1986,* pp. 84–85
HBY

27. Eight Earrings of Gilded Copper Alloy

Diameter: 3.1 cm–5 cm
Provenance: Kerkouane, in Tombs 63, 108, and 161 of the Punic necropolis
Location: Bardo Museum
Date: Fourth to third century B.C.
Numbers: Inv. 2311, 2835, 2837, and 2860

These earrings are gold-leaf plated over copper alloy. The stem of the ornament is wound around itself twice, creating a double-rolled effect. The extremities of the stem thin out and terminate with a gold thread that winds in a spiral around the central stem. The ends of one earring terminate in a gold thread wound around itself, forming two little rings for suspension, while the rest of the thread twines around in the more typical spiral. Around the two main elements of four of the earrings and over about three-quarters of the circumference is a third circular element decorated with a torsade, or twisted cord pattern.

One example contains a third circular element, an angular band over three- quarters of the circumference worked in filigree and granulation and consisting of a tress pattern enclosed between two granulated dot borders. Of all of the earrings of this group, this is the most carefully worked and shows the quality and beauty of gold products produced in the Punic workshops. Another example forms a simple ring that may have joined another element when worn.

Bibliography: Gauckler, 1915, p. 532; Pisano, 1974, p. 87; *30 Ans 1986,* p. 100, with bibliography.
ABYK

28. Two Rings Showing Isis Nursing Horus

Punic Ring (third from left in first illustration)

Diameter: 2.6 cm; *Thickness:* 0.2 cm; *Length of bezel:* 1.1 cm; *Width of setting:* 0.9 cm
Material: Gold with soldered bezel of gold
Provenance: Unknown
Location: Bardo Museum
Date: Sixth to fifth century B.C.
Number: None

Punic Ring (top left in the second illustration)

Diameter: 1.8 cm; *Greatest length of bezel:* 1.8 cm
Material: Gold with oval bezel of gold
Provenance: Unknown
Location: Bardo Museum
Date: Fourth to third century B.C.
Number: None

The Isis nurturing Horus theme appears on the bezels. In the third from the left ring in the first illustration, we see a winged Isis wearing the Atef crown or headdress; it contains the solar disk and flanking feathers. She shelters the infant with her wings. Horus wears the pschent, or double crown, symbolizing the unity of Upper and Lower Egypt. The crown has a wicker stinger in volute form at the front. Two females, who are wearing disks on their heads and raising their hands in a gesture of adoration, surround the divine pair. The crosshatchings represent the ground. The workmanship is of very high quality. The scene recalls a seventh- to sixth-century B.C. scarab from Carthage on which Isis, flanked by two falcon-headed figures, nourishes Horus.

In the second illustration and on the ring to the left, the scene is simplified; only the divine pair appears. Isis, on a seat with a back, holds Horus on her knees and suckles him. He wears the pschent. A globe is shown on both rings; on one is an incense burner (*thymiaterion*).

These rings are unpublished.

Bibliography: *De Carthage à Kairouan,* 1982, p. 52, on Isis and Horus images, with bibliography.
HBY

29. Punic Ring

Diameter: 62.8 cm; *Length of bezel:* 1.7 cm
Material: Silver
Location: Bardo Museum
Provenance: Unknown
Date: Fifth to fourth century B.C.

This ring, on the far left in the first illustration, illustrates a personage in a very schematic manner. The head is simply a hole, while the silhouette of a graceful body is shown by engraved strokes of lightly undulating form. The figure wears an ample dress decorated with striations near the base and holds its arms arched above two great wings. Behind the figure, vertical and parallel strokes occupy the field. The exergue or lower space appears to carry some Punic letters, of which can be cited a daleth. Probably one should recognize here the goddess Isis in winged form with the head surmounted either by a crescent with points facing up or by Hathoric horns or two uraei. The goddess Isis alone or accompanied by Horus counts among the Egyptian themes enormously expanded throughout the Punic world. The date is suggested pending further information. The nurturing scene occurs on scarabs and on the Carthaginian hatchets/razors.

The success of this theme would be in part due to the confusion which certainly existed in the popular mind regarding Tanit and Isis and the role of the nursing mother goddess. The theme of the goddess nourishing an infant is shown by many terra cotta Punic figurines. The ring is unpublished.

HBY

30. Punic Ring

Diameter: 2.5 cm; *Bezel height:* 0.95 cm
Provenance: Unkown
Location: Bardo Museum
Material: Faience (?)
Date: Punic period

The ring on the far right of the first illustration features an oval bezel that comes to an upper and lower point. It contains a fine band that has been stipple-decorated, enclosing a Punic inscription of six letters in two lines.

BDG/TSR

GDBRST would be the transcription, and this is a hypocristic arrangement formed with GD. J.G. Fevrier explains it as a common name that apparently means good luck or happiness as well as the name of a particular divinity. The ring is unpublished.

Bibliography: Halff, 1963–1964, pp. 63–146.

MG

31. Punic Necklace of Nine Elements

Diameter of box: 1.4 cm; *Thickness of box:* 0.6 cm
Material: Various
Provenance: Kerkouane, in Tomb 200 of the necropolis
Location: Bardo Museum
Date: Sixth century B.C.
Number: Inv. 2846

This necklace of exceptional quality is made up of nine different elements, the first of which is a round gold box. The necklace has twenty-nine pieces in all. In the center is a round box; one face is flat; the reverse is slightly domical. The flat face is decorated with a rosette of six petals made

up of simple joined fillets separated by little triangles, each formed of three beads. They enclose a seventh central circle surrounded by beads. The central circle is decorated with seven beads, the other circles have six beads, except for one that has only five. Two twisted threads form the border of the jewel. Its apertures are decorated with a simple fillet.

The opposite side of the jewel bears a rosette with seven petals grouped around a central circle. The outline of the petals and circle is emphasized on the interior by a line of granulation. *(Length:* 1.3 cm; *Width:* 1.2 cm; *Thickness:* 0.5 cm)

In addition to the central round box just described are two rectangular gold boxes. The apertures are decorated with a twisted thread design. One box carries on its two faces the right eye of Horus, known as the Oudja; the second box carries the Oudja on one face and the left eye on the other. Details are rendered through the use of filigree and granulation. *(Length:* 1.3 cm; *Width:* 1.2 cm; *Thickness:* 0.5 cm)

Near the end of the necklace is a single faience scarab containing poorly preserved hieroglyphs. *(Length:* 1.4 cm; *Width:* 1.5 cm; *Thickness:* 0.8 cm)

There are two scaraboid figures; one is in jade and the second in faience. Both contain hieroglyphs. *(Length:* 1.3 cm; *Width:* 1.1 cm; *Thickness:* 0.8 cm)

Two amulets in greenish faience illustrate the Oudja and Bastet. *(Height:* 1.2 cm) (See the entry on amulets)

One rectangular amulet, made of bone, represents the Oudja, the sacred eye, on one of its faces. *(Height:* 1.3 cm)

Four tubular pearls, several of which are in poor condition, have everted openings. The two that are best preserved taper in at the ends but swell out slightly in the center. *(Length:* 1.7 cm; *Diameter:* 0.7 cm; *Material:* silver)

There are eight pearls in carnelian. Six are biconic; one is olive shaped; and one is cylindrical *(Diameter:* 0.85 cm; *Height of cylindrical and olive shapes:* 1.1 and 1.5 cm, respectively)

There are eight pearls in gold. Four are biconic, and four are annular and of small dimension. *(Diameter:* 1.1 cm–0.7 cm)

This colorful Punic necklace combines purely decorative forms with prophylactic elements such as amulets and scarabs. These elements make this necklace a beautiful talisman. Furthermore, in this necklace there are elements typical of Punic jewelry: the circular gold box and the rectangular/parallelopiped boxes of gold. The circular gold boxes are always typified by a reverse of slightly domical shape.

Bibliography: *30 Ans 1986,* p. 97, with full bibliography; for Punic amulets in general, see Cintas, 1946; for Egyptian motifs at Carthage, see Vercoutter, 1945.
HBY

32. Gold Earrings

Diameter: 1 x 1.1 cm (small) and 1.6 cm (large)
Material: Gold
Provenance: Kerkouane, in Tombs 110 and 199 of the necropolis
Location: Bardo Museum
Date: Fourth to third century B.C.
Number: Inv. 2849 (small) and 2877 (large)

These four gold earrings (upper right and lower left in the illustration) are typical of Punic workmanship and are formed by the curvature of a cylindrical rod of which the extremities thin out, cross each other, and end up by winding into a series of spirals. These earrings may have been suspended from the ear by means of a thread.

Bibliography: *30 Ans 1986,* p. 100, with full bibliography.
HBY

33. Punic Coins

Provenance: Unknown
Location: Cathage Antiquarium
Number: All coins are without number;

One-Tenth of a Stater (small coin, right of center)

Weight: 0.8 g
Obverse: Palm, stippled edge
Reverse: Head of horse facing right. Before the neck, a globule;
Date: 350 to 320 B.C.

One-Fifth of a Stater (lower left)

Weight: 2.05 g
Obverse: Feminine head facing left
Reverse: Standing horse with palm behind it
Date: 350 to 320 B.C.

The feminine head on the obverse is crowned with wheat; two sprigs are visible on the forehead, and two leaves may be seen in the hair. She also wears an earring. On the reverse, the ground is shown by a straight line.

Stater (right of center)

Obverse: Similar to the preceding
Reverse: Standing horse facing right
Date: 350 to 320 B.C.

On the obverse, the female head has a distinct necklace around the neck and the coin is stippled. On the reverse, the ground is again rendered by a straight line, and the edge is stippled.

One and One-Half Stater (center)

Weight: 12.48 g
Obverse: Like the preceding, and stippled
Reverse: Horse standing right, turning head left; stippled
Date: 270 to 260 B.C.

Electrum Stater (bottom)

Weight: 10.87 g
Obverse: Like the preceding
Reverse: Horse standing to the right
Date: 260 to 246 B.C.

The ground is rendered in the same fashion on the reverse, but a rayonnant globe appears above flanked by two uraei with disks. Between the legs of the horse are three aligned globules.

The following group is entirely of silver.

Tetradrachm (upper right)

Weight: 16.34 g
Obverse: Feminine head
Reverse: Horse advancing left before date palm
Date: Circa 350 B.C.

The obverse features the head crowned with wheat as in lower left unit, and the necklace and earring are carefully shown. The ground on the reverse is again indicated by a straight line. (The reverse is shown here.)

Tetradrachm (left)

Weight: 16.48 g
Obverse: Similar to the preceding
Reverse: Head and neck of horse
Date: Probably 314 to 311 B.C.

The obverse features dolphins swimming around the head in the manner of the coins of Syracuse, on which this is modeled. The reverse again features the palm behind the horse. Under the horse's neck is the Punic inscription MMHNT, which means "those who constitute the army in the country."

Tetradrachm (upper left)

Weight: 13.19 g
Obverse: As above
Reverse: Horse moving right
Date: 200 to 146 B.C.

This tetradrachm has a dentillated border. The reverse, with its typical ground line, also shows a circular line border and a globule, the latter placed before the horse.

Shekel (lower right)

Weight: 7.34 g
Obverse: As above, without the necklace
Reverse: Horse standing right
Date: 300 to 260 B.C.

The horse is turning its head back and standing before a palm, while an eight-branched star is shown before him. The circular border is stippled on the reverse.

The Carthaginians began to use money well after many other communities of the Mediterranean did—probably not before the end of the fifth century B.C. The Carthaginian coins have a startling Hellenic character when compared with the rest of the Carthaginian artistic output. The coinage types seem to have followed Sicilian models closely—due to the island's proximity, Carthage's ambition in Sicily, and the desire to trade with the Greek world, which was already accustomed to using Greek currency. In fact, the money of Carthage is often termed Siculo-Punic. Although pure gold coins were issued, a mixture of gold and silver known as electrum was also popularly employed. Bronze issues were also known.

The nature of the female head on the obverse of many Punic coins has been the object of much speculation. Suggestions range from Hellenic divinities such as Kore or Persephone, daughter of Demeter, the vegetation goddess, to Queen Dido/Elyssa herself, and even to a Hellenized Tanit. Images of the female head surrounded by dolphins are clearly modeled on the Syracusan four-drachma coin (tetradrachm) showing the nymph Arethusa (whose fountain may still be visited at Syracuse). The coin with the Punic inscription would seem to be a special issue for the military, which included many mercenaries; it may have to do with Punic military operations in Sicily. The Carthaginians also used the shekel, commonly associated with ancient Phoenicia, homeland of the Carthaginian people.

Bibliography: Jenkins and Lewis, 1963, Numbers 3, 9, 13, 15–17, 112, 136, 337, and 428; *De Carthage à Kairouan*, 1982, pp. 87-95.

HBY

34. The Lupercus Stele

Height: 28 cm; *Length:* 43 cm; *Thickness:* 9 cm
Material: Yellowish limestone
Provenance: Ancient Gigthis (Henchir bou Ghrara)
Location: Bardo Museum
Date: First century A.D.
Number: None

One of the surest signs of the Romanization process in Carthage is this bilingual Punic and Latin inscription discovered in 1914. This famous stele is an irregular quadrilateral in form. It features three lines of carefully engraved text. The first two lines are in Neo-Punic and give the nomenclature of a person and his family connections:

> Himilk, the son of Shofet, son of Hannibal—Line 1
>
> Of Shabo—Line 2

The final line gives this same individual's surname in Latin: Lupercus. Comparison with epitaphs from Carthage, where the name of the deceased appears in the nominative case without indication of age or anything else affirms that this is a funerary monument. The carving of the letters is in an archaic style. But—most interesting about the Gigthis stele—it is bilingual without saying the same thing in each part. In both Punic and Latin, this is a unique occurrence; it suggests that the area is in the middle of its Romanization process so that an individual would have to employ a Latin surname in his Punic pedigree. We have, thus, happened upon a moment in the evolution of Gigthis at the beginning of the Roman Empire, a community reputed to have been founded by Phoenicians.

Bibliography: *De Carthage à Kairuoan,* 1982, p. 98, with bibliography; Constans, 1915, pp. CLXXI, CXCV; Ben Abdallah, 1986, p. 10.

ZBA

35. Mosaic of Silenus and the Ass

Provenance: Thysdrus (El Jem) in a Roman house
Location: El Jem Museum
Date: First half of the third century A.D.
Number: None

This panel was part of a much larger mosaic that decorated the reception room of the House of Silenus and the Ass. Located in the central area of the city where space was limited, the house was of modest proportions and had a small courtyard rather than a peristyle. It was, in fact, the residence of artisans who lived with a certain comfort, probably about the beginning of the third century A.D. Most of the rooms were paved in polychrome mosaics with figural motifs that are considered among the most beautiful of El Jem. But while possessing the luxury and elegance of sumptuous houses, this residence was barely the size of one of the reception rooms of the Thysdrusian aristocracy. This mosaic is one of the most splendid African creations in the exquisite vegetal style, and it also features fascinating figural scenes. The composition of the entire mosaic, of which only one small section is illustrated, is enclosed by a rinceau border of a sinusoidal form that outlines an impressive series of alternating figures, birds, and extremely diverse animal protomes: a deer, hare, lion, panther, antelope, lioness, wild boar, etc. This border frames a large rectangular field whose interior corners are filled with acanthus leaves; from them rises luxuriant vegetation whose branches, populated with birds, spreads over most of the pavement. This abundant vegetal decoration enframes a double series of scenes—one in five rectangular pictures, the other in eight circular medallions.

The rectangular scene shown occupies the central position in the mosaic. Surrounded by a braid border, the picture shows a sandy, barren landscape where only a tree is growing and a scene in three aspects. The left third is occupied by a winged Victory, who is placing a crown on the head of the young god Dionysus, who holds a ribboned thyrsus. The central part illustrates two satyrs and a bacchante carrying Silenus, potbellied and completely drunk, toward an ass. In the background is a winged Bacchus or Cupid fluttering about and holding a thyrsus and kantharos. In advance of these two groups, a bacchante or follower of Dionysus bears an offering basket and stands by the side of the ass, which is braying in unhappy anticipation of receiving Silenus on its back.

On the outer sides of this large central panel (not shown) are four smaller rectangular pictures. They are organized to be viewed with the other mosaic medallions by making a complete circuit of the pavement. The arrangement and order of the scenes follow the cult rituals and life of Dionysus. The picture at the left illustrates an ichthyocentaur (satyr face, animal ears, head surmounted by lobster antennae) carrying a Nereid and advancing nude in a sea represented by parallel lines broken by small slashes. The basket which the centaur carries appears to be a sacred winnowing basket (*liknon*), Dionysus's first cradle. Thus, the scene depicts the god's birth and first days. Beneath the central panel, the second picture illustrates an ichthyocentaur waving a torch and carrying a Nereid on his back. She holds a cloth-covered basket, allowing the viewer only to guess at the projecting object (a cake, perhaps, in the form of a phallus). The activity, which seems to accelerate on the sea, simulates the marches of torchbearers as the scene terminates in revelry, sacrifice, and sexual union. To the right of the large panel, the third picture shows the ichthyocentaur blowing into a long conch while the Nereid, flaunting her nudity, suggests the relationship's pleasures. The fourth depicts the ichthyocentaur holding a shepherd's crook and caressing the breast of the Nereid stretched out on his back; she gazes at him with a face inflamed with passion. This scene is characterized by a considerable sense of intimacy, and from one picture to another, the Nereid is presented by turns—at first shy, then agitated, quiescent, and impassioned.

While the four pictures illustrating ichthyocentaurs and Nereids are set in a Dionysiac atmosphere, the eight circular medallions are filled with subjects whose association with the god is even more evident. The four located in the lower half of the pavement toward the entrance of the room treat the childhood of Dionysus primarily.

The first circle at the left (beneath the ichthyocentaur with the torch) represents an enormous lion ridden by a very young Dionysus, holding a large bunch of grapes and supported by a bacchante who is carrying a tambourine and thyrsus. The second circle to the right also depicts an extremely young Dionysus, this time perched on the shoulder of a satyr who is accompanied by a dancing bacchante holding a tambourine and thyrsus. Above this, the circular medallion on the left shows a bacchante and a nude, very short-legged, extraordinarily ugly and grotesque Silenus; he is holding a large lyre in his left hand. The theme of the musical Silenus, as one knows, is rare. The fourth medallion to the right illustrates a tranquil Silenus riding a panther and holding a shepherd's crook; a bacchante with a thyrsus in the right hand supports him with her left. Thus, three of the four scenes show the divine infant having tamed the wild beasts, particularly the lion, which is the symbol of the death that devours us all.

The other circular medallions in the upper part of the pavement above the central panel celebrate the victory of Dionysus. To the right is a bacchante playing cymbals and dancing; she is followed by Pan, who is carrying a shepherd's staff on his right arm. To the left, a naked bacchante bearing a thyrsus and an offering basket casts a glance toward a besotted and staggering Hercules, who holds his club and the lion skin. As a hero, he symbolizes virtue and is associated with the victory of Dionysus.

These last two scenes are illustrated in medallions placed between leaves of acanthus. That at the right shows two Indian captives, their hands manacled behind their backs, seated on an elephant. The elephant is a symbol of eternity because of its longevity and often linked to Dionysus, whose influence spread as far as the Ganges, assisted by his followers and Hercules. That at the left represents a naked satyr carrying a leopardlike animal and a shepherd's crook and leading a goat—doubtlessly to sacrifice. Consecrated to the god, the goat has a garland of leaves around its neck. Behind the animal, a bacchante plays the double flute. According to Virgil, the goat was sacrificed to protect the vineyards against the depredations of the herd.

The sacrifice underscored the power of the god and transferred to the pavement's owner the benefits of the magic contained in the act. Thus, the landlord enjoyed not only the beauty of the decorations and mythological scenes but was assured of the god's favor. This mosaic is unpublished and is considered one of the masterpieces of Tunisian art.

36. The Infant Bacchus

Height: 62 cm
Material: Copper alloy
Location: Bardo Museum
Date: Second century A.D.(?)
Number: Inv. 2779

One of the most popular deities in Roman Africa was the wine god Dionysus, also known as Bacchus. He and his train of ecstatic women (Maenads) and fun-loving satyrs and Silenus figures became symbols of the bounty of the fields and the love of the good life. This extraordinary bronze, one of the most renowned in the Bardo Museum, illustrates the god as a child. He is nude and stands on an elegant circular socle.

He wears sandals and rests the weight of his body gracefully on his right foot; his left leg is slightly bent and placed behind the right. In his left hand, he holds the thyrsus, the sacred wand of the god normally twined round with ivy and vine leaves. The left arm is held nearly at the side, but the right arm is bent and holds up a rhyton, or animal-headed drinking vessel. The animal in question appears to be a panther, another frequent companion of the god.

His head is turned slightly to the right, toward the drinking vessel. The face is oval in shape with fine features: inlaid eyes, ear lobes pierced for earrings, and beautiful long hair parted in the middle and flowing down to the back and sides of the neck. Representations in bronze of the young Bacchus are rare; often they lack the details from which identification can be made. The presence of the rhyton in place of a cornucopia is even more rare.

The overall quality of the workmanship is outstanding; the bronze worker rendered perfectly the slightly plump form of the child who has not matured physically. He has even given the child the long hair of the adult Bacchus, and the calmness of the pose adds to the feeling of majesty that the god merits.

Bibliography: Yacoub, 1969, p. 90; Mitten, 1969, Number 252; *De Carthage à Kairouan,* 1983, p. 125.
NAO

37. Lamp of Drunken Silenus

Height: 2.4 cm; *Length:* 11.6 cm; *Diameter:* 8.4 cm
Material: Terra cotta
Provenance: Bulla Regia
Location: Bardo Museum
Date: Third century A.D.
Number: K167

The Romans never tired of celebrating the exploits of Dionysus or depicting drunken figures such as Silenus, the tutor and attendant of Bacchus, readily distinguishable by his bald head, his

donkey, and his drunkenness. These images were popular on oil lamps that could be fitted with flax wicks and used for illuminating social gatherings. This type of lamp has a simple rounded spout and a full handle. (See lamp to the right in the illustration.) The spout is marked by an incised arc, and a filling hole is placed to one side of the discus so as not to disturb the decoration. Another small hole, perhaps for cleaning, appears above the spout. On the shoulder is a decoration of alternating grapes and vine leaves. The back is slightly concave and carries a stamp within two concentric circles: CHELIAN. This is obviously the name of the maker; such markings commonly appear on Roman lamps.

The discus features a detailed scene of a nude and drunken Silenus passing before a tetrastyle temple (fronted by four columns). On the right, he is supported by a faun, a mythical forest deity. On the left, a bacchante, a female follower of Dionysus, helps him along. She is bare breasted and holds an object (a cane?). In the field to the right is a vine shoot.

According to mythology, Silenus was a sage, philosopher, and prophet. He is always represented as a jovial old man and voluptuary.

Bibliography: Deneauve, 1969, p. 202, No. 981.

MK

38. Bacchic Lamp

Height: 3.8 cm; *Length:* 10.5 cm; *Diameter:* 7.6 cm
Material: Terra cotta
Provenance: Unknown
Location: Bardo Museum
Date: Early first century A.D.
Number: K1879

This lamp (on the far left in the illustration) without a handle and with a triangular spout decorated with simple volutes again shows the popularity of Dionysus. There is a filling hole on the discus. The narrow base lacks a maker's mark.

On the discus, the god Bacchus appears nude, not as a young boy but as a young man, standing in a three-quarters view with his head in profile to the left. He holds the thyrsus with his right hand down at his side, similar to the way in which the young bronze Dionysus grasps his thyrsus in the elegant statue also included in this exhibition. An animal skin is draped on his left arm, while his left hand holds an indistinct object. A drinking cup, or cantharus, appears in the field before him.

Bibliography: Deneauve, 1969, Type IV A.

MK

39. The Rape of Ganymede

Length: 4.70 m; *Width:* 3.64 m
Material: Mosaic of polychrome marble and limestone
Provenance: El Jem (Thysdrus), in the Domus Sollertiana
Location: El Jem
Date: A.D. 200 to 250
Number: None

Rarely in the Roman period can the proprietor of a house be identified, but here an inscription allows us not only to know that Sollertius was master but also that the family was happy: "Sollertiana Domus Semper Felix Cum Suis." The inscription is in the west wing antechamber reserved for bedrooms and a chapel for the family and ancestral cult (*lararium*).

The building occupies 1,120 square meters in a zone in the southeast quarter of Thysdrus at the limit of the city. It is the smallest of a group of large villas with peristyles in this area. Its proprietors, the Sollertii, are certainly representative of the Thysdrus bourgeoisie at the end of the second or beginning of the third century A.D. Located in a wing inaccessible to outsiders, the antechamber with the inscription is intended to function with two bedrooms, whose privacy it assures.

The first room is decorated with a pavement featuring unexceptional geometric motifs. The second is a large bedroom of 28 square meters (5.95 by 4.75). It is divided into two parts by a banquette that is raised up 20 centimeters, serving for the emplacement of a bed. It is 2.2 by 5 meters and contains a simple geometric mosaic. But the second part of the room is decorated with this mosaic depicting the rape of Ganymede.

Preserved in an excellent state, it forms a complex figural tableau surrounded by a band containing an intricate pattern of facing arcs of a circle, each filled with a pelta and two smaller arcs. A polychrome cross is placed in between each group of four of these. The arc pattern exceeds a semicircle at the four corners. The effect is elegant and the workmanship careful, each arc carefully color-coordinated in stones of red, green, and yellow in a tapestry effect. Outside this band, on two sides, is a decorative vegetal rinceau pattern also rendered in delicate polychromy.

In the central area, a swarming array of motifs dazzles the eyes—geometric images, figures, and vegetal ornament. These motifs are arranged around and inside a broad cross pattern of laurel made up of four half-circles linked by trapezoidal sections of laurel. A laurel crown frames the central scene in medallion form. A series of squares and rectangles of various sizes fills the spaces on all four sides.

The central medallion shows the theme of the rape of Ganymede by Zeus. Around this medallion are the four seasons. Spring is depicted as a woman crowned with flowers, dressed in a transparent robe and holding a hare in one hand and a basket of flowers in the other. Summer has her classic attributes: wheat sheaves and a sickle. She wears a light veil that leaves her breast, torso, and most of her thighs and legs exposed. Autumn exhibits even greater nudity and holds a bunch of grapes. Winter, her body enveloped in a long robe, is placed before a sprig of millet from which a duck is suspended. In the curvilinear trapezoidal area below each season are two masks.

The four angles of the tableau contain squares decorated with floral motifs of four leaves. On either side of each square is a charming combat scene between a serpent and a griffin. The confrontation is in eight successive phases and seems to end with the triumph of the griffin, traditional ally of Nemesis. To the side of these scenes and within the interior curve of garlands hanging in festoons from the laurel cross are four scenes of divine courtship (*scènes galantes*) shown within rectangles.

Each scene is flanked by two rectangles that are filled with roses and surmounted by birds that are generally looking back. In each figural rectangle, a divine figure with apparently amorous intentions encounters a damsel who may be said to be in distress. First, a satyr removes the clothing from a sleeping woman, and then Leda appears reclining as she becomes possessed by the swan. Leda was a beautiful woman whom Zeus, in the form of a swan, seduced. In the third panel, a satyr tries to seduce a bacchante, female follower of Dionysus. In the fourth, a satyr terrifies another baccchante with a snake.

This extraordinary tableau seems almost overloaded with elements, but its concentration on episodes from mythology, primarily Bacchic, does provide a certain unity. The scenes were probably deliberately chosen for their specific location. One may speculate that scenes of nudity and dalliance were concentrated in proximity to the bed.

Bibliography: M. Alexander, 1987, with full bibliography.

HS

40. Relief of the Dancing Maenads

Height: 39 cm; *Width:* 57 cm; *Thickness:* 4.5 cm
Material: White marble with fine crystals, gold patina
Provenance: Thuburbo Maius, in the area of the Portico of the Petronii
Location: Bardo Museum
Date: Circa. A.D. 150 to 200
Number: Inv. 125

This beautiful relief was found in excavations conducted by the Department of Antiquities. It was discovered at Thuburbo Maius in the "quarter of the Maenads" about 30 meters north of the Portico of the Petronii, which adjoins the well-known Summer Baths. Thuburbo Maius is located some 35 miles from Tunis in the plain of El Fahs; it is one of Tunisia's largest archaeological sites. The buildings include a large capitolium (principal Roman temple to Jupiter) in the forum, numerous baths, a market (with Temple of Mercury, god of commerce, nearby), and a major temple (perhaps dedicated to Saturn). Numerous private houses, such as the House of Neptune, have produced elegant mosaics recently published by a Tunisian-American team in *Corpus des Mosaiques de Tunisie: Thuburbo Maius.*

This particularly fine work shows the light use of a stoneworker's trepan, traces of chisel work, and considerable polishing. The relief is bordered on the long side by a slightly projecting rim on which three Maenads, female followers of Dionysus, are dancing. Multiple restorations cover the relief's surface, and there are multiple fractures as well. Of the first Maenad, only a bit of flaring drapery and one hand holding a knife survive. A second Maenad is shown in profile and moving to the left. Her hair is bound in a headband, and she is dancing on her toes. In her left hand she is holding behind her the lower torso of a goat that has been neatly sliced in two; with her right hand, she is swinging a large knife behind her head. She is wearing a long diaphanous chiton; her left breast and left arm are exposed. From the belt at the waist, the garment clings closely to the legs, and its folds at the ankles suggest wild dancing movement. A veil billowing out from over the right shoulder further accentuates the activity.

The third Maenad, shown in profile and looking up, is moving to the right and executing the same dance step in the opposite direction. Her hair is arranged in a chignon, but a number of loose locks are flying out and up behind her. In her right hand, she is holding the thyrsus in front of her; the left hand is holding the upper half of the goat's torso behind her. She is also wearing a long, transparent chiton that reveals her shapely body. A heavier scarflike drape is flaring out from her left shoulder and behind her body.

The scene shows a traditional procession in honor of Bacchus. The Maenads have torn apart a sacrificial victim (*disasparagmos*) and eaten it on the spot (*omophagy*). This theme was enormously popular and was present in the fifth century B.C., notably on an amphora by the Amasis painter. The prototype of these dancing Maenads may be found toward the end of the fifth century B.C. in the work of Kallimachos, a Greek sculptor. His model has been consistently imitated since the second century B.C. and continued to be popular in the period of the Roman Empire, when it was followed by artists working in the Neo-Attic style.

The accent is particularly on the transparent drapery typical of the later fifth century B.C. in Athens. W. Fuchs has noted no fewer than nineteen examples of this type, and this relief is faithful to the prototype. A similar Maenad, lacking the knife and goat, appears on the large marble crater found in Tunisia at Mahdia at the site of an ancient shipwreck. Another close parallel occurs on the famous Borghese Vase in Rome.

This relief, produced in a Neo-Attic workshop, is impressive because of its excellent workmanship and the gilt patina of its marble. Despite the relief's damaged state, a viewer recognizes that the sculptor has captured the rhythm of the dance, the movement of the draperies, the attitude of the bodies, the gestures of the arms, and the composition of the procession. The movements, although still and elegant, suggest excitement and abandon.

The relief may have decorated the wall of a public building or that of a wealthy person's private home. The context of its discovery suggests that it may be dated in the second half of the second century although the workmanship suggests a second or third century A.D. date.

Bibliography: Lezine, 1968, p. 19; *De Carthage à Kairouan*, 1983, p. 115, with full bibliography; Richter; 1965, pp. 242 –245.

NAO

41. Glass Cinerary Urn and Cover

Height: 30 cm; *Diameter of body:* 26.5 cm
Height of cover: 6.5 cm; *Diameter:* 13.3 cm
Material: Glass
Provenance: Unknown
Location: Bardo Museum
Date: Latter first to second century A.D.

This cinerary urn has been mended and lacks some elements in one of its handle areas. It is a two-handled piece with spherical body, turned-out lip, annular foot, and slightly concave base. The cover is circular and flat and has a knob with a button in the center for removing the lid.

Cremation was the most common burial rite during the first three centuries of the Roman Empire, although inhumation became popular in the second century A.D in Italy. The body was burned either in a burning area (*ustrinum*) or at the spot where the tomb would be erected. Once the pyre was extinguished, the remains were placed in a receptacle that was interred in the tomb or placed in a niche of a mausoleum or columbarium such as the funerary monuments found at Thysdrus as well as Pompeii.

The urns were of many types and materials, most often pottery or limestone, although marble, lead, and glass examples have been found. Vessels like this were not uncommon; this could just as conceivably be a cookie jar. However, given the fact that this example was found in Tunisia and is complete, the hypothesis that it is a cremation urn is persuasive. The object is unpublished.

MK

42. Funerary Stele

Height: 0.69 m; *Width:* 0.435 m; *Thickness:* 0.145 m
Material: White limestone
Provenance: Possibly Sbeitla [Sufetula]
Location: Bardo Museum
Date: Second century A.D.
Number: None

Funerary steles had a long life, evolving from the Punic period and continuing well into the time of the Roman conquest—as this example reveals. The style is provincial, simple, and frontal; many details of this low relief were executed by incision. The stele is rectangular. Its pedimental top follows a tradition begun in Carthage as a result of Greek influence in the last Classical period, but the overall impression is that of a temple façade. A band (perhaps a cornice) surrounds the pediment, which rests on two columns or pilasters with summarily indicated capitals. An extra band running just above the capitals and below the pediment may be the architrave under which, between the capitals, runs what appears to be a molding with a simplified bead-and-reel decoration.

In the tympanum of the pediment are two rosettes with incised interiors in a pattern of eight rays. A crescent with its points facing up surrounds a disk. Under the temple pediment stands a male figure. The face is rounded, the eyes are almond-shaped, the nose is straight and prominent, and the body is draped in a mantle with many folds. The right hand is holding a diagonal draping of the mantle; the left hand appears to be holding a rectangular object.

The eyes, long neck (deformed with respect to the body), and the seemingly atrophied limbs associate this work with the African iconographic repertoire. The drapery and architectural background of a sanctuary façade with a pediment supported by fluted columns are typical of Roman influence and may be dated roughly to the second century A.D. Because of the absence of an archaeological context for the object, its precise use is difficult to determine, but it shows parallels with funerary steles such as those found in the museum at Maktar.

Bibliography: Picard, Musée Alaoui, plates CVII to CXII, several examples dated in the second century A.D.

ABYK

43. Neo-Punic Funerary Stele

Height: 60.5 cm; *Width:* 26 cm; *Thickness:* 1.2 –1.65 cm
Material: White limestone
Provenance: Area of Segermes (?)
Location: Bardo Museum
Date: Probably first century A.D.
Number: None

This quadrangular stele with a lightly rounded summit contains an incised surface decoration. At the top is a crescent with the end points facing upwards; stylized palm branches appear on either side. Below is a rare anthropomorphized sign of the Punic goddess Tanit; it features the typical triangle form surmounted not by the usual circle but by a head in the form of a disk with rays and containing highly simplified eyes and mouth. At the interior of the triangle, two tiny punctures represent breasts and a third indicates the goddess's sex. Two arms emerge from the triangle; each contains a stylized five-finger hand. The rays around the head may indicate hair or, more likely, a radiant solar image.

This most unusual stele is an example of one of the very last steps in the evolution toward anthropomorphism of Tanit's sign and the rayonnant solar disk; it represents an individual standing nude with two hands upraised.

Bibliography: Picard, Musée Alaoui, plate CVIII for the anthropomorphized Tanit and plate CXIX for anthropomorphized solar disks.

ABYK

44. Votive Stele to Saturn

Material: Limestone
Provenance: Oued Leya, region of Sousse
Location: Depository of the Institut National d'Archéologie et d'Art
Date: Later second century A.D.
Number: None

This quadrangular stele shows the façade of a temple with pediment, but the columns are replaced with two palms, each with five palm branches and two date fruits in place of capitals. In the central area (*tympanum*) of the pediment is a large fir cone symbolizing Saturn. At either of the upper limits of the stele is a radiate solar genius and a lunar genius with crescent symbol.

To the right of a blazing altar is a priest whose skull appears to be shaved. Dressed in a large mantle with large folds descending to the knees, he holds a pyxis in his left hand; with his right, he pours some incense on the altar. To the left, a ram faces the altar.

Under the entablature is engraved a dedication showing the donor of the votive:

L(UCIUS) MARIUS PAVLINUS - V (OTUM) SOLVTI

Artistically; the stele is quite schematic but not lacking in originality. It is previously unpublished.

ABABK

45. Seated Goddess

Height: 11 cm; *Thickness:* 7 cm
Material: Plaster
Provenance: Thysdrus (El Jem), in a cemetery reserved for children
Location: Reserves of El Jem
Date: Later first to early second century A.D.
Number: None

This statuette comes from a cemetery reserved for infants—rare in antiquity and now. It is a sacred cemetery, and the infants interred here are those who have been admitted into the secrets and religious practices of their protecting divinities. The statuette represents one of these divinities. Enthroned in a majestic chair with elbow rests, she has a grave and solemn air. Her elaborate and imposing coiffure is in the style of Roman women between the Flavian and the Hadrianic period. Her hair comes to a point at the top of her head and forms a chignon at the back of the head. Her drapery features rigid folds and descends to her feet without covering them. In her left hand, she holds a round fruit, possibly an enormous quince or pomegranate, which she grasps with difficulty. The fingers of her right hand are closed around a sceptre or wheat stalk that has long since disappeared.

This statuette is finely executed, and it had a beneficent presence over the deceased. The goddess is actually invoked on one of the epitaphs discovered there: "May you receive the blessing of this goddess' favor by being deterred from violating this sepulchre." No doubt this moving plea is made to ensure the protection of the gods of this place and the fragile infants interred here. The funerary enclosure recalls the Tophet, where the Carthaginians sacrificed their infants to Baal and Tanit to obtain their blessing. The goddess represented here may be related to Tanit or her Roman-epoch substitutes. The statue is unpublished.

Bibliography: *30 Ans 1986*, p. 166

LS

46. Herm Featuring the Head of a Black African

Height: 88 cm; *Height of head:* 23 cm; *Width of head:* 14.5 cm
Material: Black schist
Provenance: Carthage, in the 1946 excavations of the Antonine Baths
Location: Bardo Museum
Date: Circa A.D. 150
Number: Inv. 3018

This beautifully chiseled, highly polished piece is a companion to the herm featuring the head of a Libyan (Catalogue 1). It probably dates to the middle of the second century A.D., when the Antonine Baths at Carthage were apparently built. It is a herm figure of a black African with long hair arranged in long fringelike braids. The lips are thick, the nose is broad and flat, and the face is alert and powerful. This figure and its companion were intended to decorate the Bath's principal polygonal room, and they may have commemorated Roman victories against Saharan

and Libyan tribes around A.D. 144 to 149. The portrait is realistic and carefully executed—probably in the same atelier where its companion piece was made.

Bibliography: Picard, *De Carthage a Kairouan*, 1983, p. 119, with full bibliography.
NAO

47. Banquet in the Amphitheater

Dimensions: 1.45 m x 1.31 m
Provenance: Thysdrus (El Jem), about 500 meters west of the amphitheater
Location: Bardo Museum
Date: Circa A.D. 200 to 220
Number: Inv. 3361

El Jem is known for its amphitheater, comparable in beauty and dramatic setting to the Colosseum in Rome, and for its mosaics depicting games and combats in the arena. The most famous mosaic is often called "Fancy Dress Banquet" and was discovered in 1954. The panel is framed by four millet stalks, traditional good luck symbols, and depicts five men seated around a curved banquet table and engaged in animated conversation.

The men's words are placed over their heads. All have been drinking. The man at the extreme right is wearing a white tunic decorated with vertical red bands that start from the shoulders; in his left hand, he holds a staff topped with a crescent, the symbol of the Telegenii group. Shown in a three-quarters view, he is raising his right arm and addressing his companions, who are looking at him earnestly: NOS TRES TENEMUS. ("We three, we are getting along most comfortably.") His neighbor, dressed in a red tunic banded with green, is carrying millet, the emblem of the Leontii group associated with the games of the arena. He responds: AVOCEMUR. ("Let us amuse ourselves.") The third man is wearing a green tunic with black stripes and a gold crown with five points and a fish on its top. This is the badge of the powerful Pentasii group. He is gesturing with his arms as he replies to the man at the right: IA(M) MULTU(M) LOQUIMINI. ("Enough talk.") Before him on the table is a glass with a round foot.

The fourth figure is in three-quarters view but more sideways than the first. He is wearing a black-striped tunic and a gold three-pointed crown that has at its summit a capital letter *S* atop a horizontal bar, the sign of the Sinematii group. With this right arm raised, palm

upward, he proclaims: BIBERE VENIMUS. ("We have come to drink.") The last guest wears a white tunic banded with brown with an ivy leaf on the right sleeve. He is leaning back, his left leg casually raised and his head resting on his right hand in devil-may-care fashion. In his left hand, he is holding a cup; his right hand is holding a sprig of ivy. He makes a suggestion to his companions: (N)OS NUDI (F)IEMUS. ("We shall become naked.") The ivy leaf and the numeral II are the symbol of the Taurisci fellowship, to which this individual is usually assumed to belong; close examination reveals it may be the numeral III that is just visible above his head. The ivy leaf and III are the emblems of the Crescentii group.

In front of the table are three containers of wine. The large one is on the ground; the two smaller ones are resting on a little table. Two slaves wearing short white green-striped tunics are approaching the banqueters. One is hurrying to serve a drink; the other, holding his left hand to his mouth, calls out for silence: SILENTIU(M) DORMIANT TAURI. ("Silence, let the bulls sleep.") In the foreground, five zebus, or Indian oxen, seem to be sleeping and stirring slightly. Some of them appear to be branded on the rump with a gladiator, a sistrum, or Egyptian rattle.

This scene evidently pertains directly to the amphitheater, whose form is suggested by the shape of the table. The lower area of the table is supported by colonnettes. The games are evoked by amusing figures who are probably venatores or professional hunters belonging to different teams or professional organizations. A scene of a similar nature from Uzitta bears the legend AT DORMIANT TAURI. ("Don't wake the sleeping bulls.") The two inscriptions suggest that this may be a formula with magic value that is designed to ensure the defeat of the opposing team, which is the Tauriscii in this example.

Bibliography: *De Carthage à Kairouan*, 1983, p. 170, with full bibliography; Yacoub, 1970, pp. 70-71.

ME

48. The Young Wrestlers Mosaic

Dimensions: 1.71 m x 0.77 m
Provenance: Utica, in the House of Wrestlers
Location: Bardo Museum
Date: A.D. 200 to 250

This mosaic, found in 1913, is bordered by a double yellow fillet and the main scene surrounded by black and white fillets. The border between these fillets is a polychrome wave pattern of pale red, rose, white, black, olive green, brown, and blue-green mosaic tesserae. Two pairs of wrestlers are confronting each other in an earnest combat on either side of a table on top of which the rewards are enthroned for the victor: a weighty agonistic crown flanked by two palms. The four young wrestlers are naked, their skins subtly rendered with the tones of light yellow, dark yellow, brown or white, and light or dark pink or dark red.

Their hair is tied up in a lock at the top of their heads, a coiffure (*cirrus*) characteristic of athletes of that profession. The theme of Etruscan wrestlers contending for prizes is shown on the sixth-century-B.C. Tomb of the Augurs in Tarquinia, Italy.

Most Roman cities had athletic guilds, often with patron divinities such as Mercury/ Hermes. These charged membership fees and were led by a xystarch, who managed entries into sacred games as well as local competitions. Boys' wrestling had been an official competition at the great games at Olympia since 632 B.C. Even boys' wrestling required strenuous training. Practice such as tripping and throwing a person down was encouraged, particularly in "standing wrestling" (the type shown here) as opposed to "ground wrestling." Three out of five falls was the normal duration, and the atheletes oiled themseves for the competition. The most famous boy wrestler of antiquity was Milo of Croton, who lived in the sixth century B.C. As a

prize, the palm branch indicated victory. In the final awards procession, it was carried in the right hand. This was a practice relating to the sacred palm of Apollo, who is said to have instituted games at Delos. Crowns, usually of olive leaves, were also awarded.

Bibliography: Alexander, 1976, p. 2, No. 246, Plate II; Yalouris, 1976, p.30; Drees, 1968 pp. 76,81,85–86.

OBOB

49. Thin-Walled Goblet

Height: 15 cm; *Maximum diameter:* 10 cm
Material: Ceramic
Provenance: Unknown
Location: Bardo Museum
Date: A.D. 225 to 250
Number: None

In the later first century A.D., Tunisia became a major pottery-producing center; and products were exported to all parts of the Roman world. One of the most beautiful styles was produced in the third century A.D. at El-Aouja in the El Jem region. This example is a typical goblet, having the characteristic pear shape and featuring very thin walls. The vessel has a circular foot and a high arching handle that is usually decorated with a spray of leaves on this type of pottery. Appliqué relief decorations are typical; this one includes three shells across the top and under this a molding that runs around the goblet's upper part. Three palms divide its surface vertically. In one, a lion is leaping to the right; a crown decorated with ribbons is shown, and a bull's horn bears the inscription TAURISCI NIKA. Finally, a venator is raising his right hand in a victory sign and holding in his left hand the carcass of an animal that he no doubt killed in the arena. Above the lion and the venator are some ornamental motifs in the form of an arch.

This goblet is an excellent companion to the "Fancy Dress Banquet" mosaic. If that mosaic illustrates the banquet on the day before the great arena fights, this goblet shows the happy result for the winning Taurisci group. Such vessels could be sold or given as gifts—members of the competing teams and their followers would be proud owners of these souvenirs, just like baseball and football fans today. The goblet is unpublished.

Bibliography: Hayes, 1972, pp. 193–200.

AE

50. Cylindrical Jug with Relief Decoration

Height: 25 cm
Material: Ceramic
Provenance: El Aouja, in a Roman necropolis
Location: Bardo Museum
Date: Third century A.D.
Number: CMA 1209

This cylindrical jug has a small neck and two handles joining the neck and top of the jug's shoulder. It bears an inscription indicating that its maker was the Navigius firm: EX OFFICINA NAVIGIUS. This atelier was one of the finest in the El Aouja area in the third century A.D.; it was responsible for some of the most unusual vases produced in ancient Tunisia.

Under the inscription are two concentric grooves, and central motifs surrounded by ancillary scenes in several registers are shown on each vertical side. Three pairs of double grooves appear on the body at regular intervals. On one side in the center is the god Apollo. He is wearing a mantle and Phrygian cap. He is seated on an altar decorated with a garland and playing his cithara. (Apollo Citharoedos was long known in the Greek and Roman world, where Apollo was the sun god and the lord of the Sanctuary of Delphi.) He had invented the cithara, a lyre-like stringed instrument with a sounding board and two side pieces and, usually, seven strings. Silenus is seated to the side, holding a bunch of grapes. Below him is the god Mercury, divinity of commerce and messenger of the gods. He is carrying his caduceus (a magic wand that can bring blessings and prosperity) and a purse. Below Apollo is a bacchante between two satyrs; to the right of this is an erotic scene taking place under two stalks of wheat. Above is a hovering Victory with a crown and a palm.

On the other side, Mars is standing in the center; he is nude but is wearing a helmet and carrying a spear. On his right, a Silenus holding a thyrsus is moving to the left; below, another Silenus with a staff is moving to the right. Below Mars are two cupids wearing helmets. Venus, the goddess of love, is seated next to them; her garment has fallen from her upper body. Next comes another bacchante draped in a long tunic and carrying a thyrsus. Next to the top of Mars' spear is another flying Victory with a crown and palm.

The Navigius factory must have been in north central Tunisia in the area of El Aouja, some 20 miles south of Kairouan.

Bibliography: *De Carthage à Kairouan*, 1983, p. 147, with bibliography.
AE

51. Head Vase from the Navigius Workshop

Height: 25 cm; *Width:* 13 cm
Material: Ceramic
Provenance: El Aouja
Location: Bardo Museum
Date: Third century A.D.
Number: H25

Another unusual offering from the ever-inventive Navigius workshop is this pouring vessel (*oinochoe*) in the form of a female head. The young woman has a round, full face, heavy eyebrows, a pronounced dimple in her chin and hair parted in the middle and coming down in front and in back of each ear. A curious cap that has a basket-weave design and is fronted by six beads or knots terminates in the neck of the vase. A segmented necklace completes the image. The neck of the vessel is inscribed EX OFFICINA NAVIGIUS ("from the workshop of Navigius"). The strap handle is made of three adjacent fillets.

Bibliography: *De Carthage à Kairouan*, 1982, pp. 148, with full bibliography.
AE

52. North African Ceramics: Red Slip Wares

Beaker with Stamped Decoration (left)

Height: 8.8 cm
Provenance: El Jem
Location: Bardo Museum
Date: Late first to early second century A.D.
Number: None

This simple but rare beaker usually has two handles attached from the rim to the belly. The sides flare out gently into a cone with a slight curve, and the extension is stamped with three rough rows of lozenge decorations. There are three horizontal moldings or fillets on the exterior, one of which is neatly rouletted. A low ring foot is provided.

Although not an elegant vase, the fabric is thin and the gloss handsome, making this a good example of typical ancient Tunisian Roman pottery.

Bibliography: Hayes, 1972, Form 144, p.184.

Feeder Vase (center)

Height: 9 cm
Provenance: Bulla Regia
Location: Bardo Museum
Date: Later first to early second century A.D.
Number: CMA M.211

This little pouring vessel with horizontal flutes on a roughly cylindrical body is particularly attractive, yet simple and functional. It has a closed dome top with a projecting neck and mouth on one side and a loop handle on the other. It is also a rare piece and rests precariously on a low ring foot.

Bibliography: Hayes, 1972, Form 122, p.175

Red Slip Bowl (right)

Height: 6.0 cm; *Diameter:* 15 cm
Provenance: Dougga
Location: Bardo Museum
Date: Circa mid-second century A.D.
Number: CMA M.1047

Found in the French excavations of 1913, this is a popular bowl form with sides slightly sloping from the vertical and a lustrous gloss. This form is undecorated, with a slight carination from the base to the side wall.

These ceramics are unpublished.

Bibliography: Hayes, 1972, Form 14, p.41.

AE

53. North African Red Slip Dishes

Red Slip Dish (bottom left)

Height: 4.5 cm; *Diameter:* 18.5 cm
Provenance: Sidi El Hani (Sousse area)
Location: Bardo Museum
Date: A.D. 150 to 200
Number: B19

Discovered in excavations of 1910, this typical small dish was an enormously popular form in ancient Tunisia and is found throughout the country and in other areas, such as Spain and Algeria. This is the simple later version with no decorations, carinated side, and horizontal lip with a single groove.

Bibliography; Hayes, 1972, Form 6, p.29.

Feather Rouletted Bowl (bottom right)

Height: 6 cm; *Diameter:* 15 cm
Provenance: Dougga
Location: Bardo Museum
Date: Fifth century A.D.
Number: CMA M.1047

Found in 1913, this is a typical example of late Roman African Red Slip, formerly known as Late Roman D ware. It is a small bowl with a dull red-orange gloss and a distinctive feather rouletted interior characteristic of the period.

Bibliography: Hayes, 1972, See Forms 81, 85, and 91 for similar types of which this may be a variant.

Large Flat-Based Dish (rear right)

Height: 3 cm; *Diameter:* 30 cm
Provenance: La Skhira
Location: Bardo Museum
Date: A.D. 350 to 425
Number: B19

This common large dish with curved wall and plain rim has a central decoration that includes four stamped palmettes radially displayed around a circular groove with four rosettes placed between. A rouletted band runs around the edge of the floor.

Bibliography: Hayes, Form 62A, No. 3, p.107.

Large Flat-Based Dish (rear left)
Height: 3.5 cm; *Diameter:* 30 cm
Provenance: La Skhira
Location: Bardo Museum
Date: A.D. 350 to 425
Number: A28

Another plate or large dish like the preceding in orange-red fine ware. Note the twig marks on the underside where the slip was brushed on. It is decorated with nine quintuple circles dispersed radially around a central groove. There is a rouletted band around the edge of the floor.

These dishes are unpublished.

Bibliography: Hayes, Form 62A, No.6, p.108.

AE

54. Lead-Glazed Ceramic Cup

Height: 9.5 cm; *Diameter of mouth:* 9.5 cm
Provenance: El Jem
Location: Bardo Museum
Date: Third century A.D. (?)
Number: 2615

This cup with a footed base has two handles bent into S shapes to conform to the user's fingers. A molding that runs the length of these two handles divides each in half. The upper edge of this vase is encircled by a groove passing just above the two handles. The globular body is decorated with three rows of plump pointed leaves arranged in a "pine cone" style of decoration.

A groove defines the junction of the body with the base and the foot, which flares out at the bottom. The base is convex on the outside and slightly concave on the inside.

On the exterior of the vase and on the bottom of the base is a glaze of green lead that forms an iridescent coat of metallic luster. The grooved interior of the vase is lead-glazed with a mustard-yellow color. Two drops of glaze on the edge of the cup show that this glaze was baked on in an oven with the cup inverted.

This technique of applying lead glaze has very ancient origins. It could have begun in Mesopotamia, where vases were made this way around 1000 B.C. Later this technique is found in Egypt, then in Asia Minor. In western Europe, ceramics with lead glazing have been found principally in areas that are now France, Belgium, Great Britain, and perhaps Germany. Discoveries in North African excavations are rare and from widely scattered locations. A few years ago, the discovery at El Jem (Thysdrus) of numerous lead-glazed fragments indicates that this technique was used in Roman Africa in the first half of the third century A.D. Most examples made in Asia Minor date between the first century B.C. and the first century A.D. In the light of these discoveries, a new study is needed.

The series of vases found on this site seems to prove that it was a production center. This cup is another indication of the economic development and diversification of a Roman African city such as Thysdrus. The cup is unpublished.

Bibliography: For green-glazed pottery in general, see Toll, 1943.

LS

55. The Rape of Europa

Length: 10.7 cm; *Diameter:* 7 cm; *Height:* 3.2 cm
Material: Ceramic
Provenance: Bulla Regia
Location: Bardo Museum
Date: Third century A.D.
Number: K127

This lamp has a heart-shaped spout and a plain handle. A ventilation hole has been placed off center to avoid intrusion on the motif of the discus. A raised shoulder inclines toward the exterior and is decorated by an ovolo molding. The flat back has the fabricant's mark bound by three concentric circles: PULL/AENO(RUM)/PU(?). This mark belonged to the Pullaenii, one of the richest families in the region, known through numerous epigraphic texts.

On the discus a young woman holding a flower in her right hand is sitting sidesaddle on a bull that is running (in profile) to the right. The subject is Zeus's rape of Europa, daughter of Agenor (the king of Phoenicia) and future father of Minos (the king of Crete). Zeus has transformed himself into a white bull with golden horns to seduce Europa and to escape the vigilance of his wife, Hera. The loves of the gods was a delightful subject, one that proved quite popular on Roman lamps.

Bibliography: See Deneauve, 1969, pp. 182-187, for the Pullaeni.
MK

56. Bilychnis Lamp with Two Spouts

Height: 5.8 cm; *Length:* 26.8 cm; *Diameter:* 12 cm
Material: Ceramic
Provenance: Neighborhood of Mateur (ancient Matera)
Location: Bardo Museum
Date: Fifth to sixth century A.D.
Number: K46

This large lamp has a spout at each end; both spouts have been blackened by usage. There is a suspension ring at the beginning of each channel leading to the spout. One of the rings is partially broken. On the discus is a crudely engraved six-pointed star formed by two overlapping triangles. In the center of the six small triangles formed by this overlap is a vent hole. The circumference of the lamp is crudely engraved with hatch marks. The bottom bears the artisan's workshop trademark: a cross in a ring. The date is based partly on the parallels between the channel/spout arrangement here and a similar arrangement on Hayes African Lamp Types IIA and B. The lamp is unpublished.

57. Tragic Poet and Actor Mosaic

Dimensions of floor: 6 x 6
Dimensions of panel: 2.11 x 1.45
Provenance: Sousse (Hadrumetum), in the House of the Masks
Location: Museum of Sousse
Date: Third century A.D.
Number: None

African citizens were almost all patrons of the theater, which presented plays, mime shows, poetry readings, music, and other types of performances. These performances inspired the mosaicists. They presented scenes from the works of Plautus (Hadrumetum, Inv. 57010) and Virgil (Hadrumetum, Inv. 57104) or simply evoked the theater by illustrating the Muses and masks. This mosaic falls into this latter category. Discovered in the House of the Masks at Sousse, this mosaic was located about 50 meters south of the ancient theater.

The mosaic shows an illusionistic circle designed like a shield. Adjacent *trompe l'oeil* cubical forms surround a circular or central picture (*pseudo emblema*). In the rear is a pensive poet, dressed in a white tunic and wearing sandals. He has a round face that is framed by a beard. He is seated, holding a scroll (*volumen*) in his left hand, and with his right hand he holds a reed pen (*calamus*) to his chin. Before him is a box (*capsa* or *cista*) containing twelve manuscripts (*volumina*). From the height of his platform, the poet appears to be helping a clean-shaven actor (seen full face and with his right elbow leaning on a stand or console) choose between two masks, the one he is holding and a second mask on a table at the far left.

The actor, standing, is dressed in a greenish tunic and a red cape with a white band at the shoulder. He is wearing sandals. The scene described fits perfectly into the decor of the building in which it was found; the structure is dominated by dramatic art, which has led L. Foucher to call this the location of a brotherhood of actors.

Close examination of the tableau does not lead to identification of the figures as famous artists. Perhaps the mosaicist based his creation on familiar surroundings; he seems to have tried to individualize the faces, for example. Was he portraying a local poet and an actor who were popular at the time? Or is it a portrait of the owner of the House of Masks or a patron who wished to be identified with the famous Hadrumetum artists' group?

Masks were essential ingredients of the Greek and Roman theater, and the exaggerated masks told the audience much about the roles being played; open-mouthed masks expressed agony or laughter, for example. In the Hellenistic period, the hair was built up to a high crest. The mask on the viewer's left indicates a mature adult and may be for the performance of a tragedy; the beardless mask on the right may be more appropriate to tragic youth. The latter has also been identified by several scholars, including Yacoub, as a comic mask.

Because the playwright is sitting remote and almost statuelike on what might even be thought of as a throne, he has been identified as one of various great writers of the past, but who it might be is anyone's guess.

Bibliography: Yacoub, 1978, pp. 149–151; Foucher, 1965, pp. 15–16.
ME

58. Tragic Mask

Height: 21 cm; *Width:* 15 cm
Material: Lead
Provenance: Carthage, near the cisterns of Borj-Jedid
Location: National Museum of Carthage (storage)
Date: Roman era
Number: CMA H56

This lead mask may have served as a wall decoration. It is the slightly elongated face of a beardless young man surmounted by a headdress with five horizontal layers, made almost three-dimensional by apparently overlapping vertical lines of tresses. Each layer of this complicated wig is carefully arranged. A curly lock of hair hangs from each side, covering the ears; the curls are represented by small circles set close together.

The almond-shaped eyes do not protrude but are actually deep, slightly asymmetrical hollows that give the face a disconcerting and serious look. Oblique dash marks indicate the thick eyebrows. Above a slightly jutting chin, the wide-open mouth seems to shout, absorbing the lips and occupying a large part of the cheek area.

The use of masks dates back to the most remote antiquity. The Egyptians used them, as did the Greeks. During their Lupercalian and Saturnalian celebrations, the Romans put on masks and ran through the streets, disguised. Masks were also used in funeral ceremonies. Metal and especially terra cotta masks have been found in Punic tombs; the masks were designed to ward off evil spirits and to appease the good spirits necessary to the eternal rest of the deceased. Masks were also used in theatrical scenic representations. During the Roman era, they were called *personae*. Inherited from the Greek tradition, these masks were of a standard type and varied in expression according to the comic, satiric, or tragic nature of the scenes and the sex and age of those represented. The standard types (forty-three types of comic masks, thirty types of tragic and satiric masks) always have the same traits.

The Carthage mask apparently related to young Greeks, eighteen to twenty years of age, who received religious, civic, and military instruction (*ephebes*); and a Greek-tragedy juvenile type that includes several varieties, such as those that have a high curly-haired wig, straight eyebrows and a severe, haughty expression (*oulos*). This type recalls portraits of proud young heroes like Hippolytus or Achilles. The oulos mask types have been found in the mosaics of Sousse (Hadrumetum) and of El Jem (Thysdrus).

The considerable quantity of masks in African mosaics indicates the African enthusiasm for spectacles, especially in Carthage. Writing in the second century A.D., the philosopher Apuleius praises the architecture of the theater and describes the varied cultural events given there: "It is no longer a dream that here at various times we can attend the expressive dances of pantomime, the dialogues of comedy, the booming monologues of tragedy, the daring leaps of the high wire artist..." (*Florides* 4 XVIII).

The proximity of the theater, 150 meters to the southeast, may mean that the mosaic was part of a location where actors met. A tragic mask in Carthage discovered in the cisterns of Borj-Jedid, not far from the Roman theater, evokes a hypothesis that may be applied to this example; the mask could have served as decoration on a door or wall as a gargoyle. Nevertheless, the material found here, lead—the least noble and the least pure of all metals—was used especially in funeral and magic ceremonies. Perhaps this was a funeral mask destined for an actor's tomb. The mask is unpublished

Bibliography: Bieber, 1971, discusses personae throughout the book and illustrates numerous examples.

LLS

59. The Great Nile Pygmy Hunt

Dimensions: 2.15 m x 1.45 m
Provenance: Hadrumetum (Sousse), in a Roman house
Location: Archaeological Museum of Sousse
Date: A.D. 200 to 250
Number: 57.027

The dining room (*triclinium*) of a sumptuous Roman house in ancient Tunisia was a showplace for mosaics. The pavement was often composed of two mosaics, separated by a border. One mosaic, in the form of a U, corresponded to the area reserved for the banqueting couches which were placed around the side and back walls. It was usually decorated with geometric designs. The second mosaic, in the form of a T, was often decorated with scenes designed to provide banqueters facing in different directions with interesting views. This scene of hunting and fishing on the Nile formed part of the hast of the T. A swampy area filled with lotuses, papyri, fish, and ducks is the background for a stone and trident attack on a feisty hippo, a successful fishing venture, and a cast net about to trap a fish. The mosaic, excavated in 1883, offers a fine glimpse of a fishing boat of the period— pronounced stern and low prow; however, it does not seem to be of typical Egyptian reed construction and crescent shape. The low prow with lower projecting hull was designed to cut the water and act as a ram against other boats—a type known since the third millennium in the Cyclades and Crete. The fanlike stern ornament (*aphlaston*) is known from the sixth century B.C. This type of boat was probably intended to be a sort of merchant galley, but the lack of sails may indicate a smaller craft; size and proportion are not necessarily to be taken in absolute terms.

The fish do not appear to be Nile types, and above the gesturing oarsman is a parrotfish. The hippo is *Hippopotamus amphibius*. The duck to the viewer's left may be a mallard (*Anas platarhyncos*), while its companion may be a teal (*Nettion crecca*). The pygmy with trident is sexually well endowed and boasts a green, yellow, red, and olive shield. The stone hurler is wearing a loin cloth and pointed cap, while his companion—more concerned about sun—sports a wide-brimmed *petasus* of felt that resembles a cowboy hat. The pointed cap appears to be a brimless *pilleus* of felt, the Roman cap of freedom, especially of sailors and fishermen.

Bibliography: Yacoub, 1967, p. 14; Foucher, 1960, pp. 9–11.
ME

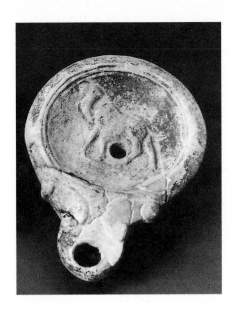

60. Lamp with Image of Camel

Length: 12 cm; *Width:* 8.5 cm; *Height:* 3.2 cm
Material: Ceramic
Provenance: Ksar-es-Zit (ancient Siagu)
Location: Bardo Museum
Date: A.D. 50 to 100
Number: Inv. 2973

This lamp lacks a handle and has a pointed spout decorated with double volutes. The flat bottom bears the artisan's trademark: OMI. On the discus is the profile of a camel.

The one-humped dromedary was brought to North Africa at a relatively recent date—the beginning of the Roman Empire. It has since become the one indispensable domestic animal in the daily life of desert and semidesert residents. The considerable role it has played in the history of these regions has made it worthy of being called the "ship of the desert." The animal is considered native to both India and North Africa; it is perfectly adapted to the Sahara regions because it can lose up to 25 percent of its body weight in water and regain its normal appearance within ten minutes after quenching its thirst. This lamp is unpublished.

Bibliography: Deneauve, 1969, Type VA.

MK

61. Running Hare and Dog

Dimensions: 100 cm x 60 cm
Provenance: El Jem, in the House of the Dionysiac Procession
Location: El Jem depot
Date: Circa A.D. 150–200
Number: None

This fragment of a mosaic border comes from the same house as Catalogue 79 and 80. It is part of a border decorated with acanthus rinceau enclosing a hare and a dog.

Bibliography: *30 Ans 1986*, p. 170, with bibliography.

HS

62. Basket of Fish

Dimensions: 2.05 m x 1.48 m
Provenance: Environs of Sousse (Hadrumetum), from a Roman house
Location: Sousse Museum
Date: Third century A.D.

Despite surface damage, this mosaic found in 1952 presents a fisherman's delight: a basket overflowing with fruits of the sea, including catfish, perch, mullet, daurade, eel, pike, cod, electric ray (*Torpedo inidae*), giant shrimp, and goatfish such as bearded mullet (*Mullus barbatus*). The white background is decorated by a rectangular pattern of swastikas. The straw basket is braided with yellow, white, and green loops. The mosaic is invaluable for showing the daily diet possible for fish lovers of ancient Tunisia and as a document for those interested in Roman weaving—of which precious little survives.

Bibliography: Foucher, 1960, p.117, No. 57260, Plate LXIV, with bibliography.
OBOB

63. Balance with Hooks

Length of the lever: 21.5 cm; *Length of the chains:* 26.0 cm
Material: Copper alloy
Provenance: Dougga (ancient Thugga), west of the Temple of Tellus
Location: Bardo Museum
Date: Roman period

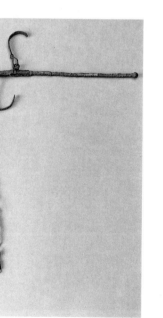

Found with an identical example at Dougga in 1917, this is an example of a Roman balance. The principal elements can be recognized. The beam hangs from a hook. From one end (*jugum*) hang two small chains terminating in two hooks (one in this example) to hold objects to be weighed. From the other end hang identical chains and hooks to hold counterweights. A scale is marked on the beam, and a counterbalance (*aequipondium*) is slid back and forth along the marked beam to bring the counterweights and the jugum object into balance. Once they are in balance, the position of the counterbalance on the beam's scale provides the correct weight. (Only traces of the beam markings remain in this example—evidence of heavy use?) The goods to be weighed were hooked to the jugum chains, or placed in a pan that was hooked to the chains. This balance, which was easily and quickly employed, was known as a stater. Numerous examples of balances of varying degrees of sophistication have been found throughout the Roman Empire. Because of the simplified design and the size of the hooks in this example, merchandise of low density could be weighed.

The invention of the balance dates back to the earliest antiquity, and representations of it appear in all periods. Exchange is found at the beginning of every social order, however primitive, and Egyptians and Greeks are known to have been using the balance long before the Roman period. As early as the Mycenaean period, the Greeks were using it as we do today; their balance consisted of a beam and two pans. And, as can be seen on an ex-voto from Carthage, the Punic people used the balance with pans at least as early as the third century B.C. and probably before that. Goldsmiths, money-changers, and tradesmen used it, and it could even be a cult instrument used in sanctuaries to weigh animal parts awarded to the clergy after the sacrifice and to the donors of the offerings.

The Dougga balance was discovered with its companion on a commercial street of ancient Thugga (that leading to the market, west of the Temple of Tellus) and perhaps originally belonged to a shop; it is valuable evidence of the economic life of an African city during the

Roman period. Working-class Tunisians in certain old city areas (*medinas*) still use the so-called Roman balance. The object is unpublished.

ZBA

64. The Kiss

Height: 5.5 cm; *Length:* 17.7 cm
Material: Ceramic
Provenance: El Aouja
Location: Bardo Museum
Date: Third century A.D.
Number: Inv. 121

This stylized depiction of embracing lovers is one of the most tender and charming Tunisian scenes. The lamp has an elongated spout bordered with double volutes and an extended channel, or reservoir, a reflecting plate (rear handle) decorated with a wreath, and a flat back that carries no mark. At the base of the reflector plate is a ventilator hole surrounded by a wreath. The upper part of the reservoir illustrates two figures in the act of embracing. The figure on the right is a man. He is beardless, has curly hair, and apparently wears no clothing. He is resting his right hand on the cheek of the young woman facing him. She is dressed in a tunic, her hair coiffed in a chignon. She is offering her lips to her partner and placing her left hand on his neck.

The nozzle channel decorated with a segmented floral pattern such as the one shown on this lamp is characteristic of a type of lamp produced between about A.D. 200 and 250 and often characterized by unique decoration of the discus. One example features a fierce lion reclining on discus and shoulder. This object is unpublished.

Bibliography: Deneauve, 1969, Type XB.

MK

65. Stucco Relief of the Monokinied Ladies

1. Profile of a Standing Woman

Height: 34.5 cm; *Height of head:* 9 cm

2. Seated [?] Figure

Height: 40.5 cm

3. Bust in Profile

Height: 22 cm

4. Full-Face Bust

Height: 20 cm

5. Figure Seated on a Basket

Height: 45 cm; *Width:* 33.5 cm

6. Standing Figure, Legs Crossed Diagonally

Height: 40 cm

7. Youth or Putto Atlantid

Height: 15 cm

8–10. Three Apparently Female Heads

Height: 12.5 cm

Material: Stucco painted black and ochre
Provenance: Dougga
Location: Bardo Museum
Date: Third century A.D.(?)
Number: C68/C1497

For the most part, these fragments are in a bad state of repair and require a restoration. Of some figures, only the head has survived. Three figures are shown frontally, two are shown com-

pletely in profile, and two are presented in three-quarters profile. They are reposing or about to move. One profile figure is standing, her body leaning slightly forward, reaching out with her right arm. The other, standing on the left leg, is holding her right foot up against her left thigh as if examining the sole of her right foot. The third, seated on a basket, is folding her left leg under her extended right leg. The fourth is standing full front, her weight on her right leg and her left leg extended slightly.

All of these lean, sturdy young women are wearing black net pants made of two form-fitting pieces held together by ties from which ribbons dangle to their knees. Their upper arms are decorated with yellow ochre bracelets. Their faces are oval. Their arched foreheads are high. Fine eyebrows shelter slightly protruding eyes that have hollowed pupils. Their drooping upper eyelids are underlined by fine grooves. Their cheekbones are prominent, their mouths delicate, and their lips full. Their chins jut out slightly, and their hair is parted in the middle and drawn back into buns on top of their heads or swept up in soft waves at the side.

These scantily clad young women are not bathers, as one would think from their surroundings and as was thought at first, but they are probably gymnasts. Unfortunately, no athletic gear or objects have been preserved, if they ever existed. Women athletes perform gymnastics on the Piazza Armerina mosaics, but—unlike the Dougga athletes—they are clad in more conservative bikinis. On a mosaic from Cherchel in the private baths of a Roman villa, three entirely nude women are performing. On mosaics, female athletes are rarer than male athletes, which makes this relief all the more important.

These women athletes were part of a wall revetment that probably decorated a private bath, perhaps in an elegant palaestra or exercise ground. The relief is the work of a sculptor who knew how to translate precise movements and well-defined positions by using softened planes and well-shaped masses. The moderate use of a trepan suggests the second half of the second century as a date for the relief, but the context of the discovery places it in the third century, if the dating of the Trifolium house is to be trusted.

In addition to the female athletes, there are three more apparently female heads and a figure that looks like a boy whose long and tousled hair hangs down across what may be part of a wing. He is carrying an object that has four nostril-like perforations in it. The boy is almost smiling with his mouth slightly open. If he is a cupid, or putto, normally in the entourage of

199

Venus, goddess of love, a reevaluation of who the women are may be necessary; certainly the revealing black net panties worn by the female athletes go one step beyond the bikinis worn by the Piazza Armerina females. The latter seem modest by comparison.

Bibliography: Carandini, Ricci, and de Vos, 1982, p. 154–155; *De Carthage à Kairouan*, 1982, p.140, with bibliography.

NAO

66. Erotic Lamp

Length: 10.3 cm; *Width:* 8 cm; *Height:* 2.5 cm
Material: Ceramic
Provenance: Haidra (ancient Ammaedara)
Location: Bardo Museum
Date: Later second to third century A.D.
Number: K971

This lamp with a heart-shaped nozzle and a perforated handle has a filling hole and a vent hole. The outer perimeter is turned up to the outside and is decorated with alternating grape leaves and bunches of grapes. The flat bottom bears the fabricant's trademark: three palm trees surrounded by two concentric circles.

Within the discus is an erotic scene shown in right profile. The scene presents a standing naked man in the act of making love to a woman who is offering him her hindquarters. This type of erotic scene is very common in Roman art and may be noted not only in such locations as the House of the Vetti in Pompeii but also in the Archaic Etruscan tomb painting of Tarquinia. The find spot is also of interest, since Ammaedara was the first military headquarters of the Third Augustan Legion, pacifiers of Africa. This piece is unpublished.

Bibliography: Deneauve, 1969, Type VIII B.

MK

67. The Drunken Hercules

Height: 52 cm
Material: Copper alloy (cast bronze)
Provenance: Thibar
Location: Bardo Museum
Date: Second century A.D. (?)
Number: Inv. 2778

The region of Thibar, near Beja, is known for extraordinary wines. It was also an important ancient agricultural and Christian center. The site was sporadically excavated in the 1930s.

From the 1939 excavations by Father Lepeyre came this humorous, muscular, and drunken Hercules. He is standing naked, in the act of urinating. His trunk is thrown back, the legs are apart, and the stomach is thrust forward. The left arm is raised and bent back; the right hand grips a gnarled club. The head is powerful; the facial features are heavy, strong, and well-delineated, and he has a very bushy beard. The hair is comprised of short, sleek, tight locks bound by a fillet. His muscles are knotted and well-defined. This is an example of the type known as "Hercules *mingens*" (in the act of urinating), in which the hero is represented in a state of intoxication. The quality of the work strongly recalls that of Lysippos.

An almost identical Hercules in marble was discovered in the House of the Stags in Herculaneum, suggesting that the drunken Hercules series evolved from an original of the Hellenistic period, perhaps from the Pergamum (Asia Minor) area. There the contrast of a powerful, muscular form with an unstable, teetering stance would have been viewed as an artistic challenge—since Hercules was associated with the Attalid dynasty.

Punic religion honored the god Melqart—"king of the city" and lord of ancient Tyre, home city of Queen Dido and the Carthaginians—well into the Classical Period. In that era, Melqart became assimilated to Herakles. The Romans called him Hercules, son of Zeus and Alcmene, a daughter of Mycenean royalty. Thus Melqart/Herakles/Hercules was popular and honored in ancient Tunisia. The name of Hamilcar, the great Carthaginian general of the First Punic War and father of Hannibal, means "servant of Melqart."

To the Dorian Greeks and the Romans, however, Hercules was a mortal struggling against untold dangers to win a place among the gods. He could make human mistakes and had to choose between a virtuous and a debauched way of life. Although he was usually accomplishing superhuman tasks and was shown in colossal statues, this image brings to mind Euripides' play *Alcestis* (circa 438 B.C.). In this play, based on an old folktale, Herakles—on one of his twelve labors—stops at the home of Admetus, a northern Greek king who was mourning the death of his wife Alcestis. In the play, Herakles is a kindly superhero agent of Apollo and noble offspring child of Zeus. Being mortal, he has flaws and is susceptible to extremely good hospitality (*xenia*). As the servant in the play says: "I have known all sorts of foreigners who have come in from all over the world here to Admetus' house, and I have served them dinner, but I never yet have had a guest as bad as this to entertain...the flame of the wine went all through him, and heated him, and then he wreathed branches of myrtle on his head and howled, off-key!"

According to the French scholar Gilbert Charles-Picard, Hercules can be a fertility figure, a phallic genius of the fecundity of springtime and a symbol of convivial banqueting and good times. This figure in a banqueting room might inspire diners to behave a little less formally than they otherwise might.

Bibliography: Yacoub, 1969, p.96, Fig. 104; *De Carthage à Kairouan*, 1983 p.125, No. 177.

NAO

68. Head of Medusa

Dimensions: 90 cm x 89 cm
Provenance: Henchir Thina, in the Roman baths (region of Sfax)
Location: Sfax Museum
Date: Third century A.D.
Number: M9

The mosaic of the head of Medusa is shown in a circular medallion with a white background. The medallion is bordered by a double line with a checkered pattern of white and black squares. Medusa is wearing two small wings on her forehead. From her thick and slightly wavy hair writhe five pairs of snakes; the two in each pair are facing each other. The tails of the last two are tied beneath her chin. The face is wide, and her large eyes are shadowed with maroon and cast a magnetic gaze on the viewer. Her nose is long, slightly thick and irregular, and her mouth is small, with well-shaped lips.

The medallion radiates white diamond shapes surrounded by cubes of white, black, yellow, and red in a three-dimensional *trompe l'oeil* effect.

Medusa was one of the Gorgons; her two sisters were Stheno and Euryale. Homer wrote that a glance from her turned humans to stone. The hero Perseus beheaded Medusa, stuck her head in his bag, and gave it to Athena. From Medusa's streaming blood, the winged horse Pegasus was born. Originally a horrid creature, Medusa was by Roman times lovely of face but still a powerful apotropaic, or protector from evil spirits, and very popular for this reason.

Bibliography: Massigli, 1912, p.6, 23; Gauckler, 1910, p.10, n. 18A, 14C.
OBOB

69. Malediction Tablet Inscribed on Two Faces

Dimensions: 0.13 m x 0.26 m
Material: Lead
Provenance: Carthage, in the Cemetery of the Officials
Location: Carthage Museum (storage)
Date: Roman period

This lead tablet, rather thick and slightly undulant on its edges, bears the following inscription engraved with styles in precise cursive Latin letters:

Face A:

TE ROGO QUI INFER

NALES PARTES TENES COM

MENDO TIBI IULIA FAUSTIL

Face B:

TE ROGO QUI INFERNAL

ES PARTES TENES COMMEN

DO TIBI IULIA FAUSTILLA

LA, MARII FILIA UT EAM CELE   UT EAM CELERIUS ABDUCA

RIUS ABDUCAS ET IBI IN NUM   S INFERNALES PARTIBUS

ERUM TU ABIAS   IN NUMERU TU ABIAS

Expansion, Face A: Te rogo qui infer/nales partes tenes com/ mendo tibi Iulia(m) Faustil/la(m), Marii filia ut eam cele/rius abducas et ibi in num/erum (defunctorum) tu a[b]ias.

Expansion, Face B: Te rogo qui infernal/es partes te es commen/do tibi Iulia(m) Faustilla(m) ut eam celerius abduca/ s infernales partibus in numeru(m defunctorum) abias.

The two texts are almost identical. The translation is:

I beseech you, you who are the master of the underworld; I commend to you Julia Faustilla, the daughter of Marius; take her to your realm as quickly as possible that she may number among the dead in hell.

This tablet is one of a number of examples found in Roman Africa and especially in Carthage and Sousse (Hadrumetum). It is associated with magic and charms, and it is representative of the malediction tablets (*execrationes, defixiones,* or *devotiones*) used by magicians to damn an enemy to the underworld, to bring about his death, or to harm him at the very least. They were used to get rid of an adversary, to check horses and drivers from an opposing stable in chariot races, or to obtain favors from someone who could not otherwise be persuaded.

Almost all the malediction tablets that have been found were inscribed on very thin lead plates. The name of the enemy was recorded. The repetition of the name was the rule and is illustrated here with the almost identical inscription on both sides. The name was usually surrounded by cabalistic signs and formulas. Following inscription, the plates were folded or rolled and slipped into tombs through prepared openings in the masonry intended for libations.

The necropolis at Sousse and the Cemetery of the Officials (slaves and imperial stewards) at Carthage have provided a good number of documents of this type. They provide valuable indication of the Africans' state of mind and superstitions during the Roman period. The rituals were evidently rigorously forbidden and severely punished by law. The celebrated criminal case brought against the noted philosopher Apuleius of the second century A.D. is well known. He was accused of the crime of magic and was forced to defend himself in Oea (Tripoli). His accusers claimed that he had bewitched the rich widow Pudentilla for the sole purpose of marrying her. In his *Apologia,* Apuleius had no difficulty proving that magic was not involved in his marriage, but his reputation as a magician was to follow him throughout many centuries. Apuleius's argument is a priceless historical document on the widespread practice of magic and witchcraft in Africa during the imperial epoch.

The adversary of Julia Faustilla (the daughter of Marius), who was probably a rejected lover or a jealous rival, did not hesitate to damn the poor woman to hell. We will never know if the sorcery bore fruit and if this unfortunate lady perished like Ennia Fructuosa of Lambaesis, who died at the age of twenty-eight, the victim of magic incantations. The epitaph engraved on her tomb: "carminibus defia iacet per tempora multa."

Bibliography: *CIL* VIII, 12505, 2756; *CLE,* 1604 Delattre, 1882, p.181; Audollent, 1984, p.300, No. 228; Apuleius, 1962.

LLS

70. Facing Cocks Mosaic

Dimension: 1.17 m x 1.17 m
Provenance: Neapolis (Nabeul), in the House of the Nymphs
Location: Nabeul Museum
Date: Fourth century A.D.
Number: None

This picture of two cocks (*Gallus phasianidae*) facing each other decorated the entrance of the triclinium of the House of the Nymphs. The name Nympharum Domus was inserted in the basin of the peristyle. This square is one panel of a group of mosaics from this location; they are considered among the most beautiful found up to that period—the grooming of Pegasus, the gift bearers, the weddings of Bellerophon and Philonoë, etc. These themes, drawn from Greek literature and mythology, show a high level of culture and refinement. It is not surprising as the town appeared very early—as far back as 413 B.C.—and is one of the oldest cities in Tunisia cited in texts. Thucydides called it the emporium of Carthage. However, its name and certain periods in its history suggest Greek and Near Eastern origin. The decoration of the house was very significant.

Two cocks are on both sides of an ovoid-bellied jar filled with gold, and each is holding a piece of money in its beak. Their crests are bright red, pink, and black marble; the hanging folds of skin below their beaks are clearly shown, as are their wings and tails. Their sharp spurs rest on a trapezoidal ground comprised of small pieces of ochre and dark brown stones; pieces of gold, escaping from the cocks' beaks, are falling onto this ground. Three stemmed leaves of ivy (*hederae*) are placed above the jar and the two cocks.

This picture, apart from its decorative value, reflects the wealth and luxury in a house that the owner wished to be sumptuous and comfortable.

The cocks facing each other suggest the combat of fighting cocks, and the gold coins suggest the prize money for the victor. Prominently placed, the panel promised victory and prosperity to the members of the household. It has even been suggested that they evoke a certain eroticism linked to the concept of marriage and amorous desire.

Bibliography: Darmon, 1980, pp. 79–84 and Plates LXXVIII and LXXIX; for the imagery.

LLS

71. Portrait Head

Height: 13 cm
Material: White marble of large translucent crystals
Provenance: Kairouan region, presented as a gift by Mr. Farrugia of Candia to the Bardo Museum
Location: Bardo Museum
Date: Circa A.D. 150
Number: Inv. 2635

Small in size but excellent in quality is this marble portrait head with drilled hair curls, tooled eyes, an emaciated face, sunken temples, and a slightly protruding chin. The high forehead is slightly flattened in the middle, the eyebrows are thin, and the large eyes are deeply set. The upper eyelid falls gently over a lightly drilled pupil, and the lower lid is outlined by rings. The cheekbones are prominent, the slightly short nose is aquiline, and the mouth, with upper lip barely indicated and tailing off at the corners, is surmounted by a long mustache that joins the beard. The beard, which was created by long, expert blows of the drill, continues to the side-burns and completely covers the chin. The hair is arranged in tight curls, with a slight fullness on the sides, accentuating the fine and sharply delineated ears. Numerous wrinkles cross the brow and deeply furrow the corners of the mouth—the individual seems to be middle-aged. The neck is thin and tautly muscled. He is looking into the distance and appears to be very pensive. The sad thoughts of this person have been masterfully captured.

This was a private-portrait head and was probably intended to be placed on a small bust, as suggested by the edge of the neck, which has a marble tenon on the nape that normally would not be visible. This may be an indication that the sculptor had insufficient time to complete the entire work.

The very moderate use of trepanning, notably in the eyes, and its absence from the hair, leads us to date the piece to about A.D. 150 . The drooping-eyelid look is found particularly between 150 and 175. Beards were not fashionable until well into the early part of the second century. This piece is unpublished.

NAO

72. Lucilla, Wife of Emperor Lucius Verus

Height: 1.74 m
Material: Cycladic marble
Provenance: Bulla Regia
Location: Bardo Museum
Date: A.D. 150 to 200
Number: 33655

This extraordinary large sculpture has undergone recent restoration, which allows a full view of the right hand and torch. The figure is a female standing on a rectangular base. The body rests on the right leg, while the left leg is bent at the knee.

A torch with entwined serpent occupies the right hand. Two poppies are in the left hand. The face is oval, with elegant drooping almond eyes in the Antonine tradition. The nose and mouth are prominent. She is veiled, and the hair has a part in the middle and a band perhaps belonging to the veil above the hair. She wears a stola covered by an ample palla that forms diagonal bands across the breasts and lower torso.

The combination of graceful pose and awkward rendering — as with the left leg — are typical of second-century sculpture in ancient Tunisia. The attributes suggest Ceres, but the coiffure and face suggest Empress Lucilla, wife of Emperor Lucius Verus, co-emperor from 161 to 169 with Marcus Aurelius, whose daughter was Lucilla. The fusion of an empress and a mother goddess was not uncommon in Roman imperial sculpture.

Bibliography: *30 Ans 1986,* pp. 159, with full bibliography.

NAO

73. Black Child with a Dove

Total height: 55 cm; *Height of head:* 13 cm; *Diameter of small tenon holes:* 15 cm
Material: Black marble with white veins
Provenance: Sousse (ancient Hadrumetum)
Location: Sousse Museum
Date: Second century A.D.
Number: 45

This statuette of a black child with a dove is one of the most charming pieces from Sousse, the ancient Hadrumetum, principal port and commercial center of the Byzacene area of eastern Tunisia since Punic times. For a long time, Sousse kept its status as one of the free cities (*oppida*

libera), and it grew as a result of the aid it gave the Romans during their war against Carthage. This child was found on the floor of a Roman house of the second century A.D. during the 1899 archaeological expedition at Trocadero, to the northwest of Sousse. The figure is in fairly good condition. The right arm and hand, the right leg from midcalf down, the left leg from the knee down, and the head of the dove are all missing. The nose and the chin are worn away. The buttocks and the genitals are mutilated. Repairs have been made to the left eye, the right side of the neck, the wrist, the left thigh, and the right leg.

Use of a trepan at the corners of the mouth can be discerned, as well as behind the ears, on the right arm and at the crotch. The back is very slightly curved, showing good knowledge of rendering weight shift. Three tenons have been placed: one is at the nape of the neck, a second is between the shoulder blades (leaving traces of bronze nails), and the third is under the buttocks. Two others have been placed: one is on the right side of the groin, the other is on the exterior surface of the right thigh. The eyes are recessed, and the whole surface is polished.

The black child is standing and leaning on the left leg. His head is leaning to the left, and he is holding a dove against his chest with his left hand, while his right hand is falling to his side. His head is large, and his face is round. The forehead is wide and flat, and the brow is prominent and smooth. His eyes are inlaid with white marble with a smaller circle of black marble for pupils. His cheeks are rounded. The mouth juts out above the chin, and the lips are thick. The right ear is pierced, and the hair is in tufts of tight curls. The huge head rests on a too-short neck. The narrow shoulders are slightly pointed, and the navel of the protruding belly is marked by a hole. The thighs are well shaped, and the right knee is knobby. His arms are long and thin, and the three fingers of his left hand—half hidden by the bird's wings—are thin with sharply defined angles. A deep depression runs the length of the arched back.

The bird's right wing is folded against the child's chest, thus using one of the tenons; the left wing is extended over the child's hand and wrist.

We often see representations of a child holding a bird in Greco-Roman art either in relief sculpture or on gravestones. For the most part, the significance is religious. One might assume the same about this child if he were not black. Since late antiquity, blacks have been a theme in art—often appearing in ceramics as caricatures on vases, cups, kitchen wares, and low reliefs and as statues of acrobats, musicians, and dancers. Artists have always attempted to emphasize racial characteristics by enlarging the head and reducing the body, which often has a strongly arched back, a large protruding belly, and thin arms and legs. Unlike the extreme caricatures seen in many other statuettes, the black child of Sousse combines realism and conventional exaggeration—seen in the sinuous posture and the lack of proportion of the limbs. In common with statuettes like the child of Tarragona and the black basalt statuette at Alexandria, this example has eyes inlaid with white marble and black pupils. Unlike other statuettes of black children, the Sousse child seems to have had a decorative rather than a utilitarian role. In fact, the tenon holes in the back suggest to some, notably L. Foucher, that this child was a part of an architectural ensemble; the care expended on executing the back leaves us unsure on this subject.

This statuette is striking in its careful execution and the liveliness of its expression. The very moderate usage of the trepan and its total absence from the hair date this work in the Hadrianic epoch, a dating also proposed by N. de Chaisemartin, contrary to the opinion of L. Foucher, who thinks it dates from the Antonine period: "This marble is without doubt a contemporary of the mosaics found in the same house and it is probable that the victories over the Saharan rebels, in whose ranks blacks fought, contributed toward bringing the presentation of blacks into fashion during the Antonine epoch."

Bibliography: Gauckler, Gouvert, and Hannezo, 1902, No. 3, p.39, plate XIII; Beondley, 1929; Foucher, 1964, p.170, Plate XII; *Carthage*, 1981, p.81, with bibliography; Foucher, 1967, p.30, Fig.37.

NAO

74. Intaglio of a Port

Length: 1.6 cm; *Width:* 1.2 cm; *Thickness:* 0.2 cm
Material: Heliotrope
Provenance: Unknown
Location: Bardo Museum
Date: Late Roman
Number: Inv. 148

This unique oval intaglio is made of heliotrope, a variety of green jasper characterized by its dull green color and scattered red spots. The flat face is engraved with a port scene and associated ships and buildings. V. Chavanne discovered it at Carthage and gave it to the Bardo Museum.

Pierre Cintas has suggested that it is a Punic vision of the Carthage port, done in the fourth or third century B.C., when this type of jasper was popular. He based his idea on Appian's literary description, but the Punic port was a double one with a rectangular commercial port and a round military port adjacent to it. The port was located on the Le Kram shoreline.

J. Debergh took exception to this interpretation, noting that the same scene appears on a number of intaglios in the Berlin Antiquarium—an observation already made by Raymond Lantier, who published the gem first in 1922. Although the gems vary in details, they belong to the Roman period; since green jasper came back in vogue in the later Empire, our piece may be of that date, perhaps fourth century A.D.

The scene may depict three sailing ships in a harbor. On the viewer's left is a curved portico such as is found on Neronian coins that show the harbor of Ostia, port of Rome. In th upper left are several buildings; the foremost may be a sacred round building (*tholos*). To the right is a mysterious structure that might be a temple on an island, a projecting mole, or eve lighthouse. The island idea is supported by the fact that one ship is sailing in rear view betv the object and the portico (the only such Roman view of a ship known to the authors). Th lighthouse idea is suggested because it may be guiding the ship. However, lighthouses on ancient reliefs usually show their flames and are shown as squares set on larger squares. The cross-in-square motif is very difficult to explain. Is it a bird's eye view or a side view? The multiple perspectives of Roman representations and the unrealistic presentation defeats all but the most daring art historians in cases like this. The temple hypothesis for the mysterious structure seems to be the best. The cross pattern may be a stylized version of massive bronze doors leading to a sacred complex beyond.

Bibliography: Cintas, 1973, pp.41–46; Debergh, 1975, pp.212–220, Debergh, 1977, pp.457–459; Lantier, 1922, pp.292–295.

AE

75. Gold Ring with Bird of Prey

Height: 6 cm (ring); *Diameter:* 10 cm (bezel)
Material: 18 carat gold ring and bezel of carnelians
Location: Bardo Museum
Date: Later Roman (?)

This beautiful ring (at the bottom of the illustration) has an elegant perforated crown decorated with six globules in between which is a setting containing oval carnelian shapes. The ring itself shows an intertwining pattern between borders of tiny globules. On the carnelian is carved the image of a bird of prey resting on a branch. The workmanship is less than careful since the soldering connections are visible, and roughness rather than fineness of detail is apparent throughout.

Bibliography: *Catalogue du Musée Alaoui*, 1910, p.115.

ME

76. Ring with Bust of Serapis

Diameter: 3.3 cm
Material: Gilt copper alloy
Provenance: Monastir (?)
Location: Bardo Museum
Date: Roman period
Number: 2311

On this ring (second from the left in the illustration) is the bust of Serapis. It is soldered to this massive ring, which is of unequal thickness on its upper part. The god is shown as a mature man with a grave expression, a long, full head of hair, and a bushy beard. He is clothed in a simple mantle. His head is crowned with the *modius*; this is his essential attribute and is a unit for measuring wheat (less than two gallons). The decoration is not well preserved, but it might be two stalks of wheat. This type of Serapis bust is familiar throughout Roman North Africa. We may cite briefly the image on stele Inv. A.126 from Maktar, Tunisia. Serapis became popular as a result of the Ptolemies' efforts to fuse traditional Egyptian and Hellenic divinities in Hellenistic Egypt and because of his magnificent temple in Alexandria. His cult generally involved magical healing, dream oracles, and a Zeus-like appearance.

Bibliography: Picard, 1954, p.225; Carthage, 1978, No. 37 (for the Maktar example identical to the image on the bezyl).

ABYK

77. Gold Ring with Red Glass Bezel

Height: 1.5 cm; *Width:* 2 cm; *Bezel:* 6.5 x .4 cm
Material: Gold with red glass bezel
Provenance: Carthage
Location: Bardo Museum
Date: Roman period

The bezel of this attractive small ring (center in the illustration) carries a lightly convex setting of red glass and has a double carinated ring area. Several fillets decorate the bezel, and the overall effect is of simple elegance. The ring is unpublished.

JAW

78. Orpheus Charming the Animals

Dimensions: 4.13 m x 3.59 m
Provenance: Bararus (Henchir Rougga, El Jem region), in a Roman house
Location: El Jem Museum
Date: Late second to early third century A.D.

This mosaic adorned one of the rooms of a house in Bararus, a Roman city whose ruins extend over a vast area. Among the remains are the forum, amphitheater, theater, arch, mausoleums, vast necropolises, and particularly the enormous cisterns, which are among the largest and most impressive preserved.

The house where the mosaic was found has not yet been completely excavated. It is of importance even now, however, because of its size and the fact that it does not have the classical distribution of rooms around a peristyle court. Here there is a surprising arrangement of main rooms in a lofty wing. The main salon with an interior colonnade measures almost 200 square meters and is decorated with stunning figural polychrome mosaics. An idea of the sumptuousness of the residence is provided by brief mention of the scenes displayed—amphitheater and circus sports, Diana the huntress, Helios, the fall of Phaethon, and many other motifs.

This mosaic came from a less pretentious reception hall reserved, perhaps, for intimate gatherings and enjoyment of poetry and music. In its pacific character, this mosaic is a striking contrast to the violent scenes in the salon. Our pavement depicts nine wreaths of tangent foliage linked to one another and to six half-wreaths, all arranged with interstitial grape leaves along the short sides of the row. These wreaths create a field of eight curvilinear squares and six half squares the length of the long sides. Circles, half circles, and curvilinear squares are organized in a harmonious manner around the central medallion depicting Orpheus.

In this scene, Orpheus is shown with nude torso and powerful athletic musculature standing in the center of the scene. He is holding his lyre at his left shoulder, and his meditative expression indicates his absorption in the music. Even the landscape seems charmed: the trees are bending perceptibly to better hear him, and the rocks themselves appear to be following the music. His music also charms wild beasts—a lion, tiger, panther, wild boar, antelope, stag as well as a bull and horse. In the half-wreaths are more unusual animals. A snake prepared to bite (an allusion to the reptile that tried to bite off Orpheus's head and was transformed into a stone by Apollo) and animals such as hares and jackals are not surprising. But the depiction of a Greek tortoise (*Testudo graeca*), a hedgehog (*Erinaceus algirus*), and a lizard is .

The mosaic is halfway between the total schematization found in certain Tunisian (and other) pavements in which medallions with animals or busts are arranged around a central medallion portraying Orpheus and the detailed mosaics in which the composition brings together Orpheus and the animals he charms in the same conventional landscape. The Rougga artist has included figural motifs in the wreaths and squares but given them animation (flexible postures, ears cocked to hear the music). The mosaic is enhanced by the vegetal component present in the circles, half-circles, and interior of the central medallion and by the four marginal squares containing trees.

The choice of theme is explained by decorative and cultural considerations. The mosaicist had the opportunity to create an elaborate composition in which vegetal decoration frames very diverse motifs—trees, birds, and animals. The artist also has for a subject one of the greatest legendary and mythological figures. Orpheus is one of the most romantic of characters. Born to a king and a Muse, he was endowed with tremendous gifts. His music charmed the most insensitive creatures and objects. In response to him, wild beasts lost their ferocity, the winds changed their direction, and rivers interrupted their course. In short, he brought civilization from a savage to a refined state. Poet and sage, he founded many sciences and methodologies, and his reputation spread throughout the ancient world. Possessing human weaknesses, he fell desperately in love with the nymph Eurydice, who died the day of their wedding. His descent to the underworld in search of his bride is a celebrated tale: the music from his lyre captivated even the infernal gods, who were moved by its sweetness and permitted Eurydice to leave with her husband. But his impatience to look back at her on their return to Earth resulted in his loss of her. Other women tried to console him. When they were rejected, they tore him to pieces and threw his head into a river. But his lips continued to call Eurydice, and her name was echoed on both shores. In fury, the gods visited a plague on the lands of those who had killed Orpheus. In expiation, the inhabitants built a temple where Orpheus was honored as a god and women were not permitted to enter.

With all these advantages, Orpheus could only have been favored by the mosaicists and those who commissioned their works. The Orpheus subject testified to the sophistication of homeowners and helped them gain access to immortality, for his music was believed to deflect the infernal forces. The theme had remarkable longevity during late antiquity. Before renouncing him, the Christians regarded him benignly, syncretizing him with the Good Shepherd.

The mosaic is previously unpublished.

HS

79. Tiger Attacking Two Onagers

Dimensions: 2.30 m x 1.61 m
Provenance: El Jem (Thysdrus) in the House of the Dionysiac Procession
Location: Museum of El Jem
Date: A.D. 150 to 200
Number: None

This panel was part of a large Dionysiac mosaic paving the triclinium of the elegant house of an aristocrat of Thysdrus. Certain particularities of plan and decoration have led to the hypothesis, not accepted by everyone, that the structure was the seat of a group dedicated to the cult of Bacchus.

In a rocky landscape, a tiger (*Panthera tigris*) is straddling and biting a fleeing onager's back, and the sad-eyed victim is beginning to collapse from the tiger's bulk and ferocity. A second onager (*Equus pinctoris*) is looking back over its shoulder, sensing the danger. In the background are a rustic altar between two columns at the viewer's left, a barren tree with intertwined branches, a green plant and several rock outcroppings, one with what is possibly a palm tree.

This scene was a pendant to an even grislier mosaic from the same triclinium as the next entry (80). For more on the House of the Dionysiac Procession, see Catalogue 61.
HS

80. Lions Devouring a Wild Boar

Dimensions: 2.30 m x 1.60 m
Provenance: El Jem (Thysdrus), in the House of the Dionysiac Procession
Location: Museum of El Jem
Date: A.D. 150 to 200

Originating from the same House of the Dionysiac Procession of El Jem and making up a part of the same mosaic as the preceding panel, this tableau presents what may be an Alexandrian countryside: some trees and two columns rise above an altar and support an architrave, which forms a *szygia* on which rests a vase; in the foreground, two lions (*Panthera leo*) devour a wild boar. The boar's back and the paws of one of the lions do not rest on the ground; the scene is like a snapshot, with intense action frozen in time.

The tableaux have movement, life, and realism in the rendering of the bodies and the fineness and evocative quality of painting. They bring to mind the masterpieces of the same genre found in Hadrian's villa in Tivoli.

Bibliography: *De Carthage à Kairouan*, 1983, pp. 166-167, with bibliography.

HS

81. The Dermech Hunting Mosaic

Dimensions: Circa 8.5 m x 7 m
Material: Marble, limestone, glass
Provenance: Carthage, close to the station of Dermech
Location: Carthage Museum
Date: Terminus post quem (date after which it is). This is a coin of Maximian dated between A.D. 297 and 302. *Probable date:* the beginning of the fourth century A.D.

Since prehistory, the theme of the great hunt has been a part of the North African repertoire—even figuring in early rock painting. African horsemen loved the hunt for its opportunities to show their bravery and the spirit and quality of their steeds. The Numidian horse, small in size

and characterized by endurance and swiftness, was well suited for hunting game as were the African dogs, among them the saluki, the fabulous ancestor of the greyhound.

North Africa, in particular ancient Libya, was a land of wild beasts, especially the lion. Elephants were found as late as the fourth century A.D., but during that century became extinct due to the demands of the amphitheater and massacres by ivory traffickers.

Animals were needed for the arena combats (*venationes*), and elephants were used for military purposes. They could batter through enemy lines and were difficult to stop on flat ground. Hannibal had, much earlier, used them to cross the Alps during the Punic wars. Gradually, ways were found to spike the ground (thus disorganizing the elephants) or to move out of the way of a charge, so that the animals would continue straight ahead—uselessly.

During the third and especially the fourth centuries A.D. the great hunt was in vogue on North African mosaics. Almost a dozen such mosaics have been recovered from Carthage.

Rarely exhibited even in Tunisia and specially restored, this is one of the most extraordinary hunting mosaics ever discovered. The theme is a grand hunt involving trapping and killing large wild animals and taking them on board a ship. It was found by A. Mahjoubi in 1965 and originally was in a large rectangular room with an apsidal end. (Not all scenes are depicted here.)

How to Capture a Lion

The first scene of the hunting mosaic at the top and to the left. (*Dimensions*: 2.71 m x 1.94 m)

A hunter is kneeling on top of a wooden box. The box has a door that is vertically movable; the hunter must let the door go to capture the animal. In front of this trap is a small wheeled cart on which a goat is mounted as a lure. This scene is very damaged. Two observers (only one of whom is well preserved) are protecting themselves behind a light and dark pink shield that has a small gray circle in the center. Attracted by the goat, a roaring lioness is approaching and is followed by a roaring lion (*Panthera leo*) emerging from a rocky cave in the generally rocky landscape. Their bodies are portrayed in light tones of pink and olive green, bordered by two black dentilled lines. The hunting technique depicted here appears in Roman Africa and particularly in Mauritania.

This first scene is paralleled in a Piazza Armerina mosaic. A large cage or traveling box with bait is seen in the Great Hunt Mosaic; men protect themselves behind shields against a leopard that has been attracted to the cage. A man is ready to drop a funnel-shaped object, perhaps a mechanism for closing the lid. Four other similar boxes are seen throughout the mosaic. (The funnel-shaped object does not occur in the hunt mosaic from Carthage.) A similar box is found in a Hippo Regius hunting mosaic in Algeria; in this case, nets and fire are used in addition to shields to direct the leopards into the box. Another scene in a mosaic found at Carthage closely parallels the hunter on top of the box and the box itself. Although the scene is damaged in this area, the action follows the same pattern as the other mosaics. In still another mosaic from the Roman Antiquarium of Carthage, the hunt is focused on a large feline. The cage is made of wood and strengthened with rivets and iron forming an x, following the diagonals of the side of the box. Indistinguishable bait is suspended in the middle of the entrance. A man kneeling on top of the box is ready to drop the mobile lid. The goat on a wheeled cart being pulled by a man from behind the box has no parallel so far .

The Return from the Wild Boar Hunt

Fragment placed at the top and to the right in the hunting mosaic. (*Dimensions*: 1.62 m x 1.51 m)

Two hunters preceded by a greyhound are advancing toward the right supporting on their left shoulders a long pole to which a wild boar is attached by its feet. An alert dog with a red studded collar is sniffing the beast. The hunters are wearing short white and pink tunics and brown and pink capes. Their legs are protected by yellow-brown banded socks (*fasciae crurales*).

This scene representing the return from the boar hunt closely parallels the one found in the Piazza Armerina Little Hunt Mosaic. In that case, however, the boar is strapped to the pole and covered with a net. As in our mosaic, the men are holding the boar on their shoulders. The little dog portrayed is almost the same on both mosaics. Jocelyn Toynbee also cites a similar scene from Carthage in which she describes the dog as a "solidly built, blunt-nosed and short-eared animal, with short, cheekily upturned tail." Furthermore, describing the dogs in the Little Hunt Mosaic, she adds, " in the pavements which were probably the work of African artists and craftsmen, both of the types of hounds are represented—the slender, long-eared, long-tailed kind are for fox hunts, and the heavier, blunt-nosed variety with short upturned tail for work

with boars." She also writes that dogs depicted in North African mosaics may be local species. The perky Carthage dog wears a "sweater" of white with a black border, probably intended to protect it from the bite of a prey.

The Elephant Attacked by a Python

Fragment on top and to the right in the hunting mosaic. (*Dimensions:* 1.64 m x 1.58 m)

This is not a hunting scene but a pathetic drama between an elephant and a python. The reptile has coiled itself around the enormous body of the pachyderm and is fiercely biting the animal's abdomen. The elephant's popeyed glare portrays its anguish. The elephant is portrayed with a crisscross pattern to indicate pachydermy, the creature's wrinkled hide. Toynbee quotes Pliny, HN VIII, 10.30 about the elephant's latticelike skin (*cancellata cutis*).

The Capture of Young Wild Animals

Fragment in the center of the hunting mosaic. (*Dimensions:* 2.47 m x 1.81 m)

At the left of the scene is a hunter on horseback, his cape flying. In his arms, he is holding what may be a young tiger. (Mahjoubi believes it is a baby elephant.) He is galloping toward the gangplank of a vessel that has its sails free and is ready to depart. Inside are four men with curly hair dressed in tunics embroidered in green or pink, waiting impatiently for the hunter. One man is tending to the sails; the other three are steadying the gangplanks. Such scenes represent the point where "legend and truth mix in the dangerous hunts which the skilled suppliers took part in—attracted by the demands of oriental dynasties and the Roman arenas" (J. Aymard).

The capture of young wild animals is illustrated in several mosaics in the Roman world and in one tomb painting in Rome. Literary descriptions of the capture of young animals parallel the mosaics. Ancient writers such as Claudian (*De Raptu Proserpinae*, III, 263–268) and Pomponius Mela (III, 43) attest to the use of a mirror to distract the tigress by fooling her into believing that her reflection is one of her cubs. Another way of capturing young animals is described by Pliny (N.H., VIII, 18, 25, 66), Martial (VIII, 26, 1–2), Claudian (same as above): and

Solinus (17, 4–7): mounted hunters raided the tigress's lair, ran off, occasionally dropping a cub to distract and delay her, and finally escaped aboard a ship, leaving the tigress stranded on shore. These descriptions are paralleled in the Hunting Mosaic at Carthage, in the Great Hunt Mosaic at Piazza Armerina, in a mosaic from Antioch-on-the-Orontes, and in a painting from the Tomb of the Nasonii in Rome.

In the hunting mosaic from Dermech, the rider is fleeing up the gangway and looking back over his right shoulder at the animal that is pursuing him. (It has not been preserved.) The rider's face expresses fear vividly; his cape flying in the wind and the horse's legs extended in one last jump toward the ship depict movement and a real sense of danger.

The closest parallel to this scene is from the Tomb of the Nasonii. In the right foreground, two hunters with shields are fighting one lion(?); one of them is holding a cub up to a mounted hunter. In the background, two more riders are being pursued by two more lions(?). One of the riders is looking back over his left shoulder, and he is ready to jump into a ship with a gangway; two sailors are ready to assist him. The same idea of movement in the Dermech mosaic is portrayed in this fresco.

A close parallel with this scene, as with the rest of the mosaic, comes from the Great Hunt Mosaic at Piazza Armerina, Sicily. An almost identical scene is shown in both mosaics: a horseman is fleeing up the gangway of a ship; the gangway is being pulled by three sailors (giving the impression that when the rider reaches the ship, he will quickly escape from the pursuing animal). In the Great Hunt Mosaic, the tigress has been distracted from pursuing the rider by a mirror as was described by ancient writers. The Antioch mosaic shows the mounted hunter riding toward the right, looking back over his right shoulder at the tigress who is with two more cubs. In this scene, no ship is portrayed.

The Hunting of the Leopard

Fragment placed in the center right. (*Dimensions:* 2.47 m x 1.81 m)
This scene depicts a hunter in the act of killing an attacking leopard. Holding his spear with both hands, he is breaking the impetus of the assault and piercing the leopard's throat. The hunter is standing in three-quarters view facing right and holding the spear with both hands.

On his head is the traditional basket—symbol of fruitfulness (*calathus*) often shown as an attribute of the gods. He is wearing a short green tunic with red decoration and over it a brown mantle (*chlamys*); it is fastened with a brooch (*fibula*) at his right shoulder.

Additional Scenes

The Dermech mosaic contains a number of additional scenes—a leopard leaping on its prey, a lion seizing a horse as its rider falls, a hunter and his dogs pursuing a fox, and a man spearing a charging boar.

Bibliography: MacKendrick, 1980, p.146, Fig. 6.3; Toynbee, 1973, p.29, Plates 1, 8, 11, 12; Scullard, 1974, Plates XVIIb, XVIII; Aymard, 1951, p.452, Plate XXXII; Jennison (no date), p.148; Mahjoubi, 1967 pp.264–278; Casson, 1965, pp.31–39; Dunbabin, 1978, pp.46–64; OBOB

82. Personification of Summer

Dimensions: 1.10 m x 1.09 m
Provenance: Acholla, in the Baths of Trajan
Location: Bardo Museum
Date: Circa 200 A.D.
Number: Inv. 5597

The four seasons were an enormously popular motif not only because they fit neatly into the four corners of a floor but also because they symbolized the annual renewal of life and visible evidence of harmony and order in the universe. This medallion comes from a seasons mosaic. It is bordered by a black fillet, a white fillet, a line of truncated maroon eggs and adjacent darts, and a maroon and double black fillet. A wide-eyed woman on a white background is looking slightly to her right. She wears a crown of wheat, a green tunic that is fastened on her left shoulder, and a gold necklace. She personifies Summer. Part of Summer's head has been damaged, but the craftsmanship is of high quality.

Bibliography: G. Picard, 1959, p.82, note 2, Plate XVI; 5.
OBOB

83. Votive Stele Dedicated to African Saturn

Dimensions: Height: 1.15 m; *Length:* 50 cm; *Thickness:* 14 cm
Material: Calcareous sandstone
Provenance: El Ayaida, in the region of Zahret Mediène, not far from the site of ancient Vaga (known today as Beja)
Location: Depository of the Institut National d'Archéologie et d'Art
Date: Fourth century A.D., dedicated on November 8, 323

This charming stele is an important and unique artifact because of its late Roman date, iconography, and archaic style in the Punic/Numidian tradition.

It is divided into three registers: two are devoted to figural scenes; the third is an epigraphic field. In the upper register is a niche with a depressed arch. The niche is decorated with a tongue pattern called "rais de coeur" and framed by two pilasters that have twisted shafts and are topped by consoles. A majestic divinity sits enthroned, holding a sickle (*harpé*), a symbol identified with Saturn (the Latin name for Baal Hammon, the great god of Punic Carthage). At his right shoulder is a head with a radiate nimbus, the sun (*sol*), the symbolic expression of the Romano-African deity's solar character. In his left hand, he is holding a scepter with twisted shaft, a reminder that Saturn has been syncretized with Jupiter, head of the Roman pantheon.

The central register depicts the act of devotion, the sacrifice of a ram, performed by a knife-wielding worshipper, at a burning altar that appears to be laden with fruit.

The epigraphic field contains an inscription that concerns the figural scenes. It provides the following information:

The dedication: To glorious Saturn

The votive act: Performed by a priest named Marcus Gargilius Zabo (whose surname also indicates that he is African), who has fulfilled the vows that he pledged

The occasion: A personal act of piety (a sacrifice) performed under the direction of a high dignitary of the college of priests

The date: November 8, 323 A.D. (indicated by the two eponymous consuls)

Copy of the text:

Saturno Aug(usto) Sac(rum). M(arcus) Ga/rgilius Zabo, sacer(dos) v(otum) s(usceptum) s(olvit) /l(ibens) a(nimo) sac(rificium) sub Q(uinti) Serveni P/rimi mag(isterio) suo VI idus no(v) em (b) res Rufino et Seve/ro co(n)s (ulibus).

Translation:

Dedication to glorious Saturn. The priest, Marcus Gargilius Zabo, with heartfelt joy, has fulfilled the vow that he had promised to execute. The sacrifice, offered in his own name, under the guidance of the Superior of the college of priests, Quintus Servenius Primus, took place five days before the ides of November when Rufinus and Severus were consuls.

This document dedicated to Saturn bears the most recent date of all documents that have been found so far and that have the same dedication. It confirms that—despite the spread of Christianity—the cult of African Saturn endured and flourished into the fourth century.

The stele contributes importantly to understanding the cult of a Roman African divinity and the interplay between African, Oriental, and Roman elements.

Bibliography: Beschaouch, 1968, pp.258-268; *De Carthage à Kairouan*, 1983, p.112, Number 160.

ZBA

84. Paleo-Christian Plaques

The walls and probably the ceilings of early Christian churches in Africa were decorated with clay tiles, some of which were painted. The tiles show Biblical, floral, and animal scenes and are the work of local artisans. They indicate what constituted popular art in the Christian cities of North Africa.

The Sacrifice of Abraham

Dimensions: 25 cm per side
Material: Terra cotta
Provenance: Kasserine
Location: Bardo Museum
Date: Sixth century A.D.
Number: C.M.A. No. 7

The sacrifice takes place between two stylized columns that appear to have capitals. Abraham, with a full beard and a full head of hair, is on the left. He is clothed in a long tunic. With his right hand, he is brandishing a large knife, preparing to sacrifice his son Isaac in accordance with God's will. The blindfolded Isaac is kneeling on a small mound on the right, awaiting his father's fatal blow. Before him is a lighted altar. Above the scene and to the right are the sacrificial lamb and the hand of God. A cross can barely be distinguished outside the frame and to the upper right.

Christ and the Samaritan Woman

Dimensions: 26 cm per side
Material: Terra cotta
Provenance: Hajeb El Aioun
Location: Bardo Museum
Date: Sixth century A.D.
Number: C.M.A. 108

Again, in a wall sculpture bordered by two stylized "columns," Christ is presented frontally on the right of this scene. His head is surrounded by a radiate halo, and he is clothed in a long robe. He is holding a long cross in his left hand and making a sign with his right, probably of blessing.

The Samaritan woman takes up the left part of the scene. She is shown in profile, her face in three-quarters profile. She pulls on a rope that is connected to a simple pulley system for drawing water from a well. The rope is tied to an amphora with two handles. The well is flanked by forked stakes that suspend the crossrod for the pulley system. The Biblical account (JOHN IV : 7,9) tells of Jesus going from Judea to Galilee and stopping at Samaria at a well. There he spoke to a woman who was surprised that a Jew would speak to a Samaritan; upon recognizing him, she brought many to see Him over a period of several days, and many were converted.

Bibliography: *De Carthage à Kairouan*, 1983, p.188, No. 246 and No. 248, with full bibliography.
ABABK

85. The Historiated Table of Sbeitla

Original diameter: 1.25 m; *Width of border:* 17 cm
Material: White marble
Provenance: Sbeitla, in the baptistery of the so-called Church of Vitalis
Location: Bardo Museum
Date: Sixth century A.D.
Number: C14447

Sbeitla, the ancient Sufetula, is unquestionably of Libyan origin as scattered finds indicate. The Roman city dates from the Flavian period (A.D. 69-96). It was a free city (*municipium*), then a colony (*colonia*) governed by an administrator (*curator*) appointed by the emperor. Like the other African cities, Sufetula experienced great prosperity during the first half of the third century A.D. and again in the fourth. In the fifth, the city fell for a time under Vandal domination only to be conquered later by the Byzantines. The city appears to have been an important strategic point in the Byzantine sixth-century military system. The city passed under Arab hegemony about the middle of the seventh century.

Constructed on a regular plan (rare in Africa), the city was covered with monuments, still visible for the most part. Of particular note is the forum with its three stunning temples. Many Christian basilicas were also built. One of the monuments, the so-called Baptistery of Vitalis, contained a sixth-century marble table with a historiated edge—now in the Bardo Museum. Portions of the edge illustrate Old and New Testament scenes and stress the importance of faith in God. The table has a raised edge, defined on the exterior by a row of bead and reel decoration. Each scene is separated from the next by a tree. In one scene, Christ's raising of Lazarus is visible. Lazarus is represented standing under an arch supported by two columns, his body wrapped in a shroud. He is gazing to the right at Christ, who is standing and making a commanding gesture with his right hand.

The second scene represents Noah in his ark. Noah is extending his hand toward the dove, which has an olive branch in its beak to show that the waters had receded and God had made peace with man (GENESIS 8). Quite near, a raven is pecking one of two cadavers. The raven is often a symbol of the Devil and shown devouring spoiled flesh. Farther away Elijah is shown ascending to heaven in a (perhaps) flaming chariot guided by an angel. Elijah was said to have been last seen in a whirlwind in a chariot of fire drawn by flaming horses (2 KINGS, II). Elisha, his disciple, is running behind the cortege, and Elijah seems to be looking back in farewell. The other parts that survive are too fragmentary to be completely readable. Nevertheless, a part of Adam and Eve can be identified on either side of the Tree of Knowledge at the far right.

Bibliography: *De Carthage à Kairouan*, 1983, p.183, no. 237, with full bibliography.
ABABK

86. Byzantine Pyxis

Material: Ivory
Provenance: Iunca
Location: Bardo Museum
Date: Sixth century A.D.

The base of the body is missing; the lid was recently completely restored. The pyxis was originally closed by a bronze lock, which has been partly preserved. The surface of the body was connected to the side by metal clasps; the lid was attached by metal hinges. On the box's vertical surface are two scenes, one on either side of the lock. The scene on the viewer's left is the better

preserved; it comprises four figures. In the background are arcades, the last of which is supported by a column with twisted shaft. The arcades end in a wall composed of tightly fitted ashlar masonry in alternating rows of large square and small rectangular blocks; against the wall grows a cluster of plants.

The first of four figures is old and bearded. He is dressed in a long belted tunic and is walking to the left and brandishing a scroll-like object (*volumen*) in his right hand. The second figure is missing entirely; only the imprint is visible, and reveals that this figure was also standing and dressed in a long tunic gathered at the waist. The third figure is very mutilated. It is a bearded man dressed in a long robe. He is stepping to the right and gazing at a rectangular object, fitted out with a cross-piece, that he holds in his left hand. He is gently sliding his right hand under his left. The last figure is even more damaged but appears to be dressed as his companions are, and he seems to be rushing toward the right holding an object in his right hand. The scene probably represents the four Evangelists, as G. L. Feuille has suggested.

The second scene shows the other side of the wall, the same arcades are seen in the background. This scene is far more damaged than the first. Only the indistinct form of a central figure, rather young, gazing to the right remains. He has abundant hair, is dressed in a long tunic, and is probably Christ. The figure at the right is missing; only the legs survived. The imprint of the figure at the left suggests that he was dressed in the same manner as the figures in the preceding scene. He is raising his right hand and making a sign.

The side of the pyxis was painted in red, as traces of still existing pigment indicate. The entire box was covered by a cloth whose woof marks are visible. The poor state of preservation makes stylistic and regional assignment difficult, but this is not first-rate work. Containers with Christian iconography were popular from at least the fifth century A.D. in eastern Tunisia and often contained a variety of scenes such as Jesus and the Apostles and the Sacrifice of Isaac. The pyxis form was known in ancient Greece and was popular in the Geometric period; in Athens, a toilet box seems to have been known as a *kylichnis*. This work is previously unpublished.

Bibliography: Feuille, 1940, pp.21-45.

ABABK

87. Tomb Mosaic from Tabarka

Height: 2.35 m; *Width:* 80 cm
Provenance: Tabarka, in the so-called Cemetery Chapel of the Martyrs
Location: Bardo Museum
Date: Fifth century A.D.
Number C.M.A. A308

This mosaic, found in 1904, is an example of a rare early Christian art form: the mosaic covering of an individual tomb. Found in places like Tarragona in Spain and Uppenna and Kelibia in Tunisia from the fourth century, they were popular in the fifth and into the sixth. Figural images on these mosaics are rare, perhaps reflecting the initial Christian attitude toward graphic representation. These mosaics were often inserted in the church pavement.

This panel is bordered by a double black fillet. In the upper register are the upper body and face of a bearded man who is facing frontally and wearing a tunic with vertical bands patterned in black (*clavi*) and segmenta on the shoulders. He is wearing a white collar or necklace (*orarium*) represented by four rows of white cubes. His right hand is holding the split-reed pen (*calamus*) and writing on what may be an open scroll (*volumen*) on his desk. The letters MAI are visible. The desk is decorated with circular polychrome motifs. Flanking him are two rose branches with blooms and a pattern of two squares set on their points. The rose was, for both Romans and Christians, an especially sacred flower. For the Romans, it meant victory and love; to the Christians, it was the flower of Paradise and of the Virgin Mary (a rose without thorns). The damaged epitaph reads:

(I)N PA(CE) — in peace

The lower register shows an orant female figure in a long black-banded, green robe (*stola strisciata*) with a long white scarf over the bust and head and flanked by two doves, Christian symbols of peace and purity. To her right, two Numidian hens are picking at a rosebush. To her left is a lit church candle. On either side of her head, an inscription reads:

(VI)CTORIA FILIA S(ACRA?) IN PACE — daughter
Victoria daughter rest in peace.
Chi rho (the first two letters of Christ's name in Greek) appear above the R in Victoria's name. The man may be writing the life of a martyr and could have been a Church writer buried here with his daughter. The lead sarcophagus contained the remains of a man and woman.

Bibliography: Grabar, 1968, pp.236-237; *De Carthage à Kairouan*, 1983, p.199, with extensive bibliography; Ferguson, 1973, p.37.
ABABK

88. Amphitheater Scene

Length: 57.5 cm; *Width:* 47.7 cm
Material: Plaster
Provenance: El Jem/Kairouan region
Location: Reserves of El Jem
Date: Fifth to sixth century A.D. (?)

This rectangular serving tray is an almost unique example of its genre. The fragmentary mold and modern plaster cast provide an unusually vivid amphitheater scene in which the beast fight plays a principal role.

Stamped molds were impressed into wet ceramic (greenware); an awl was used to provide details. The scene occupies the central field of the cast, framed along the interior by a

frieze of delicately incised ovolos. Two series of raised linear areas and channels surround the frieze to form the exterior frame.

This description applies to the red-orange plaster cast. The amphitheater, presented in a rectangular field (28 cm by 13 cm), consists of four scenes. The upper central part of the tableau is occupied by three figures seated on a platform, somewhat like a private box. A column with capital is to the left; a balustrade is decorated with architectural elements in netlike and scale patterns; and herms serving as minipilasters divide the area into three parts. (This same type of parapet is found on the obelisk of Theodosius in Constantinople.) At the viewer's left of the "tribunal," or raised platform, is a post at the top of which is what may be a military banner or pennant. The central seated figure is a high dignitary (emperor? high magistrate?) in a toga. His right hand, raised against his chest, holds an object inflated at both ends—probably a purse with the winner's prize money. The two other seated figures in the "imperial" box are subordinate to the man in the center. To the viewer's left of the official platform stands another dignitary in formal attire. He is wearing a long robe with what seems to be a long scarf covered with elaborate embroiderylike decorations, and he is holding a scroll or insignia.

225

On the right is another toga-clad official who is leaning forward slightly; he is holding his arms over the arena and preparing to drop the prize that he is holding in his hands down to the victor below.

The second scene takes place in the arena before the backdrop of a schematically arched wall and an arched entry door. In the center are two beast fighters (*venatores*). One is moving toward the viewer's left and looking back over his shoulder. He is wearing a short cloak—probably a tunic with rolled-up sleeves—that has a breastplate on its right side. He appears to be wearing a protective leather sleeve on his left forearm and leather shinguards (the right extending above his knee). He is holding a large lance or pike with a large, sharp point in his right hand. An enormous gooselike creature, is running in the same direction in front of him. The clothing of this figure is a fine example of what the well-dressed amphitheater fighter wore; it is paralleled in other documents attributed to the later Roman era.

On the right is a gladiator armed with a rectangular shield that is decorated on its sides by a linear border bisected by a groove and a small square plate in the center. His left hand is on the upper part of the shield as if to better protect himself from a stag ready to charge. But he is looking away—as if toward his companion. The lower part of the register has disappeared.

The third scene is realistic and shows a fierce battle between a bear and a wild boar. The bear, bounding to the right, is attacking the boar's hindquarters. The boar is moving from the bear's grip to flee to the right while looking back at the bear and trying to loosen itself.

Below this and composing a fourth scene is a lion that is wrestling a bull to the ground.

The border of the cast (4 cm wide) provides another hunt scene in which lions and lionesses alternate. No doubt, a hunter was shown at each of the four corners, but only two have been preserved—one at the lower left, the other on the right at the upper end of the short side. One of them, armed with a lance and a large round shield, is facing a lion bounding in his direction. The other is holding a pike and menacing a lion that is ready to charge.

Along the border of one of the long sides and almost in the middle is a stylized plant, its tendril-like stems extending from a basket or vase (?); the motif probably was paralleled on the opposite side. At the middle of the two short sides, a palm leaf is inserted between the animals. The leaves are often interpreted as victory wreaths and are in keeping with amphitheater and circus scenes. The technique used for the frieze and border decorations especially was no doubt influenced by the procedures used for metal and ivory work. The plates made from this mold probably served as trays for large formal ceremonies, public and private.

The mold is of particular interest as it provides information on the manner in which such large dishes of African Red Slip Ware were made. It proves that this type of ceramic was produced in Tunisia. Further study will help to clarify the development of this type to the seventh century A.D. The mold is unpublished.

Bibliography: Hayes, 1972, Plate XIa, Forms 52 and 56, pp. 83-84.

LS

89. Bronze Seal

Measurements: 4 cm on each side
Provenance: Uncertain
Location: Bardo Museum
Date: Byzantine period

This square tablet is divided on its anterior face into four equal parts; each bears numbers and stamps in intaglio. Two are surmounted by a horizontal bar. The posterior face has a grasping tenon pierced by a hole attachment probably designed to receive a chain or seal cord or even an engraving stylus. This seal (?) could also have been used as a bronze stamp mold, an example of which has been found at Guelma (cf. *CIL* 22652,3). In this case, the impression left by the mold was unquestionably intended to be applied on wax, lead, or some other material used to designate goods. Whatever it may be, the incised numbers and abbreviation are strangely similar to the monograms inscribed on Byzantine coins.

The date for this object, which can be associated with no specific known type and whose provenance is unknown, allows only risky hypothesis but appears to be of the Byzantine period.

The seal is unpublished.

ZBA

90. Gold Ring

Setting height: 1.2 cm; *Length:* 1.1 cm; *Width:* 0.9 cm
Total Height: 2.7 cm; *Weight:* 6.95 g
Material: Gold
Provenance: Unknown
Location: Bardo Museum
Date: Byzantine epoch

The setting, projecting out from the ring, is in the form of the base of a pyramid (center in the illustration); seen from above, the setting is a rectangle (1.1 cm by 0.9 cm) with a groove (0.2 cm wide) around the circumference of the setting. The base of the setting has a trellislike design (4 cm high). On its long sides is a different floral design that ends at the setting with two palm trees. On the short sides, a double vegetal decoration is near the base of the setting; it ends in two palmettes, the middle leaf of which terminates in a small globule. The width of the ring is 0.8 cm (near the setting) to 0.3 cm at the bottom of the ring. The setting was designed for a stone, but is presently empty. The piece is unpublished.

JAW

227

91. Ring with Portrait Head

Diameter: 1.7 cms; *Height of bezel:* 1.7 cms
Material: Gold with oval gold bezel
Location: Bardo Museum
Date: Third century A.D.
Number: None

This striking piece features an oval bezel and a ring area that is flat on the interior and rounded on the exterior. A profile view of a feminine head appears on the bezel. The figure is wearing a much-effaced earring and a necklace with four jewels or perhaps stones of some kind. The hair, executed in simple curved strands, is pulled to a bun at the back of the head. The face shows Hellenistic influence, particularly the long, straight nose, but the coiffure suggests the Roman period. The necklace decoration recalls bracelets fitted out with rows of half spheres found at Pompeii and Herculaneum, and the coiffure resembles that of Plautilla, wife of Caracalla, emperor early in the third century A.D. and that of Julia Paula, wife of Emperor Elagabalus. The date cannot be fixed with any certainty due to the stylization of the form.

Bibliography: Coche de la Ferté, 1956, pp.90-92; Babelon, 1950, Plate XXII, Number 7.
JAW

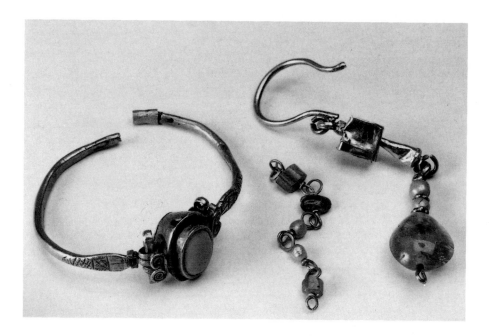

92. Late Antique Jewelry

Gold and Turquoise Earring

Diameter of the ring: 4 cm
Provenance: Unknown
Location: Bardo Museum
Date: Vandal or Byzantine epoch (?)

A beautiful earring (to the left in the illustration) in finely worked and chased gold, the setting of this piece was engraved with two serpents that recall the Egyptianizing style. The two serpent heads wrap to form a crown in which a large turquoise is set, flanked by a double spiral decoration on either side. The weight and thickness of the ring, which closes with a simple clasp, suggest that it was worn at the end of a necklace or cord.

Small Chain of Gold, Pearls, Jasper, and Rock Crystal

Length: 4.3 cm
Provenance: Carthage, in the region of the amphitheater
Location: Bardo Museum
Date: Vandal or Byzantine period

This ornament (center in the illustration) was part of a small gold chain that was perhaps part of a necklace. Between the links of chain are two pearls and three fine stones, two of green jasper and one in rock crystal. The chain was discovered in 1933 in the region of the amphitheater of Carthage in the course of the excavations made to uncover the "mosaic of the dolphins," The piece must be dated from the Vandal invasions in the fifth century or from the Byzantine epoch (sixth century A.D.).

Earrings of Gold, Pearls, and Amethyst

Length: 8 cm
Provenance: Mactar (Mactaris)
Location: Bardo Museum
Date: Vandal period
Number: Inv. 2986

These are earring pendants (right in the illustration). One of them is broken. The whole earring is composed of a simple gold hook in the form of an *S* and a long pendant on which are diverse, elegantly arranged items—at the top, a gold cube, hollowed out probably to contain a gem, and two fine pearls separated by gold rings. At the end is a large egg-shaped amethyst. The earring is mounted on a thin gold wire that ends in a small hook. The broken pendant has only the end of the oval amethyst and two fine pearls, these also are arranged on a thin gold wire. Discovered in 1945 in a tomb at Mactar, these gold earrings recall those found in the tomb of a rich Christian woman of Thuburbo Maius; they must be attached to the art of the great invasions, when—contrary to classic Roman-epoch laws—being buried with one's jewels was not forbidden.

These pieces of jewelry are unpublished.

LLS

93. Slave Collar for a Prostitute from Bulla Regia

Diameter: Varies from 14 cm to 11 cm
Material: Lead
Provenance: Bulla Regia (Hammam-Darradji)
Location: Bardo Museum
Date: Fourth century A.D. (?)
Number: None

This unusual object may not be among the most beautiful from ancient Tunisia but it is among the most fascinating historically. This lead collar weighs 300 grams and carries a Latin inscription. A number of similar objects have been found in Rome. The collars were frequently used on dogs and fugitive slaves. This collar was discovered in 1906 under the pavement of the Temple of Apollo area at Bulla Regia. It was among finds associated with the skeleton of a female about forty years of age. Formed of a large band of metal of which the ends are joined by a strong rivet fitted from the outside, this collar had been buried with her and was still attached to her neck. On its external face, the collar bears this one-line inscription:

ADULTERA MERETRIX TENE QUIA FUGIVI DE BULLA RG

ADULTERA MERETRIX TENE QUIA FUGIVI DE BULLA R(E)G(IA)

I am a dirty whore. Hold on to me because I am a runaway from Bulla Regia.

On the inside of the collar are the first four letters of the same phrase. The balance of the phrase has not been inscribed—probably because the outer face was easier to work on.

So much precise history about a slave is most unusual. The word *tene* is standard and invites the reader to recognize a fugitive slave. The inscription also indicates that the slave has fled from Bulla Regia. The woman is further described as "meretrix" i.e., a harlot or prostitute, and she is "adultera" (adulterous). The association of these terms poses some difficulties.

Most similar objects may be dated between the reigns of Constantine and Arcadius or Honorius; it is possible that our meretrix lived in the fourth century A.D., which might be a period when adultery was no longer considered the unthinkable crime of a matron but a sin condemned by the Church and forbidden to both sexes. "Adultera" could then indicate one who provokes adultery by entering into blameworthy relations with a man, especially if he is married. "Adultera" can be an insult here, a mark of reprobation relating to the courtesan's profession, referring to a woman who does not respect the requirements of her profession and who instigates debauchery and even sin. Slave, fugitive, prostitute—immoral and disgusting creature. This seems to be the distasteful message sent to us across the ages, engraved for all time on this ignoble collar.

Bibliography: Merlin, 1906, pp.366-368; Merlin, 1908, pp.10 and 11; Allard, 1924, col. 2140, Number 10; Ladjimi-Sebai, 1983, pp.88-98; Dig. XXV, 7.1.

LLS

94. Gold Leaf

Dimensions: 4.3 cm x 8.5 cm; *Weight:* 2 g
Material: 24 carat gold
Provenance: Henchir El-Faouar (Belalis Maior)
Location: Depository of the Institut National d'Archéologie et d'Art
Date: Fifth century A.D.
Number: None

This gold leaf was found in a Paleo-Christian tomb and may pertain to a tablet or object used for casting a spell or curse (*tabella difixiones*). A text of Greek appears to contain the name of demons. The piece is unpublished and, as a late addition to the exhibition, has not been studied. (See Catalogue 69.)

MBO

95. The Lady of Carthage

Dimensions: 1.08 m x 1.02 m
Provenance: Carthage, in a house on the Sayda Hill outside Sainte Monique
Location: Carthage Museum
Date: Fifth to sixth century A.D.

This mosaic lady is from the center of a room in a Carthaginian house discovered in 1953.

The border, 16 centimeters wide, is a black double line, followed by a band of squares set on their points and linked with circles. Between each circle and square are two mosaic pearl decorations. Each circle and square is outlined in black and yellow and placed on a red background. The interiors of the circles and squares are tessellated with blue and emerald green glass. The center of each pearl is emerald green and white.

In the center of the mosaic, on a background of white marble, is the bust of a young woman in formal clothing with a crown and halo. She has an oval face with regular features. Under thick black eyebrows, her huge brown eyes are circled with maroon. Her nose is straight, her mouth is small with full lips, and her chin is round. Her red and black hair frames her face and falls low on her forehead in curly bangs. On top of her head sits a diadem of gold and pearls and she wears long dangling earrings. She is dressed in a dark yellow tunic, of which we see only the right sleeve; it is decorated with transverse white bands from the wrist to the elbow. Over the tunic, she wears a purple cape, gathered at the right shoulder by a gem-encrusted fibula. The invisible left hand supports a gold scepter; the delicate right hand with its long tapering fingers, index and long finger extended and ring and little fingers closed, forms a gesture of benediction.

Who is the mysterious Lady of Carthage? She is not an archangel, because she has no wings; she is not an allegorical creation, because the name of the personification is always mentioned. It would be tempting to see in her either Galla Placidia or the Empress Theodora, because she presents numerous attributes of imperial power: the halo, the scepter, the purple cape. But to present an imperial figure on the ground would be a crime of high treason. One theory is that she was intended to be a personification of Carthage, but a diadem does not evoke the turreted crown of tutelary divinities.

The precise date of the piece is also disputed, although the inspiration of the frontal pose and wide-eyed iconic look is found in such areas as Thessalonika in Greece and Dura Europus and Palmyra in the eastern Mediterranean. A fitting end to any survey of ancient Tunisia, the Lady of Carthage turns her back on the Classical ideal and pushes Carthage into post-Classical ages. Yet the softness of the lady's cheeks, chin, and hands and the fullness of her lips show that concessions to Greco-Roman idealism of an earlier age had not yet disappeared completely and had been fused into a new style.

Bibliography: *De Carthage à Kairouan*, 1983 pp. 200-201 with full references.
OBOB

96–97. Treasure of 268 Gold Coins from the Byzantine Epoch

Dimensions: Diameters vary from 8 mm to 11.5 mm for the globular coins and 16.57 mm to 20 mm for the others; *Weight:* Varies from 4.278 g to 4.534 g
Provenance: Rougga (ancient Bararus), near El Jem
Location: Museum of El Jem
Date: A.D. 600 to 650

Coming from a Byzantine building erected on the ruins of the Roman forum, this treasure was found in 1972 in the course of an archaeological dig led by the National Institute of Archeology and Art of Tunis and the Mediterranean Archaeological Institute of Aix-en-Provence in France. The coins had been placed in a little terra cotta jug and hidden inside a building of the final Byzantine occupation. Of the 268 pieces, 194 were made in Constantinople, 70 in Carthage, 2 in Alexandria, and 2 are of undetermined origin. One is from the reign of Emperor Mauricius Tiberius (A.D. 582-602), the others are from the reigns of his successors: Phocas (83 pieces), Heraclius (120) and Constans II (64). Their dates are A.D. 602-610, A.D. 610-641 and A.D., 641-654 respectively. The coins carry inscriptions and on one side is the bust of an emperor or emperors. On the reverse is either an angel (on coins of Mauricius Tiberius and Phocas) or a cross.

Beyond its intrinsic value and its worth to numismatists, this treasure (whose owner must have been caught up in the whirlwind events of the time and unable to recover his wealth) is of significant historical value: assembled in the last years of the Byzantine occupation, it reflects the climate of insecurity that gripped the colony. Buried in 647, this find illustrates the violence and the extent of the shocks engendered by the first great Moslem raid in the country. Along with numerous other treasures of the same period, it confirms this country's reputation as a "promised land" of spoils and provides an example of the fabulous riches obtained by the victorious Moslems. Rare are the occasions when historical facts and archaeological discoveries are so perfectly in accord. With the devastation of ancient Tunisia and its subsequent transformation by the conquerors, the ancient world of Carthage and its dependencies came to an abrupt end.

Bibliography: *30 Ans 1986,* p.175; Guery, Mourisson, and Slim, 1982.
HS

Bibliography

Abun-Nasr, Jamil. *A History of the Mahgreb*. (London, 1975)

Acquaro, E. *Amuleti egiziani ed egittizzanti del Museo Nazionale di Cagliari*. (Cagliari, 1977)

Alexander, Margaret. "The Ganymede Mosaic from El Jem (Tunisia)," *IVth International Collegium on Ancient Mosaics*. (on press)

Alexander, Margaret, et al. *Corpus des mosaïques de Tunisie*. Vol. I Fascicule 3: *Utique*. (Tunis, 1976)

Allard, P. *Dictionnaire d'archéologie Chretiénne et de liturgie*. (Paris 1924–1953) Subject: Colliers d'esclaves col. 2140, No. 10.

André-Julien, Charles. *Histoire de l'Afrique du Nord*. (Paris, 1972)

Angilillo, Simonetta. *Sardinia*. (Rome, 1981)

Apuleius, Lucius. *The Golden Ass*. Edited by Harry C. Schnur; Adlington translation. (N.Y., 1962)

Audollent, A. *Definionum Tabellae*, p.300, no. 228. (Paris, 1904).

Aymard, J. *Les chasses romaines*. (Paris, 1951)

Barnes, T.D. *Tertullian*. (Oxford, 1971)

Ben Abdallah, Zeineb. *Catalogue des inscriptions latines paiennes du Musée du Bardo*. (Rome, 1986)

Ben Abed, Aicha. "Une mosaïque à pyramides vegétales de pupput," *Mosaïque, recueil d'hommages à Henri Stern*, p.61. (Paris, 1983)

―――――. "A propos des mosaïques de la maison des Protomés à Thuburbo-Majus," *IIIe Colloquio Internazionale sul Mosaico Antico*, pp.291–298. (Ravenna, 1983)

Benichou-Safar, H. *Les Tombes Puniques de Carthage*. (Paris, 1982)

Bendley, G. Hadley. *The Negro in Greek and Roman Civilization: A Study of the Ethiopian Type*. (Baltimore, 1929)

Beschaouch, Azedine; Hanoune, Roger; and Thebert, Yves. *Les ruines de Bulla Regia*. (Rome, 1977)

Bieber, Margarete. *The History of the Greek and Roman Theater*. (Princeton, 1971)

Bloesch, H. *Das Tier in der Antike*. (Zurich, 1974)

Broughton, T.R.S. *The Romanization of Africa Proconsularis*. (New York, 1968)

Brown, Peter. *Augustine of Hippo*. (New York, 1967)

Bruneau, Phillippe. "Le motif des coqs affrontés dans l'imagerie antique," *Bulletin de correspondence helléniques*, LXXXIX, 1965, pp.90–121.

Carandini, A., Ricci, A., and de Vos, M. *Filosofiana, la villa de Piazza Armerina*. (Palermo, 1982)

Casson, L. "Harbor and River Boats of Ancient Rome," *Journal of Roman Studies* 55, 1965, pp.31–39.

Casson, L. "Harbor and River Boats of Ancient Rome," *Journal of Roman Studies* 55, 1965, pp. 31–39.

Carton, L. *Sanctuaire punique découvert à Carthage.* (Tunis, 1920)

Catalogue du Musée Alaoui: Supplement. (Paris, 1910)

Chatelain, Louis. *Le Maroc des Romains.* (Paris, 1968)

Chelbi, Fethi. "Quelques aspects de la civilisation carthaginoise à l'époque hellenistique," *Cahiers des études anciennes* XVI, 1983, pp. 78–88.

Cintas, Pierre. *Amulettes puniques.* (Tunis, 1946)

_____. *Céramique punique.* (Paris, 1950)

_____. "Une ville punique au Cap Bon en Tunisie," *Comptes-rendus de l'Académie des Inscriptions et Belles-Lettres* 34, 1953, pp. 255–260.

_____. *Manuel d'archéologie punique*, I. (Paris, 1970)

_____. *Manuel d'archéologie punique*, II. (Paris, 1976)

_____. *Le port de Carthage.* (Paris, 1973)

Cornevin, Robert. *Histoire de l'Afrique.* (Paris, 1967)

Courtois, Christian. *Les Vandales et l'Afrique.* (Paris, 1955)

Darmon, J.P. "Le disciple devenu maître," *Les dossiers de l'Archéologie* 15, March–April, 1976, p. 28.

_____. *Nympharum Domus: Les pavements de la maison des nymphes à Neapolis (Nabeul, Tunisie) et leur lecture.* (London, 1980)

Debergh, Jacques. "Le port punique de Carthage sur une intaille du Musée du Bardo," *Latomus* 59, 1975, pp. 212–219.

_____. "Intaille de Carthage figurant un port," *Latomus* 61, 1977, pp. 457–459.

De Carthage à Kairouan. (Paris, 1982)

Delattre, A.L. *Carthage. La nécropole punique de Douimés. Fouilles de 1893–1894.* (Paris, 1897)

_____. *Carthage. La nécropole punique de la colline de Sainte-Monique.* (Paris, 1899)

Delattre, P. *La nécropole punique voisine de la colline de Sainte-Monique.* (Paris, 1898)

_____. *La nécropole des Rabs, prêtres et prêtresses de Carthage, 2e année.* (Paris, 1905)

_____. *La nécropole des Rabs, prêtres et prêtresses de Carthage, 3e année.* (Paris, 1906)

_____. "Une cachette de figurines de Demeter et de brûle-parfums votifs à Carthage," *Comptes-rendus de l'Académie des Inscriptions et Belles Lettres* 4, 1923, p. 361.

Delattre, R.P. *Bulletin epigraphique de la Gaule*, II, 1882, p. 181.

_____. *Nécropole punique de la colline de Saint Louis.* (Lyons, 1896).

Deneauve, Jean. *Les lampes de Carthage.* (Paris, 1969)

Dhorme, E. "Annales gravées sur des dalles de pierre au temple de Ninurta," *Revue biblique*, 1910, pp. 60–61.

Dorey, T.A., and Dudley, D.R. *Rome Against Carthage.* (New York, 1972)

Drees, Ludwig. *Olympia.* (New York, 1967)

Dunbabin, K. *The Mosaics of Roman North Africa.* (London, 1978)

Ennabli, A. "Sauvegarde, fouille et mise en valeur de Carthage," in *30 Ans 1986* (q.v.) pp. 184–190.

———, and Ben Osman, W. "Etude des pavements de la villa de la volière," *Mosaïque recueil d'hommages à Henri Stern*, p.147, Plates LXXXV, LXXXVII. (Paris, 1983)

Enneifar, Mongi. "La mosaïque de chasse d'Althiburos," *Cahiers de Tunisie* XXIII, 1975, pp. 7–16.

Fantar, M'Hamed. *Carthage, la prestigieuse cité d'Elissa.* (Tunis, 1970)

———. *Eschatologie phénicienne punique.* (Tunis, 1970)

———. "Un sarcophage en bois à couvercle anthropoïde découvert dans la nécropole punique de Kerkouane," *Comptes-rendus de l'Académie des Inscriptions et Belles Lettres* 53, 1972, pp. 340–354.

———. "Les pavements puniques," *Dossiers de l'Archéologie* 31, 1978, pp.6–11.

———. *Kerkouane, cité punique du Cap Bon.* Vols.1–3. (Tunis, 1984–1986)

Ferguson, George. *Signs and Symbols in Christian Art.* (London, 1973)

Feuille, G.L. "L'église de Iunca," *Revue Tunisienne.* 1940, pp. 21–45.

Février, J.G. "Vir Sidonius," *Semitica* IV, 1951–1952, pp. 13–18.

Flaubert, Gustave. *Salammbô.* Translation: J.C. Chartres. (New York, 1963)

Foucher, Louis. *Inventaire des mosaïque-Sousse.* (Tunis, 1960)

———. *Découvertes archéologiques à Thysdrus 1961*, pp. 15–25, Plates XV-XXVI. (Tunis, 1962)

———. *La maison de la procession dionysiaque à El Jem.* (Paris, 1963)

———. *Hadrumetum.* (Paris, 1964)

Guide du Musée de Sousse. (Tunis, 1967)

Frend, W.H.C. *The Donatist Church.* (Oxford, 1952)

Frézoul, Edmond. "Une nouvelle hypothèse sur la fondation de Carthage," *Bulletin de correspondance hellénique* LXXIX, 1955, pp. 153–176.

Gauckler, Paul. "Le Domaine des Laberii à Uthina," *Monuments et mémoires publiés par l'Académie des Inscriptions et Belles Lettres.* Fondation Piot III, 1896, pp. 177–229.

———. *Inventaire des mosaïques de Tunisie.* (Paris, 1910)

———. *Nécropoles puniques.* (Paris, 1915)

———, Gowert, E., and Hannezo, G. *Musée de Sousse.* (Paris, 1902)

Gazlan, Suzanne. "La maison de Neptune," *Monuments Piot* LIX, 1974, pp. 94–135.

Grabar, André. *Early Christian Art.* (1968)

Gsell, Stéphane. *Histoire ancienne de l'Afrique du Nord*, IV. *(Paris, 1920)*

Halff, G. "L'onomastique punique de Carthage," *Karthago* XII, 1963–1964 pp. 63–146.

Harden, D. "The Pottery from the Precinct of Tanit at Salammbô, Carthage," *Iraq* IV, 1937, pp. 59–89.

————. *The Phoenicians*. (New York, 1963)

Hayes, John. *Late Roman Pottery*. (London, 1972)

Herm, G. *The Phoenicians*. (New York, 1975)

Herodotus, *Histories*, IV, 42.

Humphrey, John. "Vandal and Byzantine Carthage: Some New Archaeological Evidence," in Pedley, *New Light on Ancient Carthage*, pp. 85–120. (Ann Arbor, 1980)

Hurst, Henry, and Stager, Lawrence. "A Metropolitan Landscape: The Late Punic Port of Carthage," *World Archaeology* 9, 1978, pp. 334–346.

Jenkins, G.K., and Lewis, R.B. *Carthaginian Gold and Electrum Coins*. (London, 1963)

Jennison, G. *Animals for Show and Pleasure in Ancient Rome*. (Manchester, no date)

Justin. XVIII, 2, 3, 4; XIX, 2, 5, 6.

Ladjimi-Sebai, L. "A propos d'un collier d'esclave en plomb trouvé à Bulla Regia," TURATI, 1983, pp. 88–98.

Lancel, Serge. *La colline de Byrsa à l'époque punique*. (Paris, 1983)

Lantier, Raymond. "Une intaille réprésentant un port," *Bulletin de la Société Nationale des Antiquaires de France*, 1922, pp. 292–295.

Lepelley, Claude. *Les cités de l'Afrique Romaine au bas-empire*. Vols. 1–2. (Paris, 1979)

Lézine, Alexandre. *Carthage-Utique*. (Paris, 1968)

————. *Thuburbo Maius*. (Tunis, 1968)

MacKendrick, Paul. *The North African Stones Speak*. (Chapel Hill, 1980)

Mahjoubi, A. "Découverte d'une nouvelle mosaïque de chasse à Carthage," *Comptes rendus de l'Académie des Inscriptions et Belles Lettres* 58, 1967, pp.264–278.

Massigli, R. *Musée de Sfax*. (Tunis, 1912)

Merlin, Alfred. "Le temple d'Apollon Bulla Regia," *Notes et Documents* I, 1908, pp.10–11.

————. "Notes," *Bulletin du comité des travaux historiques et scientifiques*, 1919, pp. 177–196.

Mitten, David, and Doeringer, Suzannah. *Master Bronzes from the Classical World*. (Mainz, 1968)

Morel, J.P. "Kerkouane, ville Punique du Cap Bon, remarques archéologiques et historiques," *Mélanges de l'Ecole Française de Rome* 83, 1971, pp. 473–518.

————. *Céramiques campaniennes. Les Formes*. (Rome, 1981)

Moscati, Sabatino. *The World of the Phoenicians*. (New York, 1965)

————. *Il mondo dei Fenici*. (Milan, 1966)

Pedley, John G. *New Light on Ancient Carthage*. (Ann Arbor, 1980)

Picard, Gilbert Charles. *Catalogue du Musée Alaoui*. Collections Puniques. (Tunis, no date)

_____. "Mactar," *Bulletin economique et sociale de la Tunisie* 90, 1954, pp. 1–18.

_____. *Les réligions de l'Afrique antique*. (Paris, 1954)

_____. *Le monde de Carthage*. (Paris, 1956)

_____, and Picard, Colette. *La vie quotidienne à Carthage au temps d'Hannibal*. (Paris, 1958)

_____. "Les mosaïques d'Acholla, annales d'est," *Etudes d'Archéologie Classique*, II, 1959, p.82.

_____. *Daily Life in Carthage*. (Paris, 1961)

_____. "Sacra Punica," *Karthago* XIII, 1965–1966, pp.61–62.

_____, and Picard, Colette. *La vie et mort de Carthage*. (Paris, 1970)

Pisano, G. Quattrochi. *I gioeilli fenici di Tharros del Museo Nazionale di Cagliari*. (Rome, 1974)

Poinssot, Claude. *Les ruines de Dougga*. (Tunis, 1983)

Polybius. VII, 9,3,3.

Pringle, Denys. *The Defense of Byzantine Africa from Justinian to the Arab Conquest*. (London, 1982)

Quillard, B. "Les etuis porte-amulettes carthaginois," *Karthago* XVI, 1970–1971 p. 10.

Raven, Susan. *Rome in Africa*. (New York, 1984)

Richter, Gisela. *The Sculpture and Sculptors of the Greeks*. (New Haven, 1965)

Sallust. *Jugurthine War,* LXXVIII, 1–5.

Saumagne, Charles. *La Numidie et Rome: Massinissa et Jugurtha*. (Paris, 1966)

Scullard, H.H. *The Elephant in the Greek and Roman World*. (London, 1974)

Seefried, Monique. *Les pendentifs en verre sur noyau des pays de la Méditerranée antique*. (Rome, 1982)

Siculus, Diodorus. V, 35; XIV, 77, 4, 5.

Snowden, F. *Blacks in Antiquity*. (Cambridge, 1970)

Stager, Lawrence. "Excavation at Carthage 1975, the Punic Project: First Interim Report," *Annual of the American Schools of Oriental Research* 43, 1978, pp. 151–189.

_____. "The Rite of Child Sacrifice at Carthage" in Pedley, *New Light on Ancient Carthage*. (Ann Arbor, 1980)

_____. "Carthage: A View from the Tophet," *Phonizier im Westen,* pp. 155–173 (Mainz, 1982).

_____, and Wolf, Samuel. "Child Sacrifice at Carthage, Religious Rite or Population Control," *Biblical Archeology Review*, Jan–Feb., 1984, pp.31–51

Stern, Henri. "Découverte de la mosaïque," *Les dossiers de l'archéologie* 15, March–April, 1976, p.12.

Sznycer, Maurice, and Massson, Olivier. *Recherches sur les Phéniciens à Chypre*. (Geneva, 1972)

30 Ans au service du patrimoine: De la Carthage des Phéniciens à la Carthage de Borguiba. (Tunis, 1986)

Tlatli, S.E. *La Carthage punique.* (Paris, 1978)

Toll, N. *The Green Glazed Pottery*, Vol. 4, part 3, Fascicule 1 of *Dura-Europus.* (New Haven, 1943)

Toynbee, Arnold. *Hannibal's Legacy.* 2 Vols. (New York, 1965)

Toynbee, J.M.C., *Animals in Roman Life and Art.* (Ithaca, 1973)

Tunisian Exposition. *Carthage.* (Tokyo, 1981)

UNESCO *Courier,* Dec. 1970, pp.14–15.

Vercoutter, J. *Objets égyptiens et égyptisants du mobilier funéraire carthaginois.* (Paris, 1945)

Warmington, B.H. *Carthage.* (London, 1960)

_____ . *The North African Provinces from Diocletian to the Vandal Conquest.* (Westport, 1971)

Wells, C.M. "The Defense of Carthage," in Pedley, *New Light on Ancient Carthage.* (Ann Arbor, 1980)

Wykes-Joyce, Max. *Cosmetics and Adornment: Ancient and Contemporary Usage.* (London, 1961)

Wightman, Edith. "The Plan of Roman Carthage: Practicalities and Politics," in Pedley, *New Light on Ancient Carthage.* (Ann Arbor, 1980)

Yacoub, Mohamed. *Chefs-d'oeuvre des musées nationaux de Tunisie.* (Tunis, 1978)

_____ . *Le Musée du Bardo.* (Tunis, 1982)

Yalouris, Nicolaos, et al. *The Olympic Games in Ancient Greece.* (Athens, 1976)